Cracking the
GRE CAT®

with Four Complete Sample Tests
on CD-ROM

THE PRINCETON REVIEW

Cracking the GRE CAT®

with Four Complete Sample Tests on CD-ROM

By
Karen Lurie

2000 EDITION

RANDOM HOUSE, INC.
NEW YORK

Princeton Review Publishing, L.L.C.
2315 Broadway
New York, NY   10024
E-mail: info@review.com

ISBN: 0-375-75408-3

Editor: Lesly Atlas
Production Editor: Kristen Azzara
Production Coordinator: Robert McCormack
Illustrations by: The Production Department of The Princeton Review

Manufactured in the United States of America on partially recycled paper.

9 8 7 6 5 4 3 2

2000 Edition

ACKNOWLEDGMENTS

The following people deserve thanks for their help with this book:

Lesly Atlas, Greta Englert, Robert "Precious" McCormack, Kristen Azzara, Joe Reddy, Becky Oliver-Remshifski, Ken Riley, Rena Rosenthal, Cathryn Still, and Clare Zagrecki.

CONTENTS

PART I

Orientation

1

Introduction

WHAT IS THE GRE CAT?

The Graduate Record Examination (GRE) Computer Adaptive Test (CAT) (ETS somtimes refers to it as a CBT, or computer-based test) is a multiple-choice admissions test intended for applicants to graduate schools. The three sections that count toward your score are (not necessarily in this order):

1. one 30-minute, 30-question "verbal ability" (vocabulary and reading) section
2. one 45-minute, 28-question "quantitative ability" (math) section
3. one 60-minute, 35-question "analytical ability" (games and arguments) section

As you can see, you won't be incredibly pressed for time on the GRE CAT. You shouldn't feel as rushed on this test as you might have on other standardized tests. The verbal section of the GRE CAT contain four types of questions:

- antonyms
- sentence completions
- analogies
- reading comprehension

The quantitative section contains 3 types of questions:
- four-choice quantitative comparisons
- five-choice problem solving questions
- charts

The analytical section contains 2 types of questions:
- analytical reasoning (games)
- logical reasoning (arguments)

Each of these question types will be dealt with in detail later in the book.

EXPERIMENTAL SECTION

You will probably have a fourth, unidentified experimental section: another Verbal, Math, or Analytic section. It can be anywhere on the test. This section will not count toward your score. You can't not do it, and you won't even recognize it. If you get two verbal sections, then one of them is experimental, but you won't know which one. So, don't worry about it. Just do your best on all questions.

RESEARCH SECTION

Occasionally you'll also be required to complete an identified, unscored research (sometimes called a "pretest") section consisting of additional experimental questions. It will probably either be a writing measure or some different math questions. If you have this section, it will be last. Fortunately, since you will have completed all scored sections of the test at this point, the use of you as a guinea pig by Educational Testing Service (ETS) can have no adverse effect on your GRE score. Data obtained from this research section will be used to continue to revise the CAT over the next few years.

All totaled, you should plan to be at the test center no longer than four and-a-half hours.

WHAT DOES A GRE CAT SCORE LOOK LIKE?

You will receive separate verbal, quantitative, and analytical scores. Scores on the GRE CAT are reported on a scale that runs from 200 to 800. GRE CAT scores can rise or fall only by multiples of ten. The third digit in a GRE CAT score is thus always a zero. You can't receive a score of 409 or 715 on a section of the GRE CAT.

WHERE DOES THE GRE CAT COME FROM?

Like most standardized tests in this country, the GRE CAT is published by ETS, a big, tax-exempt private company in New Jersey. ETS publishes the GRE under the sponsorship of the Graduate Record Examinations Board, which is an organization affiliated with the Association of Graduate Schools and the Council of Graduate Schools in the United States.

ETS is the organization that brings you the Scholastic Aptitude Test (SAT), the Graduate Management Admissions Test (GMAT), the National Teacher Examination (NTE), and licensing and certification exams in dozens of fields, including hair styling, plumbing, and golf.

WHY ON A COMPUTER?

Until a few years ago, the GRE "General" Test was only available as a paper-and-pencil test, and hadn't been modified substantially in a couple of decades. The test booklet, the answer sheet, and the three-and-a-half hour session early on a Saturday morning were all staples of the GRE experience (kind of like the SAT experience, remember?). However, the folks over at ETS decided that by transforming the GRE from paper to a computer, they could save money on printing test materials, renting facilities, and processing answer sheets.

This leads us to the trickiest CAT issue—disclosure, or your right to review the test you took and your answers, after you receive your score. Disclosure is virtually non-existent for the CAT, whereas most paper-and-pencil GREs are disclosed; with the CAT you will never know which questions you missed and how the computer arrived at your final score; you can't verify your final score, learn from your mistakes, or ever see the questions on your test again.

Cracking the GRE CAT takes a very different approach from cracking the paper-and-pencil GRE. It will require you to overcome instincts developed through a lifetime of taking tests on paper. You can't, for example, turn back to a question that gave you trouble and do more work on it later; once you've completed a question and confirmed your answer selection, you'll never see that question again.

BUT DON'T DESPAIR!

The CAT has many advantages over its paper-and-pencil cousin, not the least of which is that you have more time to answer the questions. Here are some more advantages:

- You can take the GRE CAT almost any day during the first three weeks of every month, morning or afternoon, weekday or weekend. Appointments are scheduled on a first-come, first-served basis. You may take the test only once per calendar month.

- There's no real deadline for registering for the test (technically, you can register the day before). But there's a limited number of seats available on any given day, and centers do fill up, sometimes weeks in advance. It's good to give yourself at least a couple of weeks of lead time to register.

- The CAT is technically simple: all you need to do is to point a mouse arrow at the answer and click, then click a second box to confirm your choice and move to the next question.

- You receive your scores right after you finish the exam (a modern version of immediate gratification). Scores also go out to schools more quickly.

- It's true that the lack of a physical test booklet makes it impossible to write directly on the problems themselves (to cross out incorrect answers, etc.). But, unlike paper-and-pencil testers, CAT takers get scratch paper, so your work space is limitless. No cramming your work into the margins of the test booklet. And you're going to find as you read this book that your use of scratch paper is one of the keys to scoring well on the GRE CAT.

- The CAT testing experience is much more personalized than that of the old paper-and-pencil exam with a proctor with a stopwatch at the front of a room full of coughing, squirming test-takers. You might even be the only one in the room during your test, and you will be able to begin your test when you're good and ready.

SCHEDULING A TEST

You can schedule a test session for the GRE CAT (which, by the way, will cost you $96) by calling The Sylvan Technologies National Registration Center at 800-GRE-CALL. Or, you can register online at www.gre.org. General inquiries about the GRE CAT can be made by calling Educational Testing Services at 609-771-7670. You may also call your local test center to set up an appointment (a list of centers is available from ETS; most are Sylvan Learning Centers). In order to schedule your test by phone, you must pay by VISA or Mastercard.

STAY CURRENT

ETS says that a Writing Test will be added to the GRE CAT in the fall of 1999. As of the publication of this edition, ETS has not released information about this section yet. The information in this book is accurate right now, and will be updated yearly. However, the publishing business is such that if the test changed tomorrow (which it won't), the book might be a little behind.

Therefore, obtain the most current information possible on your test by getting ETS's Registration Booklet (you should *definitely* have one of these), visiting ETS's web site at www.gre.org, or checking our web site, www.review.com, since web sites can be updated daily.

HOW THE CAT WORKS

Computer adaptive tests use your performance on one question to determine which question you will be asked next. The GRE CAT begins with ETS assuming that you have the average score in a particular category—for example, a 480 in verbal. You'll be asked a question of difficulty appropriate to this score level: if you answer correctly, the computer adjusts your score to a new level, say 550, and your next question is more difficult. If you answer incorrectly, your score will drop and your next question will be less difficult. In addition to adjusting your score, the amount your score will change with each new correct or incorrect answer is reduced as you move further into the test, so by the end the computer will have effectively zeroed in on your GRE score. That's the theory, anyway.

WHAT DOES ALL THIS MEAN?

It means that how much credit you get for a harder question depends on what you've done on the questions before you get that harder question. If you've correctly answered all the questions before it, you're going to get more credit for answering a hard question correctly than you would if you had missed a bunch of questions before you worked your way to that hard question. In a nutshell: your responses to the first questions in a section will have a greater impact on your final score than will your responses to those later in the section, after the computer has already determined your score range. So be EXTRA careful in the beginning of each section. Also, you will be penalized for not giving an answer to every question in a section. So you have to answer every question, whether you do any actual work on it or not (more on that in the next chapter).

Never, ever try to figure out how difficult a question is. Just concentrate on working carefully on each question that you get. You'll learn a lot more about pacing, as well as other general CAT strategy techniques, in the next chapter.

YOUR OWN PERSONAL CAT

The adaptive nature of the CAT means that no two people will have the same test. The question you're looking at on the screen at any given time has been "chosen" in response to how you did on the previous question.

Because the computer "decides" what to do next based on how you answer the question on the screen, you MUST answer that question. There is no skipping a question and coming back to it later. And once you answer it, it's gone forever. The computer will ask you to confirm your choice, giving you one more chance to change your answer; once you confirm, that question is out of your life forever. That means you can't afford to make any careless errors. You'll learn how to avoid making them throughout this book.

HOW TO USE THIS BOOK

This book is full of our tried-and-true GRE CAT test-taking techniques, some of which, at first, might seem to violate your gut instincts. In order to take full advantage of our methods, you will have to trust them enough to make them automatic. **The best way to do this is to practice them on real GREs.**

By "real GREs," we *don't* mean the practice tests in coaching books. The questions in such books often bear only a superficial resemblance to the questions actually used on the test; if you try our techniques on them, they won't work, because our techniques are designed for real GREs. Even the questions in this book and on the accompanying disks are not actually administered GRE questions, although we design our questions using the same methods as those used in designing real GREs. Besides, any question you do in this book, even the drills in the back, will be unrealistic in at least one way: they're printed in a book, and not on a computer screen. So, you should do everything in this book with scratch paper, to simulate the CAT experience as much as possible.

The only source of real GREs is the publisher of the test, ETS. We strongly recommend, therefore, that you purchase *GRE POWERPREP® Software—Test Preparation for the General Test*, which includes a retired GRE question pool presented in the CAT mode. The following are also available:

- *GRE Big Book* (includes 27 actually administered paper-and-pencil exams)
- *GRE POWERPREP® Software—Math Review for the GRE General Test* (extra computerized math review)
- *GRE Practicing to Take the General Test*, 9th Edition (includes 7 actually administered paper-and-pencil exams)

All of these items contain actual GRE questions. To order, call the GRE publications office at 800-537-3160. Or order from the web site at www.gre.org.

Remember, the real GREs available in printed books are paper-and-pencil tests, so use them to practice content. POWERPREP allows you to practice on a computer in the CAT style. Whatever you use, practice with scratch paper. As you prepare for the GRE CAT, work through every question you do, in this book or anywhere else, as if the question is being presented on a computer screen. That means using scratch paper, copying things down on it, and not doing ANYTHING in your head. You'll learn more about how to do that throughout this book.

TESTS ONLINE

Princeton Review Online, available on the Web at www. review.com, offers free access to Tester, the only online computer-adaptive testing engine. Using Tester, you can take a simulated GRE, get a detailed analysis of your performance, and see clear explanations for each answer choice describing how to use the techniques taught in this book. Just point your browser to tester.review.com, register, and you'll be on your way.

2

General Strategy

CRACKING THE SYSTEM

Lesson One: the GRE CAT definitely does NOT measure your intelligence, nor does it measure how well you will do in graduate school. The sooner you accept this, the better off you'll be. Despite what ETS says or admissions officers think, the GRE is less a measure of your intelligence than it is a measure of your ability to take ETS tests.

I THOUGHT THE GRE WAS COACH-PROOF

ETS has long claimed that one cannot be coached to do better on its tests. If the GRE CAT was indeed a test of intelligence, that would be true. But, the GRE CAT is NOT a measure of intelligence; it's a test of how well you handle standardized tests. And that's something that everyone can be taught. The first step in doing better on the GRE CAT is realizing that.

THIS IS GOOD NEWS FOR YOU

This means that your ability to take ETS tests can be improved. With proper instruction and sufficient practice, virtually all test-takers can raise their scores, often substantially. You don't need to make yourself smarter in order to do this; you just need to make yourself better at taking ETS tests. That's why you bought this book.

WHY SHOULD I LISTEN TO THE PRINCETON REVIEW?

Quite simply, we monitor the GRE CAT. Our teaching methods for cracking it were developed through exhaustive analysis of all available GREs and careful research into the methods by which standardized tests are constructed. Our focus is on the basic concepts that will enable you to attack any problem, strip it down to its essential components, and solve it in as little time as possible.

THINK LIKE THE TEST WRITERS

You might be surprised to learn that the GRE isn't written by distinguished professors, renowned scholars, or graduate-school admissions officers. For the most part, it's written by ordinary ETS employees, sometimes with freelance help from local graduate students. There's no reason to be intimidated by these people.

As you become more familiar with the test, you will also develop a sense of "the ETS mentality." This is a predictable kind of thinking that influences nearly every part of nearly every ETS exam. By learning to recognize the ETS mentality, you'll earn points even when you aren't sure why an answer is correct. You'll inevitably do better on the test by learning to think like the people who wrote it.

THE ONLY "CORRECT" ANSWER IS THE ONE THAT EARNS YOU POINTS

The instructions on the GRE CAT tell you to select the "best" answer to each question. ETS calls them "best" answers, or the "credited" responses, instead of "correct" answers to protect itself from the complaints of test-takers who might be tempted to quarrel with ETS's judgment. Remember, you have to choose from

Why is this test on a 200–800 scale? ETS didn't want it to look like the 0–100 scale used in schools.

the choices ETS gives you, and sometimes, especially on the Verbal section, you might not LOVE any of them. But your job is to find the one answer for which ETS gives credit.

CRACKING THE SYSTEM

"Cracking the system" is our term for getting inside the minds of the people who write these tests. The emphasis on earning points rather than on finding the "correct" answer may strike you as somewhat cynical, but it is a key to doing well on the GRE CAT. After all, the GRE leaves you no room to make explanations or justifications for your responses.

This is NOT a test of intelligence!

You'll do better on the GRE CAT by putting aside your feelings about *real* education and to surrender yourself to the strange logic of the standardized test.

HOW TO CATCH A CAT

Okay, let's start talking strategy! Come back to this chapter a few days before test day to review it.

WHAT THE CAT LOOKS LIKE

When there's a question on the screen, it will look like this:

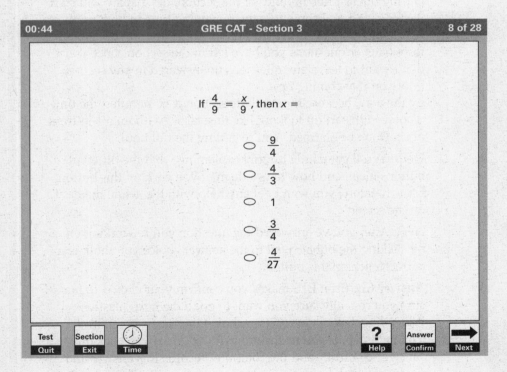

The problem you're working on will be in the middle of the screen. The answer choices will have little bubbles next to them. To choose an answer, you click on the bubble that corresponds with the choice you are picking.

A readout of the time remaining in the section will be displayed (if you want it to be displayed); the number of questions you've done and the total number of questions in the section will be displayed in the upper right corner. The bottom of the screen will contain the following buttons, from left to right:

Test Exit: You can end the test at any moment by clicking on this button. However, unless you become violently ill, we do not recommend that you ever do this. Even if you decide not to have this test scored (an option you get when you're done with the exam), you should finish the test. After all, it's great practice for when you finally want the test to count. Besides, you can't get a refund from ETS.

Section Exit: You'll be taken out of the section you're working on by clicking on this button. If you do this, you won't get a score. So even if you are lucky enough to finish early, don't exit. Just sit and rest until the next section begins.

Time: You can make visible or hide the digital countdown by clicking on this button. Some people like to have it on the screen; others like to look at their watches instead. Whatever you decide, when time is almost up, the display will appear or reappear on the screen even if you've told it to go away earlier. During the last five minutes of the section, the display will start flashing, and will show you the remaining time in both minutes AND seconds. This is a good time to guess your favorite letter for whatever questions you have left in the section, since you don't want to leave any questions unanswered in any section (more on that coming up).
By the way, because the Analytic section is 60 minutes, the time display will start off looking like this: 00:59 (without a 1 in front of it). Don't be alarmed. You're getting the full hour.

Help: You'll get a little tutorial explaining what the different buttons mean and how to use them, if you click on this button. Unfortunately, you won't get any help with the actual material on the screen!

Next: After you've answered the question you're working on by clicking the bubble next to the answer choice you think is correct, click on this button.

Answer Confirm: ETS makes you confirm your choice, to make sure you're really sure you want to go to the next question. When you click on "next" (see above) the "answer confirm" icon lights up. If you're sticking with your answer, click on "answer confirm," and the computer records this answer and gives you the next question. However, if you think you made a mistake with your answer, this is your last chance to change it.

THE ETS ELF

Remember when you were a kid, you thought that people on TV were really in the television? Well, that's sort of what's happening with the GRE CAT. It's like an irritating little ETS Elf is hanging out inside your computer, crafting your test as you go along. This is simplified, of course, but you'll see what we mean.

Say you're doing the first math question in the math section. The ETS Elf is in the computer, waiting to see what you'll pick. He's starting you out with, say, a 500 as a score. You pick your answer; you got it right! The ETS Elf bumps your score up to, say, a 550, laughs maniacally, and throws you your next question— a harder math question. He waits to see what you'll pick...oops! you got it wrong. The ETS Elf knocks your score down to, say, a 510, and gives you a slightly easier problem next. Let's say you don't know what the answer to this one is, but you make an educated guess (we'll teach you how) and get it right. The ETS Elf raises your score to a 530, and gives you a slightly harder problem. And so on, and so on.

So, when you get a correct answer, the ETS Elf "rewards" you with a harder question; when you get an incorrect answer, the ETS Elf "rewards" you with an easier question. Potentially, every tester can have a different test in terms of the questions that he or she sees. You won't know how you did on the prior question, so just focus on doing your best on each question.

SOME QUESTIONS ARE MORE EQUAL THAN OTHERS

At the beginning of your test, your score moves up and down in larger increments (sometimes as much as 80 points) than it does at the end, when the ETS Elf believes he is merely refining whether you deserve, say, a 630 or a 640.

You CAN improve your scores!

This means that the ETS Elf gives varying weights to the questions. The questions are roughly divided into thirds, and the first third of the questions in any section is weighted the most. This means that the first third to half of the questions determines the bulk of your score. The second third accounts for a lesser amount of the scaled score, and the third third counts for a relatively insignificant amount of your overall score. So, make sure you do your best on the first third of the questions in each section.

ANSWER EVERY QUESTION

So, you want to be sure about accuracy on early questions. The ETS Elf doesn't let you go backward, so do not move on to the next question until you are sure about your answer (or about your guess). You'll be penalized for incorrect answers, but the penalty becomes less strict as you get deeper into each section. But get this: you will also be penalized for not giving an answer to every question in a section.

Basically, the ETS Elf will reduce your raw score by the percentage of unanswered questions in a section (e.g., a 30-question section with 6 questions left blank will mean a 20% reduction of your raw score). So, do not leave any question unanswered.

Let the Computer Help You

Remember: All the answers you need are on your screen.

During the last five minutes of a section, the time display on the computer screen will start flashing, showing you the remaining time in both minutes and seconds. Let this be your signal to start wrapping things up by guessing your favorite letter for whatever questions you have left in the section, since you don't want to leave any questions unanswered in any section.

So, remember:

1. Don't rush

Instinct might suggest that if there's a penalty for blanks and a possibility for lost points due to incorrect answers, testers should work as quickly as possible, in order to leave enough time to see and work the final few questions. But, the impulse to rush through the early questions is dangerous, as these questions are worth considerably more points than the later ones. To maximize your score, work slowly and carefully at the beginning of the section. **A high degree of accuracy in the first third to half of each section is the single most important factor in earning the highest possible scores on the GRE CAT.**

2. Guess aggressively

Once you've worked carefully through the first third to half of the section, it is important to avoid getting bogged down in time-consuming questions. If you encounter a question that seems extremely difficult or time-consuming, eliminate answers that you know are wrong, and make an educated guess (you're about to learn more about this). This will allow you to get to subsequent questions, which may be more easily worked, with enough time to work them.

3. Respond to every question

During the last five minutes of the section, when the time display starts flashing, start guessing your favorite letter for whatever questions you have left in the section, since you don't want to leave any questions unanswered in any section.

Wait a Minute

Remember, the question you see on your screen at a particular time depends on how you answered the previous question. And, the ETS Elf picks the next question based on how you just did on the previous one. This means you can never skip a question; otherwise, how would the Elf know what to give you next?

This means you're probably going to see questions on which you'll have to guess. But we're not talking about random guessing. After all, the right answer is on the screen.

Can I Have Partial Credit?

Remember when you were in high school, and even if you got a question wrong on a test, your teacher gave you partial credit? For example, you used the right formula on a math question, but miscalculated and got the wrong result, but your teacher gave you some credit because you understood the concept?

Well, those days are over. ETS doesn't care how you got your answer; it only cares about whether you picked the right answer choice with your mouse. You might as well benefit from this by getting questions right without really knowing how to do them. And you do that with the Process of Elimination, or POE. POE is your new religion. Learn it. Live it. Love it.

THE AMAZING POWER OF POE—PROCESS OF ELIMINATION

One fabulous thing about the GRE CAT is that the "best" answer is always on the screen; you don't have to come up with it out of thin air. However, because there are roughly four times as many wrong answers as there are right answers, it's often easier to identify wrong answers than to identify the best one.

POE is your new religion.

THE IMPORTANCE OF WRONG ANSWERS

By using POE, you will be able to improve your score on the GRE by looking for wrong answers instead of for right ones on questions you're having trouble with. Why? Because, once you've found the wrong ones, picking the right one can be a piece of cake.

Wrong answers on standardized multiple-choice tests are known in the testing industry as "distracters." They are called distracters because their purpose is to distract testers away from correct choices on questions they don't understand. This keeps them from earning points accidentally, by picking the right answer for the wrong reasons.

This simple fact will be an enormous help to you. By learning to recognize these distracters, you will greatly improve your score.

IMPROVE YOUR ODDS INDIRECTLY

Every time you are able to eliminate an incorrect choice on a GRE CAT question, you improve your odds of finding the best answer. The more incorrect choices you eliminate, the better your odds.

For this reason, some of our test-taking strategies are aimed at helping you to arrive at ETS's answer indirectly. Doing this will make you much more successful at avoiding the traps laid in your path by the test writers. This is because most of the traps are designed to catch unwary test-takers who try to approach the problems directly.

POE AND GUESSING

If you guessed blindly on a five-choice GRE CAT problem, you would have one chance in five of picking ETS's answer. Eliminate one incorrect choice, and your chances improve to one in four. Eliminate three, and you have a fifty-fifty chance of earning points by guessing. Get the picture? You must answer each question to get to the next one, so you'll have to guess sometimes. Why not improve your odds?

Guess, but guess intelligently.

Use That Paper!

For POE to work, it's crucial that you keep track of what choices you're eliminating. By crossing out a clearly incorrect choice, you permanently eliminate it from consideration. If you don't cross it out, you'll keep considering it. Crossing out incorrect choices can make it much easier to find the "credited response," because there will be fewer places where it can hide. But how can you cross anything out on a computer screen?

By using your scratch paper! Even though on the GRE CAT, the answer choices have empty bubbles next to them, you're going to pretend that they are labeled A, B, C, D, and E (and so are we, throughout this book). And every time you do a question, you will write down A, B, C, D, E on your scratch paper.

A	A	A	A
B	B	B	B
C	C	C	C
D	D	D	D
E	E	E	E
A	A	A	A
B	B	B	B
C	C	C	C
D	D	D	D
E	E	E	E

Carve up at least a couple of pages (front and back) like this. This will give you a bunch of distinct work areas per page, which might be especially helpful for the math section; you don't want to get confused when your work from one question runs into your work from a previous question.

Do this and you can physically cross off choices that you're eliminating. Do it every time you do any GRE CAT question, in this book or anywhere else. Get used to not writing near the question, since you won't be able to on test day.

More About Scratch paper

Speaking of test day, you'll get about six to ten sheets of scratch paper on that fateful day, and although that may be more than enough, it couldn't hurt to have more. You don't want to run out during a section, right? So, why not ask for extra paper before the test starts? Some test centers don't like to give out extra sheets until the initial six are used up, but it couldn't hurt to ask.

Pace Yourself

Remember, you don't get points for speed; the only thing that matters is accuracy. Take as much time as is necessary to work through each problem carefully (as long as you leave some time at the end of the section to fill out the rest of it).

If you miss the question that you're looking at on the screen at any given time, you will need to get at least the next two right just to get your score back up to where it was before (roughly). But if you're making careless errors, you won't even realize you're missing questions. So, careless errors are a definite no-no! And not using POE is like being careless. Keeping track of the choices you've eliminated is being careful.

Always cross off wrong answer choices on your scratch paper.

DOUBLE-CHECK

Get in the habit of double-checking all of your answers before you choose them. Remember, there is no skipping a question and coming back to it later. And once you confirm your answer, that question is out of your life forever. That means, again, that you can't afford to make any careless errors. You must make educated guesses by eliminating as many wrong answers as you can, and making sure your thought process or calculations are sound. And don't worry—you're about to get some help in that department.

AT THE TESTING CENTER

Don't be surprised if you're the only one taking the GRE CAT, or indeed, any test, at your testing center. You'll be asked for two forms of identification; one must be a photo ID. Then an employee will take a digital photograph of you (even worse than your driver's license picture!) before taking you to the computer station where you will take the test. You get a desk, a computer, a keyboard, a mouse, about six to ten pieces of scratch paper, and a pencil. Before the test begins, make sure your desk is sturdy and you have enough light, and don't be afraid to speak up if you want to move.

If there are other people in the room, they might not be taking the GRE CAT. They could be taking a nursing test, or a licensing exam for architects. And none of the other people will have necessarily started their exams at the same time. The testing center employee will get you set up at your computer, but from then on, the computer itself will act as your proctor. It will tell you how much time you have left in a section, when time is up, and when to move on to the next section.

If you need more scratch paper, or have a question, the test center employees will be available because they will be monitoring the testing room for security purposes with closed-circuit television. But don't worry, you won't even notice. It's like you're spending a very long time at an ATM!

THE TUTORIAL

Before the actual test begins, you'll get an interactive tutorial on how to take the test, computer-wise. Even a computer novice should have no problem with this extremely simple interface. You'll learn how to use the mouse, select an answer, move on to the next question, see how much time you have left in a section, and even stop the test if you need to (but you won't need to). Take as much time as you need to practice each of these functions and get comfortable with your surroundings, the computer and mouse, and the test directions; there is no time limit on the tutorial.

Use the time you have during the tutorial to set up your scratch paper, jot down the step-by-step strategies for each section of the test, and note any math formulas or vocabulary words you always have trouble remembering. You can do whatever you want with this paper and this time, so use them both wisely.

Remember, you can ask for extra paper too. Take as much as you can get. If you have to request more scratch paper during the test, try to do so between the timed sections. But talk to the proctor at the test center before the test begins to make whatever arrangements are necessary to ensure that you will have plenty of scratch paper.

LET IT GO

When you begin a new section, focus on that section and put the last one behind you. Don't think about that pesky antonym from an earlier section while a geometry question is on your screen now. You can't go back, and besides, your impression of how you did on a section is probably much worse than reality.

THIS IS THE END

When you're done with the test, the computer will ask you (twice) if you want this test to count. If you say "no," the computer will not record your score, no schools will ever see it, and neither will you. You can't look at your score and THEN decide whether you want to keep it or not. And you can't change your mind later. If you say you want the test to count, the computer will give you your score right there on the screen. A few weeks later, you'll receive your verified score in the mail (but no copy of the test you took!). And you can't change your mind and cancel it.

TEST DAY

- Dress in layers, so that you'll be comfortable regardless of whether the room is cool or warm.

- Don't bother bringing a calculator; you're not allowed to use one.

- Be sure to have breakfast, or lunch, depending on the time for which your test is scheduled (but don't eat anything, you know, "weird"). And take it easy on the liquids and the caffeine.

- Do a few GRE practice problems to warm up your brain. Don't try to tackle difficult new questions, but review a few questions that you've done before to help you review the problem-solving strategies for each section of the GRE CAT. This will also help you put your "game-face" on and get you into test mode.

- Make sure to bring two forms of identification, one with a recent photograph, to the test center. Acceptable forms of identification include your driver's license, photo-bearing employee ID cards, and valid passports.

- If you registered by mail, you must also bring the authorization voucher sent to you by ETS.

What to Bring to the Test Center:

1. your registration ticket
2. a photo ID and one other form of ID
3. a reliable watch
4. several pencils
5. a snack

The Week Before the Test

A week before the test is not the time for any major life changes. This is NOT the week to quit smoking, start smoking, quit drinking coffee, start drinking coffee, start a relationship, end a relationship, or quit a job. Business as usual, okay?

Remember: Stay Current

The information in this book is accurate right now, and will be updated yearly. But remember, the publishing business is such that if the test changed tomorrow (which it won't), the book might be a little behind. But the web sites won't be. So, before you take your CAT, check out www.gre.org or www.review.com to see if there is any last minute CAT news.

For the latest on the GRE CAT, check www.review.com or www.gre.org.

PART ◆ II

How to Crack the Verbal Section

3

The Geography of the
Verbal Section

Every GRE CAT contains a scored verbal section, which lasts thirty minutes and contains thirty questions, in no particular order, broken down as follows:

- Six to eight analogies
- Five to seven sentence completions
- Eight to ten antonyms
- Two to four reading comprehension passages, with a total of six to ten questions

Most of the time, the verbal section starts with a few antonyms. Analogies and antonyms are classified by ETS as "vocabulary" problems, and sentence completions and reading comprehension are classified as "reading" problems. You might not see Reading Comp until question eight or twelve. Generally, the higher you're scoring, the more "vocabulary" questions you'll see. Vocabulary is a big part of all these question types, but so is strategy.

POE is your new religion

POE

There is never a "right" answer to a verbal question. ETS calls the correct answer the "credited response," or "best" answer. Think of the best answer as the one that is the least bad. So, if you can recognize the bad answers and eliminate them, you can zero in on the best answer. That's how process of elimination (POE) works. However, if you're not sure what a word in an answer choice means, *don't eliminate it*. It might be the best answer. Only eliminate answers you *know* are wrong.

SCRATCH PAPER

You're going to learn strategies for all four types of verbal questions. So the first thing you should do during the tutorial on the actual GRE CAT is write down all the strategies on your scratch paper, so you never have to think, "What should I do next?"

You may be tempted to do the verbal questions in your head. Don't. Use your scratch paper, not only for jotting down strategy, but also for POE. Always write down A, B, C, D, E on your scratch paper so you can physically cross out choices you're eliminating.

THE IMPORTANCE OF VOCABULARY

You need to get to work on your vocabulary right away, because of the heavy emphasis on vocabulary on the GRE. Most people seem to find that increasing their verbal scores is more difficult than increasing their math scores. The reason for this is that vocabulary places something of a ceiling on your score. The better your vocabulary, the higher your ceiling and the higher your possible scores.

The best way to build a good vocabulary is to read a wide variety of good books over the course of a lifetime. Since you don't have a lifetime to prepare for the GRE, you should turn ahead to page 78, the GRE CAT Hit Parade. It contains a relatively short vocabulary list of the words that are most frequently tested on the GRE. It also contains some solid vocabulary-building advice. Skim through it right now and plan a vocabulary-building program for yourself. You should work on your vocabulary a little bit every day while you work through the rest of the book.

Using your newly-strengthened vocabulary as a foundation, you will be able to take full advantage of the powerful problem-solving techniques we describe in the next four chapters. Our techniques will enable you to get as much mileage as possible from the words you do know. But the more words you know, the better.

Three kinds of words

Think of vocabulary words in terms of these three categories:

- **Words you know**—These are words you can define accurately. If you can't give a definition of a word that's pretty close to what a dictionary would say, then it's not a word you know.

- **Words you sort of know**—These are words you've seen or heard before, or maybe even used yourself, but can't define accurately. You may have a sense of how these words are used, but beware! Day-to-day usage is often different from the dictionary meanings of words, and *the only meanings that count on the GRE are those given in the dictionary*. You have to treat these words very differently from the words you can define. After you encounter a word you sort of know in this book, be sure to look it up in the dictionary, and make it a word you know from then on.

- **Words you've never seen**—You can expect to see some words in this book you've never seen before. After you encounter a word like this, *go to the dictionary and look it up!* If it's been on one GRE, there's a good bet it will show up again. If you've never seen one of the words in an answer choice, *don't eliminate that choice*. Focus on the answer choices for which you can define the words.

> Start working on your vocabulary now.

4

Analogies

WHAT YOU WILL SEE

The verbal section of your GRE CAT will contain eight to ten analogies.

ETS's Directions

ALWAYS write A, B, C, D, E on your scratch paper to represent the answer choices.

Take a minute to read the following set of directions. These are the directions exactly as they will appear on your GRE. You shouldn't even glance at them when you take the test. If you do, you will waste time and lose points. Read them now and you'll never have to read them again:

> Directions: In each of the following questions, a related pair of words or phrases is followed by five pairs of words or phrases. Select the pair that best expresses a relationship similar to that expressed in the original pair.

What Is an Analogy?

An analogy tests your ability to recognize pairs of words that have similar relationships. Your job is to figure out the relationship between the original pair of words, we'll call them the "stem words," and find an answer choice in which the words have the same relationship.

Let's look at an example.

FRICTION : ABRASION ::
- ○ sterility : cleanliness
- ○ dam : flood
- ○ laceration : wound
- ○ heat : evaporation
- ○ literacy : ignorance

Make a Sentence!

In this example, we know from the directions that a related pair of words or phrases is followed by five pairs of words or phrases. So ETS considers the words "friction" and "abrasion" related in some way. What's the relationship? If you can define both of the stem words, your first step in solving a GRE analogy is to make a simple sentence that shows the relationship between the stem words. We would say, "Friction causes abrasion." We wouldn't say, "Abrasive substances can sometimes simulate a feeling of friction." Get it? Don't tell a story. Just define one word in terms of the other. In other words, make a "defining" sentence.

PROCESS OF ELIMINATION

The best answer to an analogy will be the pair of words in an answer choice that has the same relationship as the original pair. So use Process of Elimination. The words have to fit exactly in the sentence you made for the original pair of words. If you know the words in the answer choice, and they don't fit into the sentence, eliminate that choice. Be sure to cross off answer choices on your scratch paper! If you're not sure you can define the words in an answer choice, don't eliminate that choice!

Let's look at our example:

FRICTION : ABRASION ::

- ◯ sterility : cleanliness
- ◯ dam : flood
- ◯ laceration : wound
- ◯ heat : evaporation
- ◯ literacy : ignorance

Do you know the DICTIONARY DEFINITION of the word?

(A) Does "sterility cause cleanliness"? No. So cross off choice (A) on your scratch paper.

(B) Does a "dam cause a flood"? No. Eliminate this choice.

(C) Does a "laceration cause a wound"? Nope. Get rid of this choice.

(D) Does "heat cause evaporation"? Maybe. Let's keep this choice and look at the last choice.

(E) Does "literacy cause ignorance"? No way.

So, by process of elimination, the best choice to this analogy must be (D), "heat : evaporation."

DEFINE ONE OF THE WORDS IN TERMS OF THE OTHER WORD

Always try to make your sentence define one of the words in terms of the other. Try to keep it short and simple. Let's try another example.

LISTLESS : EXCITE ::

- ◯ stuffy : brag
- ◯ skeptical : convince
- ◯ industrious : produce
- ◯ scholarly : instruct
- ◯ impenetrable : ignore

Here's how to crack it

We could express the relationship between the stem words in several different ways. We could say, "Someone listless is difficult to excite," Or we could put it, "Listless means difficult to excite." It doesn't matter which we choose. We don't need to find the *perfect* sentence. **All that matters is that you find a sentence that expresses the relationship between the stem words.**

Let's go through the answer choices.

(A) Does "stuffy" mean difficult to "brag"? No. So cross off this choice.

(B) Does "skeptical" mean difficult to "convince"? Yes, but don't stop here. You should check every answer choice.

(C) Does "industrious" mean difficult to "produce"? No. So we can eliminate this choice.

(D) Does "scholarly" mean difficult to "instruct"? No. Eliminate.

(E) Does "impenetrable" mean difficult to "ignore"? No. So this choice doesn't work either. The best answer is (B). Notice how the words in choice (B) fit *exactly* into our sentence.

DO YOU HAVE TO MAKE A SENTENCE FROM LEFT TO RIGHT?

No. Sometimes it's easier to define the second word in terms of the first. Do it! Just be sure to plug in the answer choices in the same order that you used to make your sentence.

WRITE IT DOWN!

This can't be stressed enough. If you try to make your sentence "in your head," you might forget it after you try a few answer choices. Then you would have to go back to the stem words and start all over. Even worse, if you try to "remember" your sentence, you might change it to agree with one of the answer choices. That defeats the whole purpose of Process of Elimination!

So remember, always write your sentence on your scratch paper. If you make your sentence from right to left, draw an arrow indicating this for that question to remind you to plug in the answer choices from right to left.

COMMON GRE RELATIONSHIPS

Certain relationships show up frequently on the GRE CAT. If you are very familiar with these relationships, it will be easier for you to make good sentences for the stem words on many analogies questions. Try the following drill to learn some common relationships:

DRILL

Make a sentence for each of the following pair of stem words. You don't have to make your sentence from left to right. Go in the direction that makes the most definitive sentence. (Check your work on page 38.)

STEM WORDS	YOUR SENTENCE
ORGAN : KIDNEY	_____
CENTRIFUGE : SEPARATE	_____
LASSITUDE : ENERGY	_____
FERVOR : ZEALOT	_____
EULOGY : PRAISE	_____
FRUIT: APPLE	_____
MISER : THRIFT	_____
COMPLIANT : SERVILE	_____
LUBRICANT : ABRASION	_____
INEVITABLE : CHANCE	_____

Do you know the DICTIONARY DEFINITIONS of the words in the answer choices?

Now try another example:

ETERNAL : END ::
- ⬭ precursory : beginning
- ⬭ grammatical : sentence
- ⬭ implausible : credibility
- ⬭ invaluable : worth
- ⬭ frenetic : movement

Here's how to crack it

This is a very common relationship on the GRE. "Eternal means without end," would be the perfect sentence.

(A) Does "precursory" mean without "beginning"? If you're not sure, keep this choice. By the way, take a minute to look up the word "precursor;" it's on the Hit Parade.

(B) Does "grammatical" mean without "sentence"? No, so you can definitely cross off this choice.

(C) Does "implausible" mean without "credibility"? Yes. So let's keep this choice and consider the others.

(D) Does "invaluable" mean without "worth"? No, just the opposite. Eliminate this one.

(E) Does "frenetic" mean without "movement"? No. So this choice doesn't work. The best answer is (C). Notice how the words in choice (C) fit *exactly* into our sentence.

GET MORE SPECIFIC

What happens when more than one answer choice fits your first sentence? Did you make a mistake? No, you might just need to get more specific. Your first sentence should be simple and definitive. Use it to eliminate as many answer choices as you can. But then add information to your first sentence to make it more specific.

DOLPHIN : MAMMAL ::

- ○ larva : insect
- ○ penguin : bird
- ○ sonnet : stanza
- ○ computer : machine
- ○ peninsula : island

Here's how to crack it

If you can't define a word, DON'T eliminate it.

This is another very common relationship on the GRE. "A dolphin is a type of mammal," would be the right sentence with which to begin.

(A) Is a "larva" a type of "insect"? Well, strictly speaking, no. But as always, if you're not sure, keep this choice.

(B) Is a "penguin" a type of "bird"? Definitely, let's keep this choice.

(C) Is a "sonnet" a type of "stanza"? No, so we can get rid of this one.

(D) Is a "computer" a type of "machine"? Yes, so let's keep this one, too.

(E) Is a "peninsula" a type of "island"? No. So this choice doesn't work.

Now, we're left with a few choices that all seem okay. How can we make our original sentence more specific to weed out the wrong answers? A dolphin is *what type* of mammal? A dolphin is a type of mammal that lives in the water. Is a larva a type of insect that lives in the water? No. Ditch it! Is a penguin a type of bird that lives in water? Close enough. Is a computer a type of machine that lives in the water? Not by a long shot. The best answer is (B).

PARTS OF SPEECH

If the first stem word is a verb and the second is an adjective, the first word in each answer choice will be a verb and the second will be an adjective. ETS never violates this principle. Use it to your advantage.

You may sometimes have trouble determining the part of speech of one of the words in the stem. If this happens, look at the answer choices. ETS uses one of the choices to "establish the parts of speech" when one of the stem words is ambiguous. In other words, if you aren't sure about the words in the stem, check the words in the choices. The parts of speech should be clear from at least one of the choices.

Always determine the parts of speech before you make your sentence for the stem words.

Try this example:

GREEN : EXPERIENCE ::

- ○ ungainly : grace
- ○ rank : knowledge
- ○ indolent : laziness
- ○ impassioned : ardor
- ○ dispirited : despondence

Here's how to crack it

Notice not only that "green" is an adjective, which you can see from the first answer choice, but also that a secondary meaning is being tested. The first meaning we think of is the color green. But what does it mean if a *person* is "green"? Here, green means "lacking experience."

- (A) Does "ungainly" mean lacking "grace"? If you're not sure, keep this choice.
- (B) Does "rank" mean lacking "knowledge"? No, so you can definitely cross off this choice.
- (C) Does "indolent" mean lacking "laziness"? If you're not sure, keep this choice.
- (D) Does "impassioned" mean lacking "ardor"? If you're not sure, keep this choice. But really, it means just the opposite. (If you know these words, you can eliminate this choice—so study the Hit Parade!)
- (E) Does "dispirited" mean lacking "despondence"? If you're not sure, keep this choice.

Here's where the vocabulary kicks in. If you know that "green" means lacking "experience," and "ungainly" means lacking "grace," that's what you should guess. We'll discuss guessing in greater detail below. The best answer to this one is (A).

WHAT IF I DON'T KNOW SOME OF THE WORDS IN THE ANSWER CHOICES?

Use PROCESS OF ELIMINATION. Assuming you know both words in the stem, you can still ask yourself whether *any* word could create a relationship in the choice identical to the relationship in the stem. If not, you can eliminate the choice.

Eliminate the answer choices that contain words that you can define and that you know can't be correct. But if you're not sure of the meaning of one of the words in an answer choice, don't eliminate that choice! Then see what you have left.

Example:

> DRAWL : SPEAK ::
> ○ spurt : expel
> ○ foster : develop
> ○ scintillate : flash
> ○ pare : trim
> ○ saunter : walk

Always eliminate UNRELATED answer choices.

Here's how to crack it

Our sentence defining the relationship between the stem words would be "To drawl means to speak slowly."

- (A) Does "spurt" mean to "expel" slowly? No, so eliminate this one. Think about it for a second. Could any word mean to "expel" slowly? It's not likely, since "expel" means to force out.

(B) Does "foster" mean to "develop" slowly? No, so you can definitely cross off this choice.

(C) Does "scintillate" mean to "flash" slowly? If you're not sure, keep this choice.

(D) Does "pare" mean to "trim" slowly? No, so you can eliminate this choice.

(E) Does "saunter" mean to "walk" slowly? If you're not sure, keep this choice.

Now that we're down to two choices, perhaps you know that "saunter" does mean to walk slowly, and it fits our sentence exactly, so it must be the best answer choice. Great. But also, could any word mean "to flash slowly"? No, to flash means to occur or emerge suddenly like a flame. (By the way, look up the word "scintillate.")

WHAT IF I DON'T KNOW ONE OF THE STEM WORDS?

Don't give up if you don't know the stem words!

Now you have a good understanding of the sort of relationship that must exist between stem words and correct answer choices in GRE CAT analogies. Now we're going to show you how to use the same concept to eliminate incorrect answer choices *even if you don't know the meaning of either of the words in the stem.*

REALLY?

How can it be possible to eliminate choices if you don't know the words in the stem? Think about it. Since you know that the stem words must have a relationship, and since the correct answer choice must have a relationship similar to that for the stem words, then the correct answer choice must also have a relationship between the two words. So if the words in an answer choice do NOT have a relationship, that choice cannot be correct! **An answer choice containing two words that aren't related can NEVER be the best answer.**

IMMEDIATELY ELIMINATE NON-RELATIONSHIPS

Try the example below. Notice that we've left out the words in the stem. Eliminate all the answer choices that do not have relationships. That usually won't be enough to narrow it down to only one answer choice; don't worry, you'll soon see what to do *after* you've eliminated non-relationships.

Example:

XXXXX : XXXXX ::

○ precipitous : mountain
○ judicious : system
○ dispersive : discharge
○ strident : sound
○ epidemic : disease

Here's how to crack it

(A) Are "precipitous" and "mountain" related? No. Precipitous means like a precipice, or extremely steep. Is a mountain necessarily precipitous? No. Eliminate this choice; it can't be the best answer choice.

(B) Are "judicious" and "system" related? No. Judicious means having good judgment, and it's a quality of a person, not a system. Eliminate this choice.

(C) Is there a relationship between "dispersive" and "discharge"? No. Dispersive just means tending to disperse. Is a discharge necessarily dispersive? Nope. Cross out this choice.

(D) Is there a relationship between "strident" and "sound"? Perhaps you're not sure what the dictionary definition of "strident" is, so keep this choice.

(E) Is there a relationship between "epidemic" and "disease"? Sure. An epidemic is a disease that spreads rapidly.

So even without knowing anything about the stem words in this analogy, we've gotten it down to two possible choices. There's another technique you should use right about now.

Eliminate unrelated pairs.

WORKING BACKWARDS

Once you've eliminated answer choices that don't have relationships, you may have two or three choices that do have relationships. Don't forget that the relationship between the stem words must be exactly the same relationship as the one between the words in the correct answer. So make a sentence for the words in each related answer choice and work backwards to the stem words. Would the stem words fit exactly in the sentence you make for the answer choice? If not, the relationship for that answer choice can't be the same as the one for the stem words. Eliminate that choice.

Now let's take another look at the problem we were just doing, as it would appear on the GRE CAT with the stem words. Remember, we've already eliminated the first three choices.

NOISOME : ODOR ::

- ◯ precipitous : mountain
- ◯ judicious : system
- ◯ dispersive : discharge
- ◯ strident : sound
- ◯ epidemic : disease

Here's how to crack it

(D) What's the relationship between "strident" and "sound"? If you're not sure, just start with choice (E) instead. But if you can define "strident," then your sentence for this answer choice would be "strident means having a harsh or unpleasant sound." Could "noisome" mean having an unpleasant "odor"? That's certainly possible. Let's go to choice (E). A good sentence for this choice would be "an epidemic is a rapidly spreading disease." Could "noisome" mean a rapidly spreading odor? What do you really think? Between these two choices, which one is more likely? Noisome does mean having a bad odor, so the best choice is (D).

Here's another example of how first eliminating unrelated pairs, and then working backwards, can enable you to zero in on ETS's answer:

LAMENTATION : REMORSE ::
○ reassurance : interactions
○ elegy : sorrow
○ instigation : responses
○ acknowledgment : ideas
○ ornateness : filigree

Here's how to crack it

Let's approach this assuming that you can't exactly define "lamentation."

(A) Is there a relationship between "reassurance" and "interactions"? No. You could tell a convoluted story linking these two words, but we're not going to do that! This can't be the best answer choice.

(B) Is there a relationship between "elegy" and "sorrow"? Maybe you're not exactly sure what "elegy" means at this moment (it's on the Hit Parade, so get to work learning those words). So keep this choice.

(C) Is there a relationship between "instigation" and "responses"? No. Again, you could tell a creative story linking these two words, but ... get rid of it!

(D) Is there a relationship between "acknowledgment" and "ideas"? No. This can't be the best answer choice.

(E) Is there a relationship between "ornateness" and "filigree"? A bit of a stretch, but perhaps. So let's work backwards. What would your sentence be? "Filigree" adds "ornateness" to something. Could "remorse" add "lamentation" to something? It's not likely that remorse adds anything to something.

So, Process of Elimination tells us that the best answer must be choice (B). Notice that when we made our sentence from right to left for answer choice (E), we tried the stem words from right to left in the same sentence. Remember that the best answer choice has to have a relationship just like the one between the stem words. So the stem words have to fit exactly into the sentence you make for the answer choice you're considering.

Don't Eliminate Words You Only "Sort of Know"

Never initially eliminate a choice if you can't absolutely, positively define the meanings of both words in it. You can't be certain that two words are unrelated if you are not really sure what one of them means.

Here's another example:

SUPPLICANT : BESEECHING ::
- ⭕ minister : tortured
- ⭕ coquette : flirtatious
- ⭕ benefactor : cordial
- ⭕ lawyer : articulate
- ⭕ thief : violent

If you only "sort of know" the meaning of a word, DON'T ELIMINATE IT!

Here's how to crack it

Once again, we're assuming that we don't know the meaning of one or both of the words in the stem. Let's eliminate non-related answer choices and work backwards.

(A) Is there a relationship between "minister" and "tortured"? Please. This can't be the best answer choice.

(B) Is there a relationship between "coquette" and "flirtatious"? Maybe, or maybe you're not sure. Keep this choice.

(C) Is there a relationship between "benefactor" and "cordial"? Maybe, or maybe you're not sure. Keep this choice.

(D) Is there a relationship between "lawyer" and "articulate"? No. Cross off this choice.

(E) Is there a relationship between "thief" and "violent"? No. Get rid of this choice.

Now that you're down to only two choices, use whatever you know about the words in those two choices. Focus on the choice for which you have a better sense of the words' meanings. In this case, how would you define a "benefactor"? If you know that a "benefactor" would be defined in terms of providing financial assistance, rather than in terms of some attitude, then you can eliminate choice (C). The connection between "benefactor" and "cordial" just isn't clear. Looks like the answer is (B).

If you've eliminated all the answer choices with words that you know or sort of know, and you're left with a couple of choices with words that you've never seen before, just guess and move on. Your GRE score is going to be much higher if you are guessing between two choices than it would be if you hadn't eliminated those other three choices by using our techniques.

Won't It Take Hours to Apply All These Techniques?

No. With a little practice, you'll make them your automatic way to solve GRE analogies. In fact, they'll save you time by making you much more efficient in your approach to the more difficult questions. Get to work learning the Hit Parade now!

ANSWER KEY—ANALOGIES DRILL

STEM WORDS	YOUR SENTENCE
ORGAN : KIDNEY	The kidney is a **type of** organ.
CENTRIFUGE : SEPARATE	The **function of** a centrifuge is to separate.
LASSITUDE : ENERGY	Lassitude **means a lack of** energy.
FERVOR : ZEALOT	A zealot **is characterized by** fervor.
EULOGY : PRAISE	A eulogy **is a speech** of praise.
FRUIT : APPLE	An apple is a **type of** fruit.
MISER : THRIFT	A miser uses **excessive** thrift.
COMPLIANT : SERVILE	Servile means **excessively** compliant.
LUBRICANT : ABRASION	The **function of** a lubricant is **to prevent** abrasion.
INEVITABLE : CHANCE	Inevitable **means without** chance.

Have you been learning vocabulary?

5

Sentence Completions

WHAT YOU WILL SEE

The verbal section of your GRE CAT will contain five to seven sentence completions.

ETS's DIRECTIONS

Read and learn the following set of directions. These are the directions as they will appear on your GRE CAT. You shouldn't even glance at them when you take the test. Here are the directions:

> <u>Directions</u>: Each sentence below has one or two blanks, each blank indicating that something has been omitted. Beneath the sentence are five words or sets of words. Choose the word or set of words for each blank that <u>best</u> fits the meaning of the sentence as a whole.

Remember grade school? These are like fill in the blanks.

OUR APPROACH TO SENTENCE COMPLETIONS

Our techniques for cracking sentence completions take advantage of the way that these questions are designed: All are based on POE. Sometimes you will be able to use POE to eliminate all four incorrect choices. On every sentence completion, you should be able to eliminate at least a few choices.

"I already know how to do these"

Sentence completions look very familiar—you've known them since kindergarten as *fill in the blanks*—but beware! The way ETS designs these problems is very different from the way that your elementary school or high school teachers made up vocabulary quizzes. GRE sentence completions are more than just a vocabulary test. These questions test your problem-solving skills as well as your vocabulary.

HOW ETS WRITES SENTENCE COMPLETION QUESTIONS

Let's pretend a test writer has a rough idea for a question:

> Museums are good places for students of _____.
> ○ art
> ○ science
> ○ religion
> ○ dichotomy
> ○ democracy

Here's how to crack it

As it's written, this question is unanswerable. Almost any choice could be defended (okay, probably not "dichotomy"). ETS couldn't use this question on a real test.

To make this into a real GRE question, we'd have to change the sentence so that only one of the answer choices can be defended.

Here's another try:

> Museums, which house many paintings and sculptures, are good places for students of
> _____.
>
> ○ art
> ○ science
> ○ religion
> ○ dichotomy
> ○ democracy

Here's how to crack it

Now there's only one justifiable answer: choice (A). The clause added to the original sentence makes this obvious. This clause—containing the words *paintings and sculptures*—is "the clue." The finished question is very easy. Every sentence completion has a clue.

How could this problem become more difficult? With a harder "clue"—by throwing in some moderately difficult vocabulary words:

> Museums, which house many elaborate talismans, are good places for students of _____.
>
> ○ art
> ○ science
> ○ religion
> ○ dichotomy
> ○ democracy

Here's how to crack it

The answer is choice (C). To find it, you need to know that *talismans* are religious amulets or charms.

Here's another try:

> Museums, because they house not just paintings, but paintings that depict human anatomy with great accuracy, are good places for students of _____.
>
> ○ art
> ○ science
> ○ religion
> ○ dichotomy
> ○ democracy

Always write A, B, C, D, E on your scratch paper to represent the answer choices.

Here's how to crack it

Here, the answer is choice (B). Even though you would never think of museums that house paintings as good places for students of science, you can't choose your answer according to what *you* would say. The best answer must be based on the clue in the sentence—regardless of how weird it might be in "real life." And this time, the clue is about anatomy, so the answer is "science."

Let's try another:

> Museums, because they house paintings and sculptures selected to reflect the tastes of the broadest possible segment of the population, are good places for students of _____.
>
> ○ art
> ○ science
> ○ religion
> ○ dichotomy
> ○ democracy

Find the clue(s) for the blank(s).

Here's how to crack it

Here the answer is choice (E). The average person doesn't pick it, because *democracy* is a word not usually associated with *museums*. The average person doesn't take the trouble to decipher the clue, but instead reacts according to what would be true in real life. Most people have heard of art museums and science museums, and as a result, they are strongly attracted to both of those choices.

THE CLUE—LOOK BEFORE YOU LEAP

Many testers read sentence completions quickly, then go immediately to the choices and begin plugging them into the blank(s). Don't do it.

By finding the clue, we can figure out in advance what the word in the blank has to mean. If you take the time to understand what the sentence is really about, you'll have a much easier time finding ETS's answer among the choices.

COVER THE ANSWER CHOICES ON THE SCREEN

Always physically cover the answer choices, read through the entire sentence, then find the clue and write down your own words for the blank on your scratch paper *before* you look at the answer choices.

Here's an example of what we mean. Here's a sentence completion without answer choices:

> Popular songs often _____ the history of a society in that their subjects are frequently the events that have influenced and steered the society.

Here's how to crack it

What does the blank in the sentence refer to? It's about "popular songs" and the "history of a society." Is the GRE a test of what you know about popular songs? Although you may wish it were, ask yourself what you know about popular songs *from the rest of the sentence*? We know that "their subjects are frequently the events that have influenced and steered the society."

So what would be a good word for the blank? The word in the blank has to mean something like "describe," because the clue in the sentence tells us that the subjects of popular songs are frequently the events that have influenced and steered the society. So you'd write "describe" on your scratch paper (and A, B, C, D, E, of course!).

Now that we've figured out what the word in the blank has to mean, let's uncover the answer choices.

> Popular songs often _____ the history of a society in that their subjects are frequently the events that have influenced and steered the society.
>
> ◯ confuse
> ◯ renounce
> ◯ recount
> ◯ foresee
> ◯ confront

Don't look at the answer choices until you've written something down on your scratch paper.

Here's how to crack it

(A) Does *confuse* mean describe? Nope. Eliminate this choice.

(B) Does *renounce* mean describe? No. Cross off this one.

(C) Does *recount* mean describe? Maybe. Let's keep this one.

(D) Does *foresee* mean describe? No, so this can't be the best answer.

(E) Does *confront* mean describe? Well, compare this with choice (C). Which of these comes closest to just meaning "describe"? You can also go back to the sentence. Is there any clue for a confrontational relationship of popular songs to the history of society? No. By using POE, we found out that the best answer must be choice (C).

FINDING YOUR OWN WORDS

After you've identified the clue in the sentence, don't try to think of a "GRE word" for the blank(s)—after all, "describe" is a pretty bland word, but it did the trick just now. You should try to get the proper meaning of the words that go in the blanks, but you shouldn't worry about finding the exact word that ETS will use in the best answer choice. It's perfectly fine to use a phrase to express the meaning that you know would fit. Often you can use a part of the clue from the sentence itself.

Sentence Completion Drill Part 1

In each of the following sentences, find the clue and underline it. Then see if you can anticipate ETS's answer. Write a word or phrase near the blank. It doesn't matter if your guesses are awkward or wordy. All you need to do is express the right idea.

Although a few of the plot twists in her novel were unexpected, overall, the major events depicted in the work were _____ enough.

A recent poll shows that, while 81 percent of college students are eligible for some form of financial aid, only 63 percent of these students are _____ such aid.

A business concerned about its efficiency should pay attention to the actions of its staff, because the mistakes of each of its employees often _____ the effectiveness of the organization of which they are a part.

Langston Hughes's creative works were the highlight, not the _____, of his writings; he was also a prolific writer of nonfiction and political commentary.

SENTENCE COMPLETION DRILL PART 2

Now that you've anticipated ETS's answers, look at the same four questions again, this time with the answer choices provided. Use the words you wrote above to eliminate answer choices. (You can check your answers on page 51.)

Although a few of the plot twists in her novel were unexpected, overall, the major events depicted in the work were _____ enough.

- ○ lively
- ○ well developed
- ○ predictable
- ○ complex
- ○ creative

A recent poll shows that, while 81 percent of college students are eligible for some form of financial aid, only 63 percent of these students are _____ such aid.

- ○ complaining about
- ○ recipients of
- ○ dissatisfied with
- ○ paying for
- ○ turned down for

A business concerned about its efficiency should pay attention to the actions of its staff, because the mistakes of each of its employees often _____ the effectiveness of the organization of which they are a part.

- ○ remake
- ○ provoke
- ○ celebrate
- ○ undermine
- ○ control

Langston Hughes's creative works were the highlight, not the _____, of his writings; he was also a prolific writer of nonfiction and political commentary.

- ○ peculiarity
- ○ product
- ○ initiator
- ○ average
- ○ entirety

TRIGGER WORDS

Besides the clue, certain words signal changes in the meaning or direction of a sentence. We call them trigger words. They provide important structural indicators of the meaning of the sentence, and they are often the key to figuring out which words will best fill in the blanks in a sentence completion.

Here are some of the most important sentence completion trigger words and punctuation:

- but
- although
- unless
- rather
- yet
- previously

- while
- however
- unfortunately
- in contrast
- despite

- thus
- similarly
- and
- therefore
- heretofore
- semicolon and colon

Trigger words help you to find the relationship between the two blanks. Are they the same or opposites?

Notice that words like "thus" and "and" indicate that one part of the sentence is similar in meaning to the other, whereas words like "but" and "however" indicate an opposite direction. Paying attention to trigger words is crucial to understanding the meaning of the sentence. Here's an example of a sentence completion question in which finding ETS's answer depends on understanding the function of a trigger word:

> In American film, some character actors have found it _____ to gain widespread recognition, although within the smaller community of actors, directors, and producers they are highly regarded.
>
> ○ difficult
> ○ acceptable
> ○ unsatisfactory
> ○ relatively simple
> ○ discouraging

Here's how to crack it

What does the blank refer to? The blank is describing how some actors have found gaining widespread recognition. What's the clue in the sentence that tells us how these actors have found it? We know that "within the smaller community of actors, directors, and producers they are highly regarded." So, have these actors found it easy or hard to gain recognition?

Did you notice the trigger word *although*? This indicates a contrast in the meaning of the sentence. So *although* these actors are highly regarded in the smaller community, they have found it hard to gain widespread recognition. Write the word *hard* on your scratch paper, then uncover the answer choices and use the process of elimination.

(A) Does *difficult* mean *hard*? Yes. This looks good, but be sure to check every answer choice.

(B) Does *acceptable* mean *hard*? No. Eliminate this choice.

(C) Does *unsatisfactory* mean *hard*? No. Eliminate this choice.

(D) Does *relatively simple* mean *hard*? No. Eliminate this choice.

(E) Does *discouraging* mean *hard*? No. Eliminate this choice.

So the best answer choice is (A). By the way, punctuation can also act as a trigger. For example, a semicolon would indicate something similar will follow.

POSITIVE/NEGATIVE

You should always try to come up with your own word for each blank. In some cases, however, you may think of *several* words that could go in the blanks or, you might have a "feeling" instead of a word. Rather than spend a lot of time trying to find the "perfect" word, just ask yourself whether the missing word will be a "good" word (one with positive connotations) or a "bad" word (one with negative connotations). Then write a + or a – symbol on your scratch paper.

Here's an example:

If you can't come up with exact words, write positive or negative for the blank(s) on your scratch paper.

> Despite the fact that over time the originally antagonistic response to his sculpture had lessened, to this day, hardly any individuals _____ his art.
>
> ○ applaud
> ○ castigate
> ○ evaluate
> ○ denounce
> ○ ignore

Here's how to crack it

What's the blank describing? How individuals react to the artist's work. What's the clue in the sentence? We know that "the originally antagonistic response to his sculpture had lessened." So how are people now responding? Again, notice how the trigger word in this sentence helps you decide what the word in the blank has to mean. The word "despite" indicates that even though the originally antagonistic response had lessened, hardly any individuals responded *positively* to his art. Write a + sign on your scratch paper before you uncover the answer choices.

(A) Is *applaud* a positive word? Sure, let's keep it and go to the other choices.

(B) Is *castigate* a positive word? Perhaps, or maybe you're not sure, so keep it and consider the other choices. (It's on the Hit Parade, so you should know this word before you take the GRE CAT!)

(C) Is *evaluate* a positive word? No, so eliminate this choice.

(D) Is *denounce* a positive word? No, so cross off this choice.

(E) Is *ignore* a positive word? No, so get rid of this choice.

Now that you're down to two choices, what do you do? Well, you know that *applaud* is a positive word, and you know that the word in the blank has to be a positive word; if you're not sure whether *castigate* is a positive word, then guess choice (A). In fact, choice (A) is the best answer choice. Do you see how important it is to figure out what the blank has to mean *before* you go to the answer choices?

Use POE. On two-blank sentences, eliminate entire answer choices using one blank at a time.

TWO BLANKS: ELIMINATE CHOICES ONE BLANK AT A TIME

Many sentence completions will have two blanks rather than just one. This doesn't mean that two-blank sentence completions are more difficult to solve than one-blank sentence completions. **Two-blank sentence completions are harder than one-blank sentence completions only if you insist on trying to fill in both blanks at the same time.**

You'll do much better if you concentrate on just one of the blanks at a time. A two-blank answer choice can be the best only if it works for *both* of the blanks; if you can determine that one of the words in the choice doesn't work in its blank, you can eliminate that choice without checking the other word. Which blank should you concentrate on? The one you have a better clue for. Often, this will be the second blank.

Once you've decided which blank you have a better clue for, and have written down a word for it, go to the answer choices and look *only* at the ones provided for that blank. Then eliminate any choice that doesn't work for that blank.

Here's an example of how you can crack a two-blank sentence completion by tackling it one blank at a time:

> In contrast to physicists who base their research on scientific theory, he modeled his procedure on rigorous _____; so despite the fact that his method was less sophisticated, his results were _____ sound.
>
> ◯ fiction . . methodologically
> ◯ abstraction . . arguably
> ◯ intuition . . scientifically
> ◯ observation . . factually
> ◯ speculation . . implicitly

Here's how to crack it

What is the first blank describing? It's talking about how the physicist modeled his procedure. What clue does the sentence give us for how his procedure was modeled? You know that it was modeled "in contrast to physicists who base their research on scientific theory." So, the word for the first blank has to mean something that's the opposite of *theory*. Go to the first words in the answer choices.

(A) Is *fiction* the opposite of *theory*? No. We're still talking about a physicist after all. So we can eliminate this entire choice.

(B) Is *abstraction* the opposite of *theory*? No, it's the same. So we can eliminate this whole answer choice.

(C) Is *intuition* the opposite of *theory*? No. Again, the sentence is still talking about a scientist. So we can eliminate this entire choice.

(D) Is *observation* the opposite of *theory*? Sure. Let's keep this one.

(E) Is *speculation* the opposite of *theory*? No, it's very similar. We can get rid of this answer choice too.

Have you been learning vocabulary?

Wow, the only answer left is (D)! You won't *always* be able to eliminate all four wrong answer choices using just one blank, the way we could on this example, so *always be sure to check that the second word works in the other blank.*

MORE ON TWO-BLANK QUESTIONS

Looking for positive and negative words is especially useful on two-blank sentence completions. Trigger words and punctuation are also especially important on questions with two blanks.

Trigger words like *although* and *but* show that the relationship between the two blanks involves an opposition (–/+ or +/–); trigger words like *and* and *thus* show that the relationship between the two blanks involves a similarity (–/– or +/+). Using this information, you can confidently eliminate any choice with a different arrangement. This is a useful POE technique even when you have your own words for the blanks. Cross out choices that don't fit the pattern.

Try this example:

> Although he asserted his theology was derived from _____ school of thought, it actually utilizes conventions from many religions and so it rightfully could be described as having _____ origins.
>
> ○ a particular . . diverse
> ○ a cogent . . multitalented
> ○ a prominent . . coherent
> ○ an influential . . reductive
> ○ a single . . consonant

Here's how to crack it

What are the two blanks describing? His theology. What clue does the sentence provide? We know that "it actually utilizes conventions from many religions." So the word for the second blank has to mean something like "composed of many parts." What about the first blank? Notice the trigger word *although* at the beginning of the sentence. From this trigger word, we know that the words for the two blanks will be opposites. Let's eliminate answer choices on the basis of the second blank first.

(A) Does *diverse* mean "composed of many parts"? Maybe. Let's keep it and try to eliminate other choices.

(B) Does *multitalented* mean "composed of many parts"? Maybe. Leave this in. And remember, the blanks are talking about someone's theology.

(C) Does *coherent* mean "composed of many parts"? No. Eliminate this.

(D) Does *reductive* mean "composed of many parts"? No, so we can eliminate this whole answer choice.

(E) Does *consonant* mean "composed of many parts"? If you're not sure, don't eliminate it.

Use that paper!

Now that we're down to three choices, let's look at the *relationship* between the two words in the remaining answer choices. Remember, we've determined that the two words should be nearly *opposite* in meaning.

(A) Is *a particular* the opposite of *diverse*? Yes. This choice is looking good.

(B) Is *a cogent* the opposite of *multitalented*? If you aren't sure, then you can't eliminate this choice.

(E) Is *a single* the opposite of *consonant*? Well, if you don't know exactly what *consonant* means, it's tough to say. But once again, you do know that the best answer must be two words that are opposites, and you know that *diverse* works well in the second blank, so you should guess choice (A). In fact, that's the best answer choice.

Let's try another example:

> The notion that socialism inhibits individual expression is supported by historical studies that have shown that individualism has _____ only in societies where socialist programs have been _____.
>
> ○ diminished . . debated
> ○ thrived . . abandoned
> ○ grown . . fostered
> ○ triumphed . . improved
> ○ wallowed . . restrained

Here's how to crack it

What's the clue in this sentence? Remember not to use your own knowledge to fill in the blanks. The sentence tells us, "The notion that socialism inhibits individual expression is supported by historical studies . . . . " Now, what's the relationship between the blanks? In this case, we know from the clue that the words for the two blanks are going to be opposites. It could be that the word for the first blank is positive and the one for the second blank is negative, or vice versa. No problem. Just eliminate all the answer choices for which the two words are *not opposites*.

(A) Is *diminished* the opposite of *debated*? No, so eliminate this choice.

(B) Is *thrived* the opposite of *abandoned*? Maybe. Let's keep this choice and consider the rest of the choices.

(C) Is *grown* the opposite of *fostered*? No. So eliminate this choice.

(D) Is *triumphed* the opposite of *improved*? No. So eliminate this choice.

(E) Is *wallowed* the opposite of *restrained*? Well, maybe you're not sure exactly what *wallowed* means. Again, concentrate on the information that you know for sure.

We know from the clue that socialism inhibits individualism. So would individualism *thrive* when socialism is *abandoned*? Sure. Choice (B) is the best answer.

ANSWER KEY — SENTENCE COMPLETION PART 2

1. C
2. B
3. D
4. E

6
Antonyms

WHAT YOU WILL SEE

The verbal section of your GRE CAT will contain at least eight to ten antonyms. They usually start off the section. The first five questions in the verbal section tend to mix antonyms and analogies, but you will almost always see an antonym first.

ETS's Directions

Take a minute to read the following set of directions. These are the directions as they will appear on your GRE. Read them now and you'll never have to read them again:

> Directions: Each question below consists of a word printed in capital letters, followed by five words or phrases. Choose the word or phrase that is most nearly opposite in meaning to the word in capital letters.
>
> Since some of the questions require you to distinguish fine shades of meaning, be sure to consider all the choices before deciding which one is best.

Yes, There Really are Techniques

You CAN improve your scores!

You may think that doing well on antonyms all comes down to vocabulary; that is, if you have a big vocabulary, you'll do well on antonyms, and if you have a tiny vocabulary, you'll have trouble. And, for the most part, you're right. The best way to improve your antonym score *is* to improve your GRE vocabulary. So if you haven't begun studying our GRE CAT Hit Parade (see chapter 8), definitely start now.

But even though a big vocabulary makes antonyms easier to crack, we do have techniques that can enable you to squeeze the maximum number of points out of any vocabulary. These techniques are based on our new friend POE.

Approaching Antonyms

Remember, there are three types of words on the GRE:

- Words you know
- Words you sort of know
- Words you have never seen

Your approach to antonyms will vary depending on the type of word that you are dealing with. Since you are studying the Hit Parade, you may find that you can now define some more words.

But you have to be extremely honest with yourself! It's better to be conservative, and to admit that you only "sort of" know a word, than to think you can define a word when you really can't.

WHEN YOU CAN DEFINE THE STEM WORD

When you are absolutely sure that you know what the stem word means, don't just jump at the first choice that looks right. Even ETS warns you in the directions to check all of the answer choices. Avoid careless errors by using the following steps:

- As usual, write down A, B, C, D, E on your scratch paper.

- Cover the answer choices on the screen.

- Write down your own simple opposite for the stem word.

- Uncover the answers and use POE.
    - ~ At first, eliminate the answer choices that are nowhere near your own opposite for the stem word.
    - ~ Next, make opposites for the choices that remain and work backwards to the stem word.

Try this example:

BELITTLE
- ◯ lessen
- ◯ intensify
- ◯ compliment
- ◯ begrudge
- ◯ fawn

Improving your vocabulary is the single most important thing you can do to improve your verbal score.

Here's how to crack it

We can define *belittle*, right? It means something like "to put down." So our own opposite would be a word such as "praise."

(A) Does *lessen* mean "praise"? No. Cross out (A) on your scratch paper.

(B) Does *intensify* mean "praise"? No. Cross out (B) on your scratch paper.

(C) Does *compliment* mean "praise"? Yes. Keep it.

(D) Does *begrudge* mean "praise"? No. Cross out (D) on your scratch paper.

(E) Does *fawn* mean "praise"? Well, it's close. Let's make an opposite for *fawn* just to be sure. *Fawn* means to flatter excessively. The opposite would be to ignore. So it's not quite right.

The best answer is choice (C).

Let's do another one:

PRIM
- ○ enormous
- ○ unsuitable
- ○ arid
- ○ healthy
- ○ slight

Here's how to crack it

Let's assume we can define *prim*. It means something like "proper," so our own word for the opposite would be something like "improper."

(A) Does *enormous* mean "improper"? No, so cross out (A) on your scratch paper.

(B) Does *unsuitable* mean "improper"? Yes, so hang on to this one.

(C) Does *arid* mean "improper"? No, so cross out (C) on your scratch paper.

(D) Does *healthy* mean "improper"? No, so cross out (D) on your scratch paper.

(E) Does *slight* mean "improper"? No, so cross out (E) on your scratch paper.

The answer is choice (B).

So, when you know all of the words in the problem it's pretty easy to eliminate the wrong answers, but what do you do if you don't?

WHEN YOU "SORT OF KNOW" THE STEM WORD

What do you do when you come across a word that you can correctly use in a sentence, but can't quite come up with a Webster-perfect definition for? Let's take a look.

POSITIVE/NEGATIVE

Sometimes you can't define a stem word, but you do know whether it has a positive or negative connotation. If the stem word has a positive connotation, its antonym has to be negative, so you can eliminate positive answer choices. If the stem word is negative, eliminate negative choices.

Write a + sign down on your scratch paper if the stem word is positive, and a – sign if the stem word is negative. Then write down + or – next to the A, B, C, D, E you've already written down, depending on whether the corresponding word is positive or negative. Don't forget that you're looking for the *opposite* of the stem.

Try using positive/negative on this example:

DEBILITATE
- ○ discharge
- ○ strengthen
- ○ undermine
- ○ squelch
- ○ delete

Do you really know the definition of the word? Or do you only "sort of know" it?

Here's how to crack it

Let's say we're not entirely sure what *debilitate* means, but we know it's a negative word. Since *debilitate* is negative, the antonym must be positive, so we can eliminate negative answer choices. That gets rid of choices (C), (D), and (E). Right now, we're left with (A) and (B).

WORKING BACKWARDS FROM THE ANSWER CHOICES

Instead of taking a guess here, let's take each remaining answer choice and turn it into its opposite. Then we can compare it with the word in capital letters. That way, we can see if one of those opposites could mean the same thing as "debilitate." Doing this can sometimes trigger in your memory an accurate definition of the word.

   (A) *Discharge* means to let out. Could *debilitate* mean to keep in? Not really.

   (B) Could *debilitate* mean to weaken? That's what it means. The ETS answer is choice (B).

Let's try it again:

MALADROIT
- ill-willed
- dexterous
- cowardly
- enduring
- sluggish

Here's how to crack it

Let's assume you aren't sure what *maladroit* means, but you "sort of know" that it's a negative word. That eliminates choices (A), (C), and (E). Not bad at all. Now work backwards by turning each remaining choice into its opposite and see what you have:

(B) clumsy

(D) short-lived

   After you turn each word into its opposite, compare it to the capitalized word and determine whether it could mean the same thing.

     Could *maladroit* mean *clumsy*?

     Could *maladroit* mean *short-lived*?

   If no choice presents itself yet, eliminate the least likely choices, one at a time, and try to zero in on ETS's answer. Simply spending a few extra seconds on the question often makes something click in your mind, showing you what ETS is up to. The answer to this question is choice (B). Look it up.

ELIMINATE CHOICES THAT DON'T HAVE OPPOSITES

What's the opposite of *chair*? What's the opposite of *flower*? What's the opposite of *philosophy*?

   These words have no clear opposites. If they were choices on an antonym question on the GRE, you could cross them out automatically, even if you didn't

> Down to two choices? Make opposites of the choices and work backward.

know the meaning of the word in capital letters. Why? Because if a choice *has no* opposite, the stem word can't possibly *be* its opposite.

Here's an example:

CARNAL
- ○ sensual
- ○ aural
- ○ oral
- ○ unusual
- ○ spiritual

Here's how to crack it

Have you been learning vocabulary?

Let's assume we don't know the meaning of *carnal*. Work through the choices, turning each into its opposite:

(A) There's no clear opposite. Cross it out.

(B) If you don't know this word, *don't* cross it out!

(C) There's no clear opposite. Cross it out.

(D) usual

(E) earthly

Doing this improves our guessing odds to one in three. Not bad. Our chances of finding ETS's answer now depend on whether narrowing down our choices has made anything click in our minds. By the way, the answer is (E); *carnal* means *earthly*.

WORD ASSOCIATION

Sometimes you're not sure what the stem word means, but you've heard it used with another word or phrase. Use that knowledge to help you eliminate incorrect answer choices, and maybe jog your memory of a word's meaning.

ALLEVIATE
- ○ alienate
- ○ worsen
- ○ revitalize
- ○ aerate
- ○ elevate

Here's how to crack it

You're not exactly sure what *alleviate* means. However, you've probably heard it used in the phrase "alleviate pain." Make opposites for the answer choices and plug them into your phrase.

(A) Does "welcome pain" make any sense? Not really.

(B) Does "improve pain" make any sense? Sort of.

(C) Does "debilitate pain" make any sense? Not really.

(D) Does "suffocate pain" make any sense? Not really.

(E) Does "lower pain" make any sense? Maybe.

You've narrowed it down, and maybe by now you realize choice (B) looks good. This technique won't necessarily eliminate all of the incorrect answer choices, but it can help you narrow them down.

COMBINE TECHNIQUES

Don't be afraid to combine all of these techniques. Sometimes you can eliminate a couple of choices by using positive/negative, then use word association on the choices that remain. Don't forget to work backwards when you are down to two choices.

SECONDARY MEANINGS

ETS likes to use the secondary meanings of words—in other words, a meaning of a word that doesn't come to your mind right away. (Isn't that just like them?)
Try this example:

CATHOLIC

- uncharitable
- reticent
- specialized
- irreverent
- reckless

Check parts of speech if you think the word seems "easy."

Here's how to crack it

What's the first meaning you think of? The religion? What's the opposite? It doesn't have one.

CHECK THE PARTS OF SPEECH

You can determine the parts of speech in the same way you would on analogy questions. To figure out whether the stem word is a noun, a verb, or an adjective, just check the answer choices. You can see from choice (A) in the example above that the stem word *catholic* is an adjective, because *uncharitable* is an adjective. Let's work backwards with the answer choices:

(A) Could *catholic* mean "charitable"? Sounds like a trap. ETS wants you to think about religion here, but don't fall for it.

(B) Could *catholic* mean "talkative"? Not likely.

(C) Could *catholic* mean "generalized"? Maybe.

(D) Could *catholic* mean "reverent"? Sounds like a trap. Again, don't fall for it.

(E) Could *catholic* mean "careful"? Maybe.

Well, we've eliminated three choices, so it's time to guess. Not bad for not knowing the stem word. The answer is choice (C). *Catholic* means generalized or universal.

IF YOU'VE NEVER SEEN THE WORD BEFORE

Go for the extremes. "Extreme" words are more likely to be correct than moderate words. Look at the following example. What is the most extreme answer choice? Is it correct?

Start working on your vocabulary now!

AMENABLE:
- ⭕ intrinsic
- ⭕ progressive
- ⭕ enthusiastic
- ⭕ tenuous
- ⭕ obstinate

Here's how to crack it

The most extreme answer choices are *enthusiastic* and *obstinate*. The best thing to do in this situation is to just guess one of these two choices. The answer is (E). *Amenable* means open to different possibilities, and *obstinate* means stubborn. Remember, an educated guess is better than a random guess, especially since you can't skip any questions.

7

Reading
Comprehension

WHAT YOU WILL SEE

The verbal section of your GRE will contain two to four reading passages and a total of six to ten questions. You probably won't see any reading comps until around questions eight to twelve.

THE DIRECTIONS

These are the directions as they will appear on your GRE:

> Directions: Each passage in this group is followed by questions based on its content. After reading a passage, choose the best answer to each question. Answer all questions following a passage on the basis of what is stated or implied in that passage.

Here are *our* directions:

> Directions: This is not really a test of reading, nor is it a test of comprehension. It's a treasure hunt! The answers are in the passage.

This is not a test of intelligence!

TYPES OF PASSAGES

There are two basic types of GRE reading passages: science and non-science. The science passages may be either specific or general. Knowing a little about the types will help you anticipate the main ideas.

Specific science passages deal with the "hard facts" of science. They are almost always objective or neutral in tone. The terminology may be complex, but the main idea or theme will not be. Don't be thrown into confusion by big words. If you don't understand them, neither does anyone else. If you focus on the main idea, you won't have to worry about the jargon.

General science passages deal with the history of a scientific discovery, the development of a scientific procedure or method, why science fails or succeeds in explaining certain phenomena, and similar "soft" themes. The authors of these passages often have a more definite point of view than do the authors of the specific science passages; that is, the tone may not be neutral or objective, and the author may be expressing an opinion. The main theme will be whatever point or argument the author is trying to argue.

Non-science passages will be about either humanities or social studies topics. Humanities passages typically take a specific point of view, or compare several views. The language may be abstract and dense. Social science passages usually introduce an era or event by focusing on a specific problem, topic, person, or group of persons. The tone is likely to be partisan and opinionated, although some social science passages take the form of a neutral discussion of facts.

SAMPLE PASSAGE

In the discussion that follows, we will refer again and again to the sample passage below.

Within the atmosphere are small amounts of a number of important gases, popularly called "greenhouse gases," because they alter the flow of life- and heat-energy through the atmosphere,
5 much as does the glass shell of a greenhouse. Their effect on incoming solar energy is minimal, but collectively they act as an insulating blanket around the planet. They do this by adsorbing and returning to the Earth's surface much of its
10 outgoing heat, trapping it within the lower atmosphere. A greenhouse effect is natural and essential to a livable climate on Earth.

Greenhouse gas concentrations, however, are being drastically affected by human activities.
15 One of the most important gases, carbon dioxide, is an important nutrient for plants, but it is potentially dangerous to our climate if its quantity is enormously augmented. Its concentration has increased from about 280
20 parts per million in 1850 to about 350 today, mainly because of a large increase in fossil fuel burning, forest removal, and agriculture. Other gases, such as nitrous oxide, methane, and surface ozone, although they are less abundant,
25 are also increasing rapidly and are potentially dangerous. Man-made chlorofluorocarbons (CFCs) are used as, among other things, coolants in refrigerators and air conditioners. The most common industrially produced CFCs,
30 although measured in parts per trillion, are among the most potent and the most rapidly increasing greenhouse gases in existence. One free chlorine atom, produced in the stratosphere by the effects of ultraviolet light on CFCs, can
35 eliminate 100,000 molecules of ozone.

The result? Increased concentration of greenhouse gases enhance the global greenhouse effect, trapping more heat near the Earth's surface. A warmer atmosphere can hold
40 more water vapor, which is itself a powerful greenhouse gas, and amplify the warming. On the other hand, the increase in airborne moisture may mean more clouds, which would cut off sunlight and limit or modulate warming.

45 On the basis of climate models, some scientists predict a potential increase in global

Remember, it's a treasure hunt.

surface temperature of between 1.5°C and 4.5°C in the next fifty years. This may not seem like much, but 4.5°C equals the total temperature
50 rise since the peak of the last ice age 18,000 years ago, and the increase will be even higher in some regions. The average could be slightly lower in the tropics, but at least doubled at high latitude—mainly because of the disappearance
55 of ice and snow. Snow-free land surfaces absorb more of the Sun's rays than snow-covered surfaces, so warming by the Sun will increase as the duration and area of snow cover diminishes. Moreover, the increases in temperature can be
60 quite large where there is relatively low energy from the Sun because of the very shallow, strong temperature inversions typical of the Arctic cold season. Reduced ice cover on the polar seas will also increase the heat transfer
65 from water to the overlying air.

Don't read for "comprehension." Read to find the answers.

DON'T TRY TO READ EVERY WORD

Most test takers read much too slowly and carefully on reading comp, trying to memorize all the details crammed into the passage. When they reach the end of the passage, they often realize that they have no idea what they have just read. They've wasted a lot of time and gotten nothing out of it. You'll know better.

On the GRE CAT, you read for one reason only: *to earn points*. The questions test only a tiny fraction of the boring, hard-to-remember details that are packed into each passage. So don't try to read and remember everything in the passage.

Don't read every word of the passage. Just spend a minute or two noting what the general topic of the passage is on your scratch paper, and if the passage is organized in a specific way. In other words, case the joint—get familiar with the passage. Quickly.

APPROACHING THE PASSAGE

The main idea of the passage is what the passage is *about*. The main idea may be presented immediately, in the very first sentence. Or it may be presented gradually, in the first sentences of the paragraphs. Or the main idea may come last, as a conclusion to or summary of the details or arguments that have been presented.

Just focus on the first sentence and last sentence of each paragraph. Don't try to memorize what you are reading, or learn any of the supporting details. All you should be aiming for is a general sense of the overall passage, which can be reduced to a few simple words that you can easily jot down. Remember, the passage isn't going anywhere. It will be on the screen until you answer the question. You don't have to memorize anything.

Ready to try it?

Let's try this technique on the sample passage we gave you earlier.

From the first sentence of the first paragraph, you find out that the passage is about so-called "greenhouse gases." And from the last sentence of the paragraph you see that the passage is going to discuss "the greenhouse effect."

Now let's look at the second paragraph. The first sentence talks about how greenhouse gases are affected by human activities. The last sentence is some detail about CFCs. Even though we really don't know anything about CFCs or ozone, we still can tell that they are affected by human activity.

Let's go to the third paragraph. The first sentence of the third paragraph says that the result of the CFC/ozone thing is an enhanced greenhouse effect, trapping more heat near the Earth's surface. The last sentence says "on the other hand," (a trigger phrase; remember sentence completions?) there might be more clouds cutting off sunlight.

> **Use that paper!**

On to the last paragraph. The first sentence mentions that "some scientists predict a potential increase in global surface temperature . . ." The last sentence is about reduced ice cover on the polar seas also increasing the heat transfer from water to air. Now, try to summarize the main idea of the passage. On your scratch paper, write:

possible causes and results of the greenhouse effect

That's what the whole passage is about. If we *didn't* read about something in those topic sentences of each paragraph, it definitely is *not* the main idea. Now that we've dealt with the passage, let's move on to the questions, which will pop up one at a time on your screen

THE QUESTIONS

There are two types of questions: specific and general. Most of the questions you will see will be specific.

- **Specific questions** concern specific details in the passage. You should go back to the passage to find exactly what the passage said for each specific detail question. If you don't find it immediately, skim quickly to the next place the detail is discussed.

- **General questions** ask about the main idea, the theme, or the tone of the passage *as a whole*.

SPECIFIC QUESTIONS

Most specific questions have what we call a "lead" word or phrase. These are words or phrases that will be easy to skim for in the passage. Here's how it works:

- Identify the lead word or phrase in the question. It will be the most descriptive word in the question. For example, the lead word in the question, "According to the passage, mayonnaise was invented because . . ." is *mayonnaise*.

- Quickly skim the passage to find that word or phrase.
- Scroll so that the lead words are in the middle of the screen. This should put the part of the passage that must be paraphrased to answer the question right next to the answer choices.
- If this doesn't do it, look for the next occurrence of the lead words and repeat the process.
- Read the question again and answer it in your own words, based on the information you found in the passage.
- Then use POE.

THE ANSWER CHOICES (POE)

The following techniques will help you use POE to eliminate incorrect answer choices and zero in on ETS's answer.

USE COMMON SENSE, BUT NOT OUTSIDE KNOWLEDGE

ETS takes its reading passages from textbooks, collections of essays, works of scholarship, and other sources of serious reading matter. You won't find a passage arguing that literature is stupid, or that history doesn't matter. As a result, you will often be able to eliminate answer choices simply because the facts or opinions they represent couldn't possibly be found in ETS reading passages.

However, be careful not to answer questions based on the fact that you did your undergraduate thesis on the topic at hand. This is a treasure hunt; in other words: **The answers are in the passage.**

AVOID EXTREME STATEMENTS

ETS doesn't want to spend all its time defending its answer choices. If even one percent of the people taking the GRE decided to quibble with an answer, ETS would be deluged with angry phone calls. To keep this from happening, ETS constructs correct answer choices that cannot be disputed.

What makes a choice indisputable? Take a look at the following example:

(A) Ella Fitzgerald had many fans.
(B) Everyone loved Ella Fitzgerald.

Which choice is indisputable? Choice (A). Choice (B) contains the highly disputable word *everyone*. Did *everyone* really love Ella Fitzgerald? Every person on the face of the Earth? Choice (A) is complaint-proof; choice (B) isn't.

The more extreme a choice is, the less likely it is to be ETS's answer.

Certain words make choices extreme and, therefore, easy to dispute. Here are a few of these extreme words:

- must
- the first
- each
- every
- all

- the best
- only
- totally
- always
- no

You shouldn't automatically eliminate a choice containing one of these words, but you want to turn your attention to it immediately and attack it vigorously. If you can find even one exception, you can eliminate that choice.

Other words make choices moderate, more mushy, and, therefore, hard to dispute. Here are a few of these words:

- may
- can
- some
- many
- sometimes
- often

AVOID DIRECT REPETITIONS

You should be very wary of choices that exactly reproduce a lot of the jargon from the passage. The best answer will almost always be a paraphrase, not a direct repetition. Of course, there will often have to be *some* words from the passage in the answer. But the more closely a choice resembles a substantial part of the passage, the less likely the choice is to be the best answer.

ALWAYS write A, B, C, D, E on your scratch paper to represent the answer choices.

LET'S TRY ONE

When it's time to attack a question, remember these steps:
1. Read the question and make sure you understand what it's asking.
2. Go back to the passage and read more in depth where you need to.
3. Paraphrase the answer in your own words.
4. Use POE on the answer choices.

Let's go back to the sample passage on page 63, and try a question:

It can be inferred from the passage that an increase in the levels of greenhouse gases in the atmosphere could result in

(A) a moderation of the changes in global temperature
(B) a reduction in ultraviolet radiation at the Earth's surface
(C) a long-term increase in the turbulence of weather patterns
(D) increased snow cover in higher latitudes
(E) corresponding increases in stratospheric ozone levels

Here's how to crack it

This is a typical specific question. What are the lead words? We need to go back to the passage to find out what "could result" when there's "an increase in the levels of greenhouse gases in the atmosphere." Again, don't try to answer this question using your memory or based on what you may know about the topic apart from the passage.

The third paragraph says that increased concentration of greenhouse gases "enhance the global greenhouse effect, trapping more heat near the Earth's surface. A warmer atmosphere can hold more water vapor . . . and amplify the warming. On the other hand, the increase in airborne moisture may mean more clouds, which would cut off sunlight and limit or modulate warming." So, in our own words, the increased greenhouse effect might make the Earth both warmer and cooler. Now let's use POE on the answer choices.

(A) Well, this choice has something to do with the Earth's temperature, so let's keep it.

(B) You may be tempted to keep this answer choice, because the paragraph says that increased greenhouse gases could "cut off sunlight." But there is nothing about "ultraviolet radiation" in that paragraph, and there's nothing about the effects on *temperature* in this choice. And since this isn't testing your scientific knowledge, you're not expected to bring in any outside information about sunlight and ultraviolet radiation. So eliminate this choice.

(C) There's nothing in this choice about temperature, and there's nothing in the paragraph about the "turbulence of weather patterns." Eliminate this choice.

(D) There is nothing in the third paragraph about snow cover, and there's nothing in this answer choice about temperature. If you're not sure, go to the fourth paragraph, where it says that snow-cover will diminish. Eliminate this choice.

(E) Ozone isn't mentioned in the third paragraph. We're looking for something to do with temperature. Eliminate.

The best answer is choice (A). Notice that it's a paraphrase, not a direct repetition, of what is stated in the passage.

Let's try another question.

The author refers to the last ice age primarily in order to

(A) dramatize the effect that reduced ice cover has on atmospheric temperatures

(B) show that temperatures in the tropics and polar regions are becoming more uniform

(C) illustrate the decrease in global levels of ice and snow

(D) trace the decline in surface ozone levels over an extended period

(E) emphasize the significance of an apparently minor climatic change

Remember: All the answers you need are on the screen.

■ CRACKING THE GRE CAT

Here's how to crack it

Use the lead words to go back to the right paragraph in the passage. You're looking for something about "the last ice age." It's in the fourth paragraph, the one with more details about the greenhouse effect. In the first sentence of that paragraph, it says that some scientists predict a warming of between 1.5 and 4.5°C in the next fifty years. Then it says, "This may not seem like much, but 4.5°C equals the total temperature rise since the peak of the last ice age 18,000 years ago, and the increase will be even higher in some regions."

So the author refers to the last ice age in order to, in our own words, show that a 4.5 degree change in global surface temperature can have major consequences. In any case, it's again got something to do with changes in the Earth's *temperature*, so that if an answer choice doesn't mention temperature, it can't be the best answer choice.

(A) "Reduced ice cover" is in the wrong part of the paragraph, so eliminate it.

(B) This mentions temperature, so let's keep it and try to get rid of some other choices.

(C) Nothing in this choice mentions temperature, so get rid of it.

(D) Nothing about temperature here either, so this choice is gone.

(E) This looks good. It's about what we said in our own words.

But let's go back to the passage to make sure that choice (B) is wrong. In the fourth paragraph it says, "The average could be slightly lower in the tropics, but at least doubled at high latitude." So we know that temperatures in the tropics and polar regions are *not* becoming more uniform.

The best answer choice is (E).

Let's try another question.

> Put your finger on the place in the passage where you found the answer to the question. Answer the question in your own words before you go on to the answer choices.

The passage indicates that a reduction in the amount of ice on the surface of the polar seas would result in

(A) a decrease in the frequency of Arctic temperature inversions

(B) increased transfer of heat from the sea to the polar atmosphere

(C) increased absorption of solar energy by polar land surfaces

(D) rapid reversal of the warming caused by greenhouse gases

(E) decreased heat transfer, which would cool the polar atmosphere

Here's how to crack it

This is another specific question with lead words. The lead words are "a reduction in the amount of ice on the surface of polar seas." After answering the last question, we know that we're going to go back to the fourth paragraph again.

The last sentence says, "Reduced ice cover on the polar seas will also increase the heat transfer from water to the overlying air." So the answer to the question will be a paraphrase of that sentence.

Let's use POE.

(A) You should be very suspicious of direct repetitions in answer choices like this one. The passage mentions "temperature inversions" of the typical Arctic cold season, but the question we're trying to answer is about what would happen after a reduction in the amount of ice on the surface of polar seas. Get rid of this choice.

(B) This looks like a good paraphrase of the last sentence.

(C) Use common sense! The question is about what would happen after a reduction in the amount of ice on the surface of polar seas. Eliminate.

(D) Again, use common sense. This choice would go against the main idea of the whole passage. It's also very extreme wording. Eliminate.

(E) No, the passage says that reduced ice cover will increase the heat transfer. Eliminate. The best answer is choice (B).

LINE REFERENCE QUESTIONS

These questions ask you to interpret the meaning of a certain word or phrase in the context of the passage. You will usually be referred to a specific line number in the text. These questions can be phrased in a number of ways:

> The "great orchestra" (line 29) is used as a metaphor for . . .

> The author uses the term "indigenous labor" (line 40) to mean . . .

> The author quotes Stephen Hawking (line 13) in order to . . .

Do you really think ETS is going to tell you exactly where an answer is? No way. Therefore, you will generally *not* find ETS's answer in the exact line referred to.

Read at least the five lines before the line reference, and the five lines after it as well.

Here's the best way to do these questions: Scroll so that the line referred to is in the middle of the screen. This should put the part of the passage that must be paraphrased to answer the question right next to the answer choices.

MAIN IDEA QUESTIONS

A main idea question asks you to find the main idea of the passage. It can be phrased in several different ways:

The author's main purpose is . . .

The main idea of the passage is . . .

Which of the following is the best title for the passage?

Which of the following questions does the passage answer?

> Be skeptical of answer choices that are too EXTREME.

A word about answer choices: All of these are *general* questions; therefore, they will almost always have *general* answers. That means that you can eliminate any choice that is too specific. The main idea of a passage will never be something that couldn't possibly be accomplished in a few short paragraphs. (The author's purpose in writing a 250-word essay could never be "to explain the origin of the universe.")

The incorrect choices on a question like this will probably be statements that are partly true, or are true of part of the passage, but not of the whole thing. Refer back to the sample passage on page 63 for the following question:

The author is primarily concerned with

(A) explaining the effects that ultraviolet light might have on terrestrial life
(B) illustrating the effects of greenhouse gases on solar radiation
(C) discussing the possible effects of increased levels of greenhouse gases
(D) exploding theories about the causes of global warming
(E) challenging hypotheses about the effects of temperature on the atmosphere

Here's how to crack it

This is a general question. It's asking for the "primary purpose" of the passage—in other words, the main idea. We said that the passage is about the possible causes and effects of the greenhouse effect. Let's use POE.

(A) This choice doesn't even mention the greenhouse effect, so it can't be the best answer. Eliminate it.

(B) This mentions greenhouse gases, so let's keep it and check the other choices.

(C) This also mentions greenhouse gases, so let's keep this one too. We'll consider the other choices before we come back to the ones we've kept.

(D) Nothing about greenhouse gases in this. And what are "exploding theories"? Get rid of this one.

(E) What about the greenhouse effect? Also, there was no "challenging" involved.

Now that we've eliminated three choices, let's go back to choices (B) and (C). Is there anything about "solar radiation" in our notes? No. So that can't be the primary concern of the passage. Choice (C) is right in line with what we wrote down as the main idea. It's the best choice.

You must be absolutely certain to cross out incorrect choices (of course you'll write A, B, C, D, E down on your scratch paper for this purpose) as you eliminate them. The key to doing well on reading comp is to narrow the field as rapidly as possible. Small differences between a couple of choices are easier to see once you've swept away the clutter.

Down to two choices? Go back to the place in the passage where you found the answer to the question.

QUESTIONS ABOUT TONE, ATTITUDE, OR STYLE

The second type of general question asks you to identify the author's tone, style, or overall point of view. Is the author being critical, neutral, or sympathetic? Is the passage subjective or objective? Like main idea questions, these questions can be phrased in several ways:

The author's tone is best described as . . .

The author views his subject with . . .

The author's presentation is best characterized as . . .

The passage is most likely from . . .

The author most likely thinks the reader is . . .

These questions are usually easy to spot, because the answers seldom contain many words. In fact, each choice may be just a single word. These questions are also usually easy to answer, because ETS writes them in very predictable ways. Here are the main things for you to remember:

- ETS is politically correct. Any negative or politically *incorrect* choices can quickly be eliminated.

- ETS has respect for the authors and the subjects of these reading comp passages. If an answer choice says that the purpose of a passage is "to demonstrate the intellectual dishonesty of our founding fathers," you can safely eliminate it without so much as glancing at the passage.

- You can eliminate any choice that is too negative or too extreme. ETS's reading passages have no strong emotions. ETS is middle-of-the-road, responsible, and establishment—i.e., boring. The tone of a passage will never be scathing. An author's style would never be violent. An author will never be irrational.

POE is your new religion.

LEAST/EXCEPT/NOT QUESTIONS

Lots of careless errors are made on these questions. In order for you to avoid making them, you need to keep reminding yourself that ETS's answer will be the choice that is *wrong*. Here are some of the ways these questions are phrased:

> Which of the following statements would the author be LEAST likely to agree with?

> According to the passage, all of the following are true EXCEPT ...

> Which of the following does NOT support the defense?

Always cross off wrong answer choices on your scratch paper.

The best answer will be the wrong answer, the crazy choice that normally would be the first choice to eliminate.

For EXCEPT questions, look for "correct" answers (there should be four of them)—and eliminate them. That is, refer back to the passage with each remaining choice and see if the passage supports it. If it does, it's no good. You're looking for the one choice that doesn't make sense.

I, II, III QUESTIONS

These time-consuming questions, in which you are asked to deal with three statements identified with Roman numerals, are a good place to use POE. Start with the shortest of the Roman-numeral statements and go back to the passage to find out if it's true or false.

When you find a false statement, be sure to eliminate all appropriate answer choices on your scratch paper that include the Roman numeral for that statement. When you find a true statement, cross out any answer choice that does not include its Roman numeral on your scratch paper. Don't do more work than you have to.

Let's try an example from our sample passage on page 63.

Use that paper!

The discussion of water vapor in the passage suggests which of the following conclusions?

I. Water vapor in the atmosphere helps to create an insulating layer that traps heat in the atmosphere.

II. Water vapor in the upper levels of the atmosphere can have a significant effect on ozone levels.

III. Water vapor in the atmosphere could act to decrease as well as increase global temperatures.

(A) I only
(B) III only
(C) I and II only
(D) I and III only
(E) I, II, and III

Here's how to crack it

Notice that this is another specific question with lead words. Let's go back to the passage to find out what it said about "water vapor." Water vapor is mentioned in the third paragraph. There it says, "A warmer atmosphere can hold more water vapor, which is itself a powerful greenhouse gas, and amplify the warming." Let's use this information to cancel some of the answer choices.

For the latest on the GRE CAT, check www.review.coom or www.gre.org.

Roman numeral I seems like a good paraphrase of the sentence in the passage, so this Roman numeral must be part of the best answer, and we can eliminate all the choices that don't include it—eliminate choice (B).

There was nothing in the passage connecting water vapor and ozone levels. Eliminate all the choices that contain Roman numeral II. That gets rid of choices (C) and (E).

Now let's consider Roman numeral III. Go back to the third paragraph again. Read the last sentence of that paragraph. Remember what we learned when we answered the second question, that the greenhouse effect might have both warming and cooling effects on temperature. So if water vapor is itself a greenhouse gas, then it could have both of these effects as well. The best answer is choice (D).

8

Vocabulary for the GRE CAT

Vocab, Vocab, Vocab

The techniques for cracking the verbal section on the GRE CAT are very effective, but how helpful they are to you will depend on the quality of your vocabulary. Again, our techniques can help you get maximum possible mileage out of the words you do know. The more words you know, the more help the techniques can be.

The Hit Parade

Improving your vocabulary is the single most important thing you can do to improve your verbal score.

The Princeton Review has compiled a vocabulary list that contains the most frequently tested words on the GRE CAT. We made this list, which we call the Hit Parade, by analyzing released GREs with our computers. Keep in mind that Hit Parade words make very good guesses on questions where you don't know what else to pick.

Get to Work!

Learning the GRE Hit Parade may be the single most important thing you do to prepare for the GRE CAT. Learning these words will give you a solid background in the vocabulary most likely to appear on your test. It will also give you a better idea of the kinds of words that crop up again and again on the GRE. Learning the Hit Parade will give you a feel for the level of vocabulary that ETS likes to test. Then it will be easier to spot other possible GRE words in your everyday life.

Each word on the Hit Parade is followed by the part of speech and a brief definition. Most of the words on the list have other meanings as well, but the definitions we have given are the ones you are most likely to find on the GRE CAT.

Learning New Words

How will you remember all these words? By developing a standard routine for learning new words. Here are some tips:

- When you come across a word you don't know, look it up. If you don't have a dictionary handy, write down the new word and look it up later. If you have somehow managed to make it through college without owning a dictionary, go buy one right now.

- When you look up the word, say it out loud, being careful to pronounce it correctly. Saying the word to yourself isn't enough. You'll remember it better if you make a little noise.

- When you look up your word in the dictionary, don't assume that the first definition is the one that applies. The first definition may be an archaic one, or one that applies only in a particular context. Scan through all the definitions, looking for the one that fits the context in which you found your word.

- Now that you've learned the dictionary's definition of your new word, restate it in your own words. You'll find it much easier to remember a word's meaning if you make it your own. You'll have to be certain, of course, that your definition is consistent with the one in the dictionary.

- Mnemonics—Use your imagination to create a mental image to fix the new word in your mind. For example, if you're trying to remember the word "dogmatic," which means stubborn, picture in your mind a stubborn dog who keeps pulling you toward a tree he wants to sniff even though you don't want him to go there. The crazier the image, the better.

- Keep a vocabulary notebook. Simply having a notebook with you will remind you to be on the lookout for new words, and using it will help you to remember the ones you encounter. Writing something down makes it easier to memorize. Jot down the word when you find it, note its pronunciation and definition (in your own words) when you look it up, and jot down your mnemonic or mental image. You might also copy the sentence in which you originally found the word, to remind yourself of how the word looks in context.

- Do the same thing with flash cards. Write the word on one side and the pronunciation, meaning, and perhaps a mental image on the other. Stick five or six of your flash cards in your pocket every morning and use them when you can.

- Use your new word every chance you get. Make it part of your life. Insert it into your speech at every opportunity. A powerful vocabulary requires lots of exercise. Make it burn!

Learn new words little by little; don't try to learn a ton at once!

THE GRE CAT HIT PARADE

abate	verb	to lessen in intensity or degree
aberrant	adjective	deviating from the norm
abscond	verb	to depart clandestinely; to steal away and hide
accolade	noun	an expression of praise
acerbic	adjective	having a sour or bitter taste or character
acumen	noun	quick, keen, or accurate knowledge or insight
adulation	noun	excessive praise; intense adoration
adulterate	verb	to reduce purity by combining with inferior ingredients
aesthetic	adjective	dealing with, appreciative of, or responsive to art or the beautiful
aggrandize	verb	to increase in intensity, power, or prestige
alacrity	noun	eager and enthusiastic willingness
alchemy	noun	a medieval science aimed at the transmutation of metals, especially base metals into gold
amalgamate	verb	to combine several elements into a whole
ameliorate	verb	to make better or more tolerable
amenable	adjective	agreeable; responsive to suggestion
anachronism	noun	something or someone out of place in terms of its historical or chronological context
anomaly	noun	deviation from the normal order, form, or rule; abnormality
approbation	noun	an expression of approval or praise
archaic	adjective	outdated; associated with an earlier, perhaps more primitive, time
arduous	adjective	strenuous, taxing, requiring significant effort
ascetic	noun	one who practices rigid self-denial, especially as an act of religious devotion

Start working on your vocabulary now!

assuage	verb	to ease or lessen; to appease or pacify
astringent	adjective	having a tightening effect on living tissue; harsh; severe
audacious	adjective	daring and fearless; recklessly bold
austere	adjective	without adornment; bare; severely simple; ascetic
avarice	noun	greed, especially for wealth
aver	verb	to state as a fact; to confirm or support
axiom/axiomatic	noun/adjective	a universally recognized principle; taken as a given; possessing self-evident truth
bolster	verb	to provide support or reinforcement
bombast/bombastic	noun/adjective	self-evident or pompous writing or speech; pompous; grandiloquent
bucolic	adjective	rustic and pastoral; characteristic of rural areas and their inhabitants
burgeon	verb	to grow rapidly; to flourish
cacophony	noun	harsh, jarring, discordant sound; dissonance
canon	noun	an established set of principles or code of laws, often religious in nature
canonical	adjective	following or in agreement with orthodox requirements
capricious	adjective	inclined to change one's mind impulsively; erratic; unpredictable
castigation	noun	severe criticism or punishment
catalyst	noun	a substance that accelerates the rate of a chemical reaction without itself changing; a person or thing that causes change
caustic	adjective	burning or stinging; causing corrosion
censure	verb	to criticize severely; to officially rebuke

Try using these vocabulary words in your everyday conversations.

chary	adjective	wary; cautious
chicanery	noun	trickery or subterfuge
cogent	adjective	appealing forcibly to the mind or reason; convincing
complaisance	noun	the willingness to comply with the wishes of others
connoisseur	noun	an informed and astute judge in matters of taste; expert
contentious	adjective	argumentative; quarrelsome; causing controversy or disagreement
contrite	adjective	regretful; penitent; seeking forgiveness
convention	noun	a generally agreed-upon practice or attitude
convoluted	adjective	complex or complicated
credulous	adjective	tending to believe too readily; gullible
culpable	adjective	deserving blame
cynicism	noun	an attitude or quality of belief that all people are motivated by selfishness
dearth	noun	smallness of quantity or number; scarcity; a lack
decorum	noun	polite or appropriate conduct or behavior
demur	verb	to question or oppose
derision	noun	scorn, ridicule, contemptuous treatment
desiccate	verb	to dry out or dehydrate; to make dry or dull
diatribe	noun	a harsh denunciation
didactic	adjective	intended to teach or instruct
dilettante	noun	one with an amateurish or superficial interest in the arts or a branch of knowledge
disabuse	verb	to undeceive; to set right
discordant	adjective	conflicting; dissonant or harsh in sound

discretion	noun	cautious reserve in speech; ability to make responsible decisions
disinterested	adjective	indifferent; free from self-interest
disparage	verb	to slight or belittle
disparate	adjective	fundamentally distinct or dissimilar
dissemble	verb	to disguise or conceal; to mislead
divulge	verb	to disclose something secret
dogmatic	adjective	stubbornly opinionated
ebullience	adjective	the quality of lively or enthusiastic expression of thoughts and feelings
eccentric	adjective	departing from norms or conventions
eclectic	adjective	composed of elements drawn from various sources
effrontery	noun	extreme boldness; presumptuousness
elegy	noun	a mournful poem, especially one lamenting the dead
eloquent	adjective	well-spoken; expressive; articulate
emollient	adjective	soothing, especially to the skin; making less harsh; mollifying
empirical	adjective	based on observation or experiment
endemic	adjective	characteristic of or often found in a particular locality, region, or people
enervate	verb	to weaken; to reduce in vitality
enigmatic	adjective	mysterious; obscure; difficult to understand
ennui	noun	dissatisfaction and restlessness resulting from boredom or apathy
ephemeral	adjective	brief; fleeting
equivocate	verb	to use ambiguous language with a deceptive intent
erudite	adjective	very learned; scholarly
esoteric	adjective	intended for or understood by a small, specific group
eulogy	noun	a speech honoring the dead

evanescent	adjective	tending to disappear like vapor; vanishing
exacerbate	verb	to make worse or more severe
exculpate	verb	exonerate; to clear of blame
exigent	adjective	urgent; pressing; requiring immediate action or attention
exonerate	verb	to remove blame
extemporaneous	adjective	improvised; done without preparation
facetious	adjective	playful; humorous
fallacy	noun	an invalid or incorrect notion; a mistaken belief
fawn	verb	to flatter or praise excessively
fervent	adjective	greatly emotional or zealous
filibuster	noun	intentional obstruction, especially using prolonged speechmaking to delay legislative action
flout	verb	to demonstrate contempt for, as in a rule or convention
fortuitous	adjective	happening by fortunate accident or chance
fulminate	verb	to loudly attack or denounce
furtive	adjective	marked by stealth; covert; surreptitious
garrulous	adjective	pointlessly talkative, talking too much
germane	adjective	relevant to the subject at hand; appropriate in subject matter
glib	adjective	marked by ease or informality; nonchalant; lacking in depth; superficial
grandiloquence	noun	pompous speech or expression
gregarious	adjective	sociable; outgoing; enjoying the company of other people
hackneyed	adjective	rendered trite or commonplace by frequent usage
halcyon	adjective	calm and peaceful

harangue	verb	to deliver a pompous speech or tirade
hedonism	noun	devotion to pleasurable pursuits, especially to the pleasures of the senses
hegemony	noun	the consistent dominance of one state or ideology over others
heretical	adjective	violating accepted dogma or convention
hubris	noun	arrogant presumption or pride
hyperbole	noun	an exaggerated statement, often used as a figure of speech
iconoclast	noun	one who attacks or undermines traditional conventions or institutions
idolatrous	adjective	given to intense or excessive devotion to something
imminent	adjective	about to happen; impending
immutable	adjective	not capable of change
impassive	adjective	revealing no emotion
impecunious	adjective	lacking funds; without money
imperturbable	adjective	marked by extreme calm, impassivity, and steadiness
impetuous	adjective	hastily or rashly energetic; impulsive and vehement
implacable	adjective	not capable of being appeased or significantly changed
impunity	noun	immunity from punishment or penalty
inchoate	adjective	in an initial stage; not fully formed
incipient	adjective	beginning to come into being or to become apparent
indifferent	adjective	having no interest or concern; showing no bias or prejudice
inert	adjective	unmoving; lethargic; sluggish
infelicitous	adjective	unfortunate; inappropriate
ingenuous	adjective	artless; frank and candid; lacking in sophistication

inimical	adjective	damaging; harmful; malevolent
innocuous	adjective	harmless; causing no damage
insipid	adjective	without taste or flavor; lacking in spirit; bland
intractable	adjective	not easily managed or directed; stubborn, obstinate
intransigent	adjective	refusing to compromise
intrepid	adjective	steadfast and courageous
inured	adjective	accustomed to accepting something undesirable
inveigle	verb	to obtain by deception or flattery
irascible	adjective	easily angered; prone to temperamental outbursts
laconic	adjective	using few words; terse
laud	verb	to praise highly
loquacious	adjective	extremely talkative
lucid	adjective	clear; easily understood
luminous	adjective	characterized by brightness and the emission of light
magnanimity	noun	the quality of being generously noble in mind and heart, especially in forgiving
malevolent	adjective	having or showing often vicious ill will, spite, or hatred
malleable	adjective	capable of being shaped or formed; tractable; pliable
martial	adjective	associated with war and the armed forces
maverick	noun	an independent individual who does not go along with a group or party
mendacity	noun	the condition of being untruthful; dishonesty
mercurial	adjective	characterized by rapid and unpredictable change in mood
meticulous	adjective	characterized by extreme care and precision; attentive to detail
misanthrope	noun	one who hates all other humans

Learn new words little by little; don't try to learn a ton at once!

mitigate	verb	to make or become less severe or intense; to moderate
mollify	verb	to calm or soothe; to reduce in emotional intensity
morose	adjective	sad; sullen; melancholy
mundane	adjective	of the world; typical of or concerned with the ordinary
nascent	adjective	coming into being; in early developmental stages
nebulous	adjective	vague; cloudy; lacking clearly defined form
neologism	noun	a new word, expression, or usage; the creation or use of new words or senses
neophyte	noun	a recent convert; a beginner; novice
noxious	adjective	harmful; injurious
obdurate	adjective	unyielding; hardhearted; intractable
obfuscate	verb	to deliberately obscure; to make confusing
obsequious	adjective	exhibiting a fawning attentiveness
obstinate	adjective	stubborn; hardheaded; uncompromising
obtuse	adjective	lacking sharpness of intellect; not clear or precise in thought or expression
obviate	verb	to anticipate and make unnecessary
occlude	verb	to obstruct or block
odious	adjective	evoking intense aversion or dislike
onerous	adjective	troubling; burdensome
opaque	adjective	impenetrable by light; not reflecting light
opprobrium	noun	disgrace; contempt; scorn
oscillation	noun	the act or state of swinging back and forth with a steady, uninterrupted rhythm
ostentatious	adjective	characterized by or given to pretentiousness

Try using these vocabulary words in your everyday conversations.

paean	noun	a song or hymn of praise and thanksgiving
parody	noun	a humorous imitation intended for ridicule or comic effect, especially in literature and art
pedagogy	noun	the art or profession of training, teaching, or instructing
pedantic	adjective	the parading of learning; excessive attention to minutiae and formal rules
penurious	adjective	penny-pinching; excessively thrifty; ungenerous
penury	noun	poverty; destitution
perennial	adjective	recurrent through the year or many years; happening repeatedly
perfidy	noun	intentional breach of faith; treachery
perfunctory	adjective	cursory; done without care or interest
pernicious	adjective	extremely harmful; potentially causing death
perspicacious	adjective	acutely perceptive; having keen discernment
peruse	verb	to examine with great care
pervade	verb	to permeate throughout
pervasive	adjective	having the tendency to permeate or spread throughout
phlegmatic	adjective	calm; sluggish; unemotional
pine	verb	to yearn intensely; to languish; to lose vigor
pious	adjective	extremely reverent or devout; showing strong religious devotion
pirate	verb	to illegally use or reproduce
pith/pithy	noun/adjective	the essential or central part; precise and brief
placate	verb	to appease; to calm by making concessions
platitude	noun	a superficial remark, especially one offered as meaningful

plethora	noun	an overabundance; a surplus
plummet	verb	to plunge or drop straight down
polemical	adjective	controversial; argumentative
pragmatic	adjective	practical rather than idealistic
prattle	verb	to babble meaninglessly; to talk in an empty and idle manner
precipitate	verb/adjective	to cause or to happen before anticipated or required; acting with excessive haste or impulse
precursor	noun	one that indicates or announces someone or something to come
predilection	noun	a disposition in favor of something; preference
preen	verb	to dress up; to primp; to groom oneself with elaborate care
prescience	noun	foreknowledge of events; knowing of events prior to their occurring
presumptuous	adjective	overstepping due bounds (as of propriety or courtesy); taking liberties
prevaricate	verb	to deliberately avoid the truth; to mislead
pristine	adjective	pure; uncorrupted; clean
probity	noun	adherence to highest principles; uprightness
proclivity	noun	a natural predisposition or inclination
prodigal	adjective	recklessly wasteful; extravagant; profuse; lavish
prodigious	adjective	abundant in size, force, or extent; extraordinary
profligate	adjective	excessively wasteful; recklessly extravagant
profuse	adjective	given or coming forth abundantly; extravagant
proliferate	verb	to grow or increase swiftly and abundantly
prolific	adjective	producing large volumes or amounts; productive

Try using these vocabulary words in your everyday conversations.

propensity	noun	a natural inclination or tendency; penchant
prosaic	adjective	dull; unimaginative
pungent	adjective	characterized by a strong, sharp smell or taste
putrefy	verb	to rot; to decay and give off a foul odor
quaff	verb	to drink deeply
qualm	noun	misgiving; reservation; cause for hesitancy
querulous	adjective	prone to complaining or grumbling; quarrelsome
query	noun	question; inquiry; doubt in the mind; reservation
quiescence	noun	stillness; motionlessness; quality of being at rest
quixotic	adjective	foolishly impractical; marked by lofty romantic ideals
quotidian	adjective	occurring or recurring daily; commonplace
rancorous	adjective	characterized by bitter, long-lasting resentment
rarefy	verb	to make or become thin, less dense; to refine
recalcitrant	adjective	obstinately defiant of authority; difficult to manage
recant	verb	to retract, especially a previously held belief
recondite	adjective	hidden; concealed; difficult to understand; obscure
redoubtable	adjective	awe-inspiring; worthy of honor
refulgent	adjective	radiant; shiny; brilliant
refute	verb	to disprove; to successfully argue against
relegate	verb	to forcibly assign, especially to a lower place or position
renege	verb	to fail to honor a commitment; to go back on a promise
repudiate	verb	to refuse to have anything to do with; disown

rescind	verb	to invalidate; to repeal; to retract
reticent	adjective	quiet; reserved; reluctant to express thoughts and feelings
reverent	adjective	marked by, feeling, or expressing profound awe and respect
rhetoric	noun	the art or study of effective use of language for communication and persuasion
salubrious	adjective	promoting health or well-being
sanction	noun	authoritative permission or approval; a penalty intended to enforce compliance
satire	noun	a literary work that ridicules or criticizes a human vice through humor or derision
sedulous	adjective	diligent; persistent; hard-working
shard	noun	a piece of broken pottery or glass
solicitous	adjective	concerned and attentive; eager
solvent	adjective	able to meet financial obligations; able to dissolve another substance
soporific	adjective	causing drowsiness; tending to induce sleep
sordid	adjective	characterized by filth, grime, or squalor; foul
sparse	adjective	thin; not dense; arranged at widely spaced intervals
specious	adjective	seeming true, but actually being fallacious; misleadingly attractive
spendthrift	noun	one who spends money wastefully
sporadic	adjective	occurring only occasionally, or in scattered instances
spurious	adjective	lacking authenticity or validity; false; counterfeit
squalid	adjective	sordid; wretched and dirty as from neglect
squander	verb	to waste by spending or using irresponsibly
static	adjective	not moving, active, or in motion; at rest

stoic	adjective	indifferent to or unaffected by pleasure or pain; steadfast
stupefy	verb	to stun, baffle, or amaze
stymie	verb	to block; thwart
subpoena	noun	a court order requiring appearance and/or testimony
subtle	adjective	not obvious; elusive; difficult to discern
succinct	adjective	brief; concise
superfluous	adjective	exceeding what is sufficient or necessary
supplant	verb	to take the place of; supersede
surfeit	verb	excess; overindulgence
synthesis	noun	the combination of parts to make a whole
tacit	adjective	implied; not explicitly stated
tenacity	noun	the quality of adherence or persistence to something valued
tenuous	adjective	having little substance or strength; flimsy; weak
terse	adjective	brief and concise in wording
tirade	noun	a long and extremely critical speech; a harsh denunciation
torpid	adjective	lethargic; sluggish; dormant
torque	noun	a force that causes rotation
tortuous	adjective	winding; twisting; excessively complicated
tout	verb	to publicly praise or promote
transient	adjective	fleeting; passing quickly; brief
trenchant	adjective	sharply perceptive; keen; penetrating
truculent	adjective	fierce and cruel; eager to fight
ubiquitous	adjective	existing everywhere at the same time; constantly encountered; widespread
unfeigned	adjective	genuine; not false or hypocritical
untenable	adjective	indefensible; not viable; uninhabitable

urbane	adjective	sophisticated; refined; elegant
vacillate	verb	to waver indecisively between one course of action or opinion and another
variegated	adjective	multicolored; characterized by a variety of patches of different color
veracity	noun	truthfulness; honesty
vexation	noun	annoyance; irritation
vigilant	adjective	alertly watchful
vilify	verb	to defame; to characterize harshly
virulent	adjective	extremely harmful or poisonous; bitterly hostile or antagonistic
viscous	adjective	thick; sticky
vituperate	verb	to use harsh, condemnatory language; to abuse or censure severely or abusively; berate
volatile	adjective	readily changing to a vapor; changeable; fickle; explosive
voracious	adjective	having an insatiable appetite for an activity or pursuit; ravenous
waver	verb	to move to and fro; to sway; to be unsettled in opinion
zealous	adjective	fervent; ardent; impassioned

> Improving your vocabulary is the single most important thing you can do to improve your verbal score.

PART ◆ III

How to Crack
the Math Section

9

The Geography of the Math Section

Every GRE contains a scored "quantitative ability," or math, section. This section will last forty-five minutes and contain twenty-eight questions in three question formats:

- 13 to 15 quantitative comparison questions
- 8 to 10 problem solving questions
- 4 to 6 chart questions (with 2 to 3 charts)

Practice doing simple math with your pencil in real life. Don't use a calculator as you normally would.

JUNIOR HIGH SCHOOL?

The GRE CAT mostly tests how much you remember from the math courses you took in seventh, eighth, and ninth grade. Why is a passing knowledge of eighth-grade algebra important for a future Ph.D. in English literature? Don't ask us. Apparently ETS thinks there's a connection.

But here's some good news: GRE math is easier than SAT math. Why? Because many people study little or no math in college. If the GRE tested "college-level" math, everyone but math majors would bomb.

If you're willing to do a little work, this is good news for you. By brushing up on the modest amount of math you need to know for the test, you can significantly increase your GRE math score. All you have to do is shake off the rust.

IT'S A READING TEST

In constructing the math section, ETS is limited to the math that nearly everyone has studied: arithmetic, basic algebra, basic geometry, and elementary statistics. There's no calculus (or even precalculus), no trigonometry, and no major-league algebra or geometry. Because of these limitations, ETS has to resort to traps in order to create hard problems. Even the most difficult GRE math problems are typically based on relatively simple principles. What makes the problems difficult is that these simple principles are disguised. So, this is more of a reading test than a math test.

A MATTER OF TIME

You will score higher if you spend your time working slowly and carefully at the beginning of the section. Remember, the questions you answer at the beginning of each section of the GRE CAT have a much greater impact on your final score than do the questions you answer at the end.

SCRATCH PAPER

Your use of scratch paper is crucial on the math section. Don't try to do any calculations in your head. Write it all down so you don't make careless errors. The first thing you should do for *every* question is write down A, B, C, D, E on your scratch paper (or A, B, C, D if it's a quantitative comparison—we'll get to that later).

READ AND COPY CAREFULLY

You can do all the calculations right and still get a question wrong. How? What if you solve for *x* but the question was "What is the value of *x* + 4?" Ugh. Always *reread* the question. Take your time and don't be careless. The problem will stay on the screen long enough for you to reread the question and double-check your work before answering it.

Or how about this: The radius of the circle is 5, but when you copied the picture onto your scratch paper, you accidentally made it 6. Ugh! Many of the mistakes you will make at first probably stem from copying information down incorrectly. Learn from your mistakes! You have to be extra careful when copying down information.

PROCESS OF ELIMINATION

Whenever you read a math problem, don't forget to read the answer choices *before* you start to solve the problem, because they are a part of the problem and can help guide you. Often, you will be able to eliminate a couple of answer choices before you begin to calculate the exact answer. *Physically* eliminate them on your scratch paper.

YOU KNOW MORE THAN YOU THINK

Say you were asked to find 30% of 50. Don't do any math yet. Now let's say that you glance at the answer choices and you see these:

- ⬭ 5
- ⬭ 15
- ⬭ 30
- ⬭ 80
- ⬭ 150

Think about it. Whatever 30% of 50 is, it must be less than 50, right? So any answer choice greater than 50 can't be right. That means you should eliminate both 80 and 150 before you even do any calculations! That is known as . . .

BALLPARKING

Ballparking will help you eliminate answer choices and increase your odds of zeroing in on ETS's answer. Remember to eliminate any answer choice that is "out of the ballpark."

Ballparking answers will help you eliminate choices.

HOW TO STUDY

Make sure you learn the content of each chapter cold before you go on to the next one. Don't try to cram everything in all at once. It's much better to do a small amount of studying each day over a longer period. You will master both the math concepts and the techniques if you focus on a little bit at a time.

PRACTICE, PRACTICE

Since most of us don't do much math in "real life," you can start by *not avoiding* math as you normally would. Balance your checkbook—without a calculator! Make sure your check is added correctly at a restaurant, and figure out the exact percentage you want to leave for a tip. The more you practice simple adding, subtracting, multiplying, and dividing on a day-to-day basis, the more your arithmetic skills will improve for the GRE CAT.

As you work through this book, be sure to practice on real GREs. Practice will rapidly sharpen your test-taking skills. Unless you trust our techniques, you may be reluctant to use them fully and automatically on a real administration of the GRE CAT. The best way to develop that trust is to practice before you get to the real test.

Use that paper!

10
Numbers

GRE MATH VOCABULARY

Quick—what's an integer? Is 0 even or odd? How many even prime numbers are there?

Learn this Math vocabulary!

Even though all of the math terms we will review are very simple, that doesn't mean they're not important. Every GRE CAT math question uses these simple rules and definitions. You absolutely need to know this math "vocabulary." Don't worry, we will only cover the math terms that you *must* know for the GRE CAT.

INTEGERS

The integers are the "big places" on the number line: –6, –5, –4, –3, –2, –1, 0, 1, 2, 3, 4, 5, 6.

Remember, fractions are NOT integers.

Notice that fractions, such as $\frac{1}{2}$, are not integers.

Remember that the number zero is an integer! Positive integers get bigger as they move away from 0 (6 is bigger than 5); negative integers get smaller as they move away from zero (–6 is smaller than –5).

CONSECUTIVE INTEGERS

Consecutive integers are integers listed in order of increasing value without any integers missing in between, such as:

- 0, 1, 2, 3, 4, 5
- –6, –5, –4, –3, –2, –1, 0
- –3, –2, –1, 0, 1, 2, 3

By the way, no numbers other than integers can be consecutive. However, you can list integers by type. In other words, if you were asked to list a group of consecutive even integers, you could put down: 2, 4, 6, 8, 10.

ZERO

Zero is a special little number. It is an integer, but it is neither positive nor negative. However:

- 0 is even.
- the sum of 0 and any other number is that other number.
- the product of 0 and any other number is 0.

DIGITS

There are 10 digits: 0, 1, 2, 3, 4, 5, 6, 7, 8, 9.

Simple, right? Just think of them as the numbers on your phone dial. All integers are made up of digits. For example, the integer 10,897 has 5 digits: 1, 0, 8, 9, 7. So, it's a 5-digit integer. Each of its digits has its own name:

- 7 is the units digit.
- 9 is the tens digit.
- 8 is the hundreds digit.
- 0 is the thousands digit.
- 1 is the ten thousands digit.

POSITIVE OR NEGATIVE

Numbers can be positive (+) or negative (–). For the GRE CAT, you'll need to remember what happens when you multiply positive and negative numbers:

- pos × pos = pos $2 \times 2 = 4$
- neg × neg = pos $-2 \times -2 = 4$
- pos × neg = neg $2 \times -2 = -4$

EVEN OR ODD

An even number is any integer that can be divided evenly by 2; an odd number is any integer that can't.

- Here are some even integers: –4, –2, 0, 2, 4, 6, 8, 10
- Here are some odd integers: –3, –1, 1, 3, 5, 7, 9, 11

Keep in mind

- Zero is even.
- Fractions are neither even nor odd.
- Any integer is even if its units digit is even; any integer is odd if its units digit is odd.
- The results of adding and multiplying odd and even integers:
  - even + even = even
  - odd + odd = even
  - even + odd = odd
  - even × even = even
  - odd × odd = odd
  - even × odd = even

Be careful: Don't confuse odd and even with positive and negative.

PRIME NUMBERS

A prime number is a number that is divisible only by itself and 1. Here are *all* the prime numbers less than 30: 2, 3, 5, 7, 11, 13, 17, 19, 23, 29.

- 0 is not a prime number.
- 1 is not a prime number.
- 2 is the only even prime number.

DIVISIBILITY

Here are some rules for divisibility:

- An integer is divisible by 2 if its units digit is divisible by 2. For example, we know just by glancing that 598,447,896 is divisible by 2, because the units digit, 6, is divisible evenly by 2.
- An integer is divisible by 3 if the sum of its digits is divisible by 3. For example, we know that 2,145 is divisible by 3, because $2 + 1 + 4 + 5 = 12$, and 12 is divisible by 3.
- An integer is divisible by 4 if its last two digits form a number divisible by 4. For example, 712 is divisible by 4 because 12 is divisible by 4.
- An integer is divisible by 5 if its units digit is either 0 or 5.

- An integer is divisible by 6 if it's divisible by *both* 2 *and* 3.
- An integer is divisible by 9 if the sum of its digits is divisible by 9.
- An integer is divisible by 10 if its units digit is 0.

Remainders

The remainder is the number left over when one integer cannot be divided evenly by another. The remainder is always an integer. (Remember grade school math class? It's the number that came after the big "R.")

For example, 4 divided by 2 is 2; there is nothing left over, so there's no remainder. In other words, 4 is divisible by 2. You could also say that the remainder is 0.

Five divided by 2 is 2 with 1 left over; 1 is the remainder. Six divided by 7 is 0 with 6 left over; 6 is the remainder.

You CAN improve your scores!

Factors

A number *a* is a factor of another number *b* if *b* can be divided by *a* without leaving a remainder. 1, 2, 3, 4, 6, and 12 are all factors of 12. Write the factors down systematically in pairs of numbers that when multiplied together make 12, starting with 1 and the number itself:

- 1 and 12,
- 2 and 6,
- 3 and 4.

If you always start with 1 and the number itself and work your way up, you'll remember them all.

Multiples

A multiple of a number is that number multiplied by an integer other than 0. –20, –10, 10, 20, 30, 40, 50, 60 are all multiples of 10 (10×-2, 10×-1, 10×1, 10×2, 10×3, 10×4, 10×5, 10×6).

MORE MATH VOCABULARY

Like we said, the math section is almost as much of a vocabulary test as the verbal section. Below you'll find some standard terms that you should commit to memory before you do any practice problems:

Term	Meaning
sum	the result of addition
difference	the result of subtraction
product	the result of multiplication
quotient	the result of division
numerator	the top number in a fraction
denominator	the bottom number in a fraction

ORDER OF OPERATIONS

Many problems require you to perform more than one operation to find ETS's answer. It is absolutely necessary that you perform these operations in *exactly* the right order. In many cases, the correct order will be apparent from the way the problem is written. In cases where the correct order is not apparent, you need only remember the following mnemonic:

Please Excuse My Dear Aunt Sally, or **PEMDAS**.

PEMDAS stands for **P**arentheses, **E**xponents, **M**ultiplication, **D**ivision, **A**ddition, **S**ubtraction. This is the order in which the operations are to be performed. (Exponents are numbers raised to a power; don't worry, we'll review them soon.)

Here's an example:

$$11 - (7 - 6) - (4 + 3) - 2 =$$

Here's how to crack it

Start with the parentheses. The expression inside the first pair of parentheses, $7 - 6$, equals 1. The expression inside the second pair equals 7. We can now rewrite the problem like this:

$$11 - 1 - 7 - 2 =$$
$$10 - 7 - 2 =$$
$$3 - 2 =$$
$$= 1$$

FRACTIONS

Remember elementary school? A fraction is another way of writing a division problem. For example, the fraction $\frac{2}{3}$ is just another way of writing $2 \div 3$.

A fraction is shorthand for division.

REDUCING FRACTIONS

To reduce a fraction, simply express the numerator and denominator as the products of their factors. Then cross out, or "cancel," factors that are common to both. Here's an example:

$$\frac{16}{20} = \frac{2 \times 2 \times 2 \times 2}{2 \times 2 \times 5} = \frac{\cancel{2} \times \cancel{2} \times 2 \times 2}{\cancel{2} \times \cancel{2} \times 5} = \frac{2 \times 2}{5} = \frac{4}{5}$$

You can achieve the same result by dividing numerator and denominator by the factors that are common to both. In the example you just saw, 4 is a factor of both the numerator and the denominator. That is, both the numerator and the denominator can be divided evenly (without remainder) by 4. Doing this yields the much more manageable fraction $\frac{4}{5}$.

When you confront GRE math problems involving big fractions, always reduce them before doing anything else.

Remember—you cannot reduce across an equal sign (=), a plus sign (+), or a minus sign (–).

MULTIPLYING FRACTIONS

There's nothing tricky about multiplying fractions. Just work straight across. All you have to do is place the product of the numerators over the product of the denominators. But see whether you can reduce before you multiply; then you'll be multiplying smaller numbers. Here's an example:

Always cross off wrong answer choices on your scratch paper.

$$\frac{4}{5} \times \frac{10}{12} =$$

$$\frac{\overset{1}{\cancel{4}}}{\underset{1}{\cancel{5}}} \times \frac{\overset{2}{\cancel{10}}}{\underset{3}{\cancel{12}}} =$$

$$\frac{1}{1} \times \frac{2}{3} = \frac{2}{3}$$

When one fraction is multiplied by another fraction, the product is *smaller* than either of the original fractions. What happens when you multiply $\frac{1}{2}$ by $\frac{1}{2}$? You get $\frac{1}{4}$, which is smaller than $\frac{1}{2}$.

DIVIDING FRACTIONS

Dividing fractions is just like multiplying fractions, with one crucial difference: You have to turn the second fraction upside down (that is, put its denominator over its numerator), then reduce before you multiply. Remember the word "reciprocal"? Here's an example:

$$\frac{2}{3} \div \frac{4}{5} =$$

$$\frac{2}{3} \times \frac{5}{4} =$$

$$\frac{\overset{1}{\cancel{2}}}{3} \times \frac{5}{\underset{2}{\cancel{4}}} =$$

$$\frac{1}{3} \times \frac{5}{2} = \frac{5}{6}$$

ETS sometimes gives you problems involving fractions whose numerators or denominators are themselves fractions. These problems look intimidating, but if you're careful, then you won't have any trouble with them. All you have to do is remember what we said about a fraction being shorthand for division. Always rewrite the expression horizontally. Here's an example:

$$\frac{7}{\frac{1}{4}} = 7 \div \frac{1}{4} = \frac{7}{1} \times \frac{4}{1} = \frac{28}{1} = 28$$

ADDING AND SUBTRACTING FRACTIONS

Adding and subtracting fractions that have the same (common) denominator is easy—just add up the numerators and put the sum over that common denominator. Here's an example:

$$\frac{1}{10} + \frac{2}{10} + \frac{4}{10} =$$
$$\frac{1+2+4}{10} = \frac{7}{10}$$

To add, subtract, or compare fractions, use the BOWTIE.

When you're asked to add or subtract fractions with *different* denominators, you need to fiddle around with them so that they end up with a *common* denominator. To do this, all you need to do is multiply the dominators of the two fractions and use a technique we call **the bowtie**:

$$\frac{2}{3} + \frac{3}{4} =$$

$$\overset{8}{} \qquad \overset{9}{}$$
$$\frac{2}{3} \times \frac{3}{4} = \frac{8}{12} \Big| \frac{9}{12} = \frac{8}{12} + \frac{9}{12} = \frac{17}{12}$$

In other words, multiply the denominators together to get the new denominator, and multiply diagonally up (as shown) to get the new numerators. Then just add or subtract. Using the bowtie on these fractions doesn't change the values of the terms, but it does put them in a form that's easier to handle.

COMPARING FRACTIONS

The GRE CAT often presents you with math problems in which you are asked to compare two fractions and decide which is larger. These problems are a snap if you use the bowtie. You can ignore the denominator and simply find which fraction would have a larger numerator if they had a common denominator. Just multiply the denominator of each fraction by the numerator of the other. Then compare your two products.

$$\frac{3}{7} \qquad \frac{7}{12}$$

$$\overset{36}{} \qquad \overset{49}{}$$
$$\frac{3}{7} \times \frac{7}{12}$$

Multiplying the first denominator by the second numerator gives us 49; be sure to write 49 above $\frac{7}{12}$ on your scratch paper. Multiplying the second denominator by the first numerator gives us 36; write that above $\frac{3}{7}$ on your scratch paper. Since 49 is bigger than 36, $\frac{7}{12}$ is bigger than $\frac{3}{7}$.

When using the bowtie, always work from bottom to top, in the direction of the arrows, as in the problem we just solved. Working in the other direction will give you the wrong answer!

Comparing more than two fractions

You will sometimes be asked to compare more than two fractions. On such problems, don't waste time trying to find a common denominator for all of them. Simply use the bowtie to compare two of the fractions at a time. Here's an example:

$$\frac{3}{7} \quad \frac{4}{8} \quad \frac{7}{11}$$

Here's how to crack it

ETS loves to compare fractions, especially in Quantitative Comparison questions.

Compare the first two fractions and eliminate the smaller one on your scratch paper (read the question carefully!); compare the remaining fraction with the next in line and eliminate the smaller one; and so on. In this case, $\frac{7}{11}$ wins.

$$\overset{24}{\underset{\frac{3}{7}}{}}\times\overset{28}{\underset{\frac{4}{8}}{}}$$

$$\overset{44}{\underset{\frac{4}{8}}{}}\times\overset{56}{\underset{\frac{7}{1}}{}}$$

CONVERTING MIXED NUMBERS INTO FRACTIONS

A **mixed number** is a number that is represented as an integer and a fraction, like this: $2\frac{2}{3}$. In most cases on the GRE, you should get rid of mixed fractions by converting them to fractions. How do you do this? By multiplying the denominator by the integer, adding the numerator, and putting the whole thing over the denominator. In other words $\frac{3\times2+2}{3}$ or $\frac{8}{3}$.

The result, $\frac{8}{3}$, is equivalent to $2\frac{2}{3}$. The only difference is that $\frac{8}{3}$ is easier to work with in math problems. Also, answer choices are usually in this form.

Be careful

The most common source of errors on GRE fraction problems is carelessness. You'll see problems in which finding ETS's answer will require you to perform several of the steps or operations we've described. Remember that the goal of all these steps and operations is to *simplify* the fractions. **Always write down every step! Use that scratch paper!**

DECIMALS

Decimals are just fractions in a different form. Basically, decimals and fractions are two different ways of expressing the same thing. Every decimal can be written as a fraction; every fraction can be written as a decimal. For example, the decimal .35 can be written as the fraction $\frac{35}{100}$. These two expressions, .35 and $\frac{35}{100}$, have exactly the same value.

Don't forget about decimal points when working with decimals.

To turn a fraction into its decimal equivalent, all you have to do is divide the numerator by the denominator. Here, for example, is how you would find the decimal equivalent of $\frac{3}{4}$:

$$\frac{3}{4} = 3 \div 4 = 4\overline{)\begin{array}{r} 0.75 \\ 3.00 \\ \underline{2.8} \\ 20 \\ \underline{20} \\ 0 \end{array}} = 0.75$$

ADDING AND SUBTRACTING DECIMALS

Simply line up the decimal points and proceed as you would if the decimal points weren't there. If the decimal points are missing from the numbers you need to add or subtract, put them in. You can make all your numbers line up evenly by adding zeros to the right of the ones that need them. Here, for example, is how you would add the decimals 23.4, 76, 234.567, and 0.87:

$$\begin{array}{r} 23.400 \\ 76.000 \\ 234.567 \\ + 0.870 \\ \hline 334.837 \end{array}$$

Subtraction works the same way:

$$\begin{array}{r} 16.55 \\ - 4.30 \\ \hline 12.25 \end{array}$$

MULTIPLYING DECIMALS

The only tricky part is remembering where to put the decimal point. Handle the multiplication as you would with integers. Then position the decimal point according to this simple two-step rule:

1. Count the total number of digits to the right of the decimal points in the numbers you are multiplying. If you are multiplying 2.341 and 7.8, for example, you have a total of four digits to the right of the decimal points.

Use that paper!

2. Place the decimal point in your solution so that you have the same number of digits to the right of it. Here's what you get when you multiply the numbers above:

$$\begin{array}{r} 2.341 \\ \times\ 7.8 \\ \hline 18.2598 \end{array}$$

Except for placing the decimal point, we did exactly what we would have done if we had been multiplying 2,341 and 78:

$$\begin{array}{r} 2{,}341 \\ \times\ 78 \\ \hline 182{,}598 \end{array}$$

DIVIDING DECIMALS

Before you can divide decimals, you have to convert the divisor into an integer. (Vocab review: In the division problem $10 \div 2 = 5$, the 10 is the dividend, the 2 is the divisor, and the 5 is the quotient.) Just set up the division as a fraction. All you have to do is move the decimal point all the way to the right. You must then move the decimal point in the dividend the same number of spaces to the right. Here's an example:

$$20 \div 1.2$$

Here's how to crack it

First, set up the division problem as a fraction:

$$\frac{20}{1.2}$$

Now start moving decimal points. The divisor, 1.2, has one digit to the right of the decimal point. To turn 1.2 into an integer, therefore, we need to move the decimal point one space to the right. Doing so turns 1.2 into 12.

Because we've moved the decimal point in the divisor one place, we also need to move the decimal point in the dividend one place. This turns 20 into 200. Here's what we're left with:

$$\frac{200}{12}$$

Now all we would have to do to find our answer is complete the division: 200 divided by 12 is 16.66 repeating.

COMPARING DECIMALS

Which is larger: 0.00099 or 0.001? ETS loves this sort of problem. You'll never go wrong, though, if you:

- Line up the numbers on their decimal points.
- Fill in the missing zeroes.

Here's how to answer the question we just asked. First, line up the two numbers on their decimal points:

0.00099

0.001

Now fill in the missing zeros:

0.00099

0.00100

Can you tell which number is larger? Of course you can. 0.00100 is larger than 0.00099, because 100 is larger than 99.

Convert decimals to fractions

Fractions are safer and easier to work with than decimals. When you're trying to solve a decimal problem, convert the decimals to fractions. If the answer choices are decimals, convert back to decimals when you finish the work.

> Decimals are DANGEROUS.
> Fractions are safer.

EXPONENTS AND SQUARE ROOTS

WHAT ARE EXPONENTS?

Exponents are a sort of mathematical shorthand. Instead of writing (2)(2)(2)(2) we can write 2^4. The little 4 is called an exponent and the big 2 is called a base. The following is all you need to remember about exponents: **When in doubt, expand it out!**

Multiplication with exponents

It's easy to multiply two or more numbers with the same base. All you have to do is add up the exponents. For example:

$$2^2 \times 2^4 =$$
$$2^{2+4} = 2^6$$

You can see this when you expand it out, which is just as good a way to solve the problem:

$$2^2 \times 2^4 =$$
$$2 \times 2 \times 2 \times 2 \times 2 \times 2 = 2^6$$

Be careful, though. This rule does *not* apply to addition. $2^2 + 2^4$ *does not equal* 2^6. There's no quick and easy method of adding numbers with exponents. But you'll never have to do it on the GRE CAT.

Division with exponents

Dividing two or more numbers with the same base is easy, too. All you have to do is subtract the exponents. For example:

$$2^6 \div 2^2 = 2^{6-2} = 2^4$$

You can see this easily when you expand it out.

$$2^6 \div 2^2 = \frac{2 \times 2 \times 2 \times 2 \times 2 \times 2}{2 \times 2} = 2 \times 2 \times 2 \times 2 = 2^4$$

If you EXPAND IT OUT, you'll never be in doubt.

Once again, don't assume this same shortcut applies to subtraction of numbers with exponents. It doesn't. But again, you won't have to worry about it on the GRE CAT.

Another time you might need to divide with exponents is when you see a negative exponent. You just put 1 over it and get rid of the negative. For example:

$$3^{-2}$$

should be rewritten as

$$\frac{1}{3^2}$$

That gives us

$$\frac{1}{9}$$

Please excuse...

Remember PEMDAS? Pay close attention when there are exponents inside and outside the parentheses. You can simply multiply the exponents. Here's an example:

$$(4^5)^2 =$$
$$4^{5 \times 2} =$$
$$4^{10}$$

Don't be shy about expanding these out on your scratch paper. It doesn't take too much time, and it's better to be correct than to be fast.

$$(4^5)^2 =$$
$$(4 \times 4 \times 4 \times 4 \times 4)(4 \times 4 \times 4 \times 4 \times 4) = 4^{10}$$

IF YOU ALWAYS EXPAND IT OUT, YOU'LL NEVER BE IN DOUBT

When solving problems involving exponents, it's extremely important to pay careful attention to terms within parentheses. When an exponent appears on the outside of a parenthetical expression, expanding it out is the best way to ensure that you don't make a careless mistake. For example, $(3x)^2 = (3x)(3x) = 9x^2$, not $3x^2$.

The same is true of fractions within parentheses: $\left(\frac{3}{2}\right)^2 = \left(\frac{3}{2}\right)\left(\frac{3}{2}\right) = \frac{9}{4}$.

THE PECULIAR BEHAVIOR OF EXPONENTS

- Raising a number greater than 1 to a power greater than 1 results in a *bigger* number. For example, $2^2 = 4$.

- Raising a fraction between 0 and 1 to a power greater than 1 results in a *smaller* number. For example, $\left(\frac{1}{2}\right)^2 = \frac{1}{4}$.

- A negative number raised to an even power becomes *positive*. For example, $(-2)^2 = 4$ because $(-2)(-2) = 4$.

- A negative number raised to an odd power remains *negative*. For example, $(-2)^3 = -8$ because $(-2)(-2)(-2) = -8$.

- A number raised to a negative power is equal to 1 over the number raised to the positive version of that power. For example, $2^{-2} = \frac{1}{2^2} = \frac{1}{4}$.

- A number raised to the 0 power is ALWAYS 1, no matter what the number is. For example, $1,000^0 = 1$.

- A number raised to the first power is ALWAYS the number itself. For example, $1,000^1 = 1,000$.

WHAT IS A SQUARE ROOT?

The sign $\sqrt{}$ indicates the square root of a number. For example, $\sqrt{2}$ means that something squared equals 2.

If $x^2 = 16$, then $x = \pm 4$. You must be especially careful to remember this on quantitative comparison questions. But when ETS asks you for the value $\sqrt{16}$, or the square root of any number, you are being asked for the *positive* root only. Although squaring -5 will result in 25, just as squaring 5 will, when ETS asks for $\sqrt{25}$, the only answer it's looking for is $+5$.

PLAYING WITH SQUARE ROOTS

You multiply and divide square roots just like you would any other number:

$$\sqrt{3} \times \sqrt{12} = \sqrt{36} = 6$$

$$\sqrt{\frac{16}{4}} = \frac{\sqrt{16}}{\sqrt{4}} = \frac{4}{2} = 2$$

> You can multiply and divide any square roots, but you can only add or subtract roots when they are the same.

However, you can't add or subtract them unless the roots are the same:
So $\sqrt{2} + \sqrt{2} = 2\sqrt{2}$. (Just pretend there's an invisible 1 in front of the root sign.)

But $\sqrt{2} + \sqrt{3}$ does *not* equal $\sqrt{5}$!

LEARN THESE FOUR VALUES

To use our techniques, you'll need to memorize the following values. You should be able to recite them without hesitation.

$$\sqrt{1} = 1$$
$$\sqrt{2} = 1.4$$
$$\sqrt{3} = 1.7$$
$$\sqrt{4} = 2$$

You'll see them again when we discuss geometry.

A FEW LAWS

ASSOCIATIVE LAW

There are actually two associative laws—one for addition and one for multiplication. For the sake of simplicity, we've lumped them together.

Don't worry about the word "associative." Here's all you need to know: *When you are adding a series of numbers or multiplying a series of numbers, you can regroup the numbers in any way you'd like.* Here are some examples:

$$4 + (5 + 8) = (4 + 5) + 8 = (4 + 8) + 5$$
$$(a + b) + (c + d) = a + (b + c + d)$$
$$4 \times (5 \times 8) = (4 \times 5) \times 8 = (4 \times 8) \times 5$$
$$(ab)(cd) = a(bcd)$$

DISTRIBUTIVE LAW

This is often tested on the GRE. You must know it cold. Here's what it looks like:

$$a(b + c) = ab + ac$$
$$a(b - c) = ab - ac$$

For example:

$$12(66) + 12(24) =$$

Here's how to crack it

This is really just *ab* + *ac*. Using the distributive law, this must equal 12(66 + 24), or 12(90) = 1080.

FACTORING AND UNFACTORING

When you use the distributive law to rewrite the expression $xy + xz$ in the form $x(y + z)$, you are said to be *factoring* the original expression. That is, you take the factor common to both terms of the original expression x, and "pull it out." This gives you a new, "factored" version of the expression you began with.

When you use the distributive law to rewrite the expression $x(y + z)$ in the form $xy + xz$, we say that you are *unfactoring* the original expression.

ETS is very predictable. Because of this, we can tell you that on any problem containing an expression that can be factored, you should always factor that expression. If, for example, you encounter a problem containing the expression $5x + 5y$, you should immediately factor it, to make the expression $5(x + y)$.

Similarly, whenever you find an expression that has been factored, you should immediately *un*factor it, by multiplying it out. In other words, if a problem contains the expression $5(x + y)$, you should unfactor it, yielding the expression $5x + 5y$.

Sometimes on a hard question you might see some ugly-looking thing like this that you have to simplify:

$$\frac{8^7 - 8^6}{7}$$

To simplify the numerator, you can factor out the biggest chunk that's common to both. In other words, the biggest thing that goes into both 8^7 and 8^6 is 8^6. So, you can "pull out" an 8^6, like so:

$$\frac{8^6\left(8^1 - 1\right)}{7}$$

This can be simplified even further:

$$\frac{8^6(7)}{7} = 8^6$$

PROBABILITY

If you flip a coin, what's the probability that it will land heads up? One out of two, or $\frac{1}{2}$. What is the probability that it won't land heads up? One out of two, or $\frac{1}{2}$. If you flip a coin nine times, what's the probability that the coin will land on "heads" on the tenth flip? One out of two, or $\frac{1}{2}$. Previous flips do not affect anything.

Think of probability in terms of fractions:

- If it is impossible for something to happen, the probability of it happening is equal to 0.
- If something is certain to happen, the probability is equal to 1.
- If it is possible for something to happen, but not necessary, the probability is between 0 and 1, otherwise known as a fraction.

$$\text{probability} = \frac{\text{outcome you're looking for}}{\text{total outcomes}}$$

Let's see how it works:

> Fifteen marbles are placed in a bowl; some are red, and some are blue. If the number of red marbles is one more than the number of blue marbles, what is the probability that a marble taken from the bowl is blue?
>
> ○ $\dfrac{1}{15}$
>
> ○ $\dfrac{2}{15}$
>
> ○ $\dfrac{7}{15}$
>
> ○ $\dfrac{1}{2}$
>
> ○ $\dfrac{8}{15}$

Here's how to crack it

We have 15 marbles, and there's 1 more red than blue. That means there must be 8 red marbles and 7 blue marbles. Now we need the probability that we'd pick a blue marble. That would be 7 out of a possible 15. Express it as a fraction, and you get choice (C), $\dfrac{7}{15}$.

Let's try another one:

> In a bowl containing 10 marbles, 5 are yellow and 5 are green. If 2 marbles are picked from the bowl at random, what is the probability that they will <u>both</u> be green?
>
> ○ $\dfrac{1}{5}$
>
> ○ $\dfrac{2}{9}$
>
> ○ $\dfrac{1}{4}$
>
> ○ $\dfrac{1}{2}$
>
> ○ $\dfrac{15}{18}$

Write everything down on scratch paper! Don't do anything in your head!

Here's how to crack it

Let's do this one draw at a time. On the first draw, the probability of drawing a green marble is 5 out of 10, or $\frac{1}{2}$—but now that marble is no longer in the bowl. So on the second draw, the probability of drawing a green marble is 4 out of 9. Therefore, the probability of both is equal to $\frac{1}{2} \times \frac{4}{9}$, which is $\frac{4}{18}$, or $\frac{2}{9}$. That's choice (B).

PERMUTATIONS AND COMBINATIONS

A permutation is an arrangement of things in a definite order. You may remember the word *factorial*. Four factorial, or 4!, equals $4 \times 3 \times 2 \times 1$, which is 24.

Suppose you were asked to figure out how many different ways you could arrange 5 statues on a shelf. All you have to do is multiply $5 \times 4 \times 3 \times 2 \times 1$, or 120. That's it.

The difference between a permutation and a combination is that in a combination, order doesn't matter. For example, suppose you were asked to figure out how many different three-flavor combinations of ice cream flavors you could make out of the following five flavors: vanilla, chocolate, strawberry, butter pecan, and mocha. In this case, order doesn't matter, because vanilla-chocolate-strawberry is the same as chocolate-strawberry-vanilla. So here's what you do: Use brute force; in other words, write out every combination:

VCS VCB VCM VSB VSM VBM CSB CSM CBM SBM

That's 10 combinations. Or you can use the following formula:

$$\frac{n!}{(n-r)!(r!)}.$$

This is the formula if you have n things being used r at a time. Remember, that "!" sign means "factorial." In our ice cream example, we have 5 flavors being used 3 at a time. Let's plug that into the formula.

$$\frac{5!}{(5-3)!(3!)}$$

$$\frac{5 \times 4 \times 3 \times 2 \times 1}{(2 \times 1)(3 \times 2 \times 1)}$$

Don't forget to reduce:

$$\frac{5 \times 4}{2 \times 1} =$$

$$\frac{20}{2} =$$

$$= 10$$

Bingo.

ALWAYS write down A, B, C, D for quant comps.

QUANTITATIVE COMPARISON

OUR OWN DIRECTIONS

Usually we tell you to learn ETS's directions. This time we're going to tell you to learn our own directions instead. Why? Because our directions are better than ETS's. They'll keep you out of trouble. Remember, we're using A, B, C, and D to refer to the answer choices. Here they are:

> Directions: This question consists of two quantities, one in Column A and one in Column B. You are to compare the two quantities and choose:
>
> A if the quantity in Column A is <u>always</u> greater
> B if the quantity in Column B is <u>always</u> greater
> C if the quantities are <u>always</u> equal
> D if <u>different</u> numbers would result in <u>different</u> answers

THERE IS NO FIFTH CHOICE

Quant comps have only four answer choices. That's great—A blind guess has one chance in four of being correct.

WRITE IT DOWN

Always write A, B, C, D (no "E") on your scratch paper. Then use Process of Elimination in the same way you would on questions that provide the answer choices. Cross off wrong answer choices as you go.

WHAT ABOUT THE MATH?

The content of quant comp problems is drawn from the same basic arithmetic, algebra, and geometry concepts that are used on GRE CAT math problems in other formats. In general, then, you'll apply the same techniques that you use on other types of math questions. Still, quant comps do require a few special techniques of their own.

IF A QUANT COMP QUESTION CONTAINS ONLY NUMBERS, THE ANSWER CAN'T BE D

POE is your new religion.

Any problem containing only numbers must have a single solution. Therefore, choice (D) can be eliminated immediately on all such problems. For example, if you are asked to compare $\frac{3}{2}$ and $\frac{3}{4}$, you know the answer can be determined, so the answer could never be choice (D).

IT'S NOT WHAT IT IS; BUT WHICH IS BIGGER

You don't always have to figure out what the exact values would be in both columns *before* you compare them. The prime directive is to compare the two columns. Treat the two columns as if they were the two sides of an equation.

Anything you can do to both sides of an equation, you can also do to the expressions in both columns on a quant comp. You can add the same number to both sides; you can multiply both sides by the same positive number; you can simplify a single side by multiplying it by some form of one.

Don't multiply or divide both sides by a negative number

When you multiply or divide both sides of an inequality by a negative number, the direction of the inequality symbol changes (you'll learn more about that later). If the quantity in Column A is greater than the quantity in Column B, multiplying or dividing by a negative number will make Column A smaller than Column B—so don't do it.

Always simplify

If you *can* simplify the terms in a quant comp, you should *always* do so. As is so often true on the GRE CAT, finding ETS's answer is frequently merely a matter of simplifying, reducing, factoring, or unfactoring. Here's an example:

Column A	Column B
25 × 6.28	$\dfrac{628}{4}$

- ○ the quantity in Column A is always greater
- ○ the quantity in Column B is always greater
- ○ the quantities are always equal
- ○ it cannot be determined from the information given

Here's how to crack it

First of all, you should notice that choice (D) can't be ETS's answer: There's nothing here but numbers. Cross out (D) on your scratch paper.

What should you do next? Whatever you do, *don't* do the multiplication in the first column and the division in the second. You'd find the answer that way, but it would take forever. Instead, get rid of the fraction in Column B by multiplying *both sides* by 4. Here's what you end up with:

Column A	Column B
100 × 6.28	628

- ○ the quantity in Column A is always greater
- ○ the quantity in Column B is always greater
- ○ the quantities are always equal
- ○ it cannot be determined from the information given

Notice anything? You get 628 in both columns. That means ETS's answer is choice (C), the quantities are equal.

> Always cross off wrong answer choices on your scratch paper.

Let's try another one:

Column A	Column B
$\dfrac{1}{16} + \dfrac{1}{7} + \dfrac{1}{4}$	$\dfrac{1}{4} + \dfrac{1}{16} + \dfrac{1}{6}$

○ the quantity in Column A is
  always greater
○ the quantity in Column B is
  always greater
○ the quantities are always equal
○ it cannot be determined from
  the information given

Here's how to crack it

Remember, it's not what's in each column, but which is bigger. Of course, first eliminate choice (D). Then get rid of the numbers that are common to both columns ($\dfrac{1}{16}$ and $\dfrac{1}{4}$). What's left? In Column A you have $\dfrac{1}{7}$; in Column B, $\dfrac{1}{6}$.

How do you know which is greater? Use the bowtie! The ETS answer is choice (B).

So now you're back in shape, numbers-wise. It's time to move on to letters. Yep, there are letters in math, too.

11

Variables and Equations

So far, we've been playing with numbers. But many GRE math problems involve letters, or variables (such as n, x, or y). It's time to learn how to deal with those.

SOLVING FOR ONE VARIABLE

If you have one equation with one variable, you can solve it. Try to get the variable on one side of the equation, and the numbers on the other side. To do this, you can add, subtract, multiply, or divide both sides of the equation by the same number. Just remember that anything you do to one side of an equation, you must do to the other side. Be sure to write down every step. Let's look at a simple example:

$$3x - 4 = 5$$

Always write A B C D E on your scratch paper to represent the answer choices (or A B C D if it's quant comp)

Here's how to crack it

You can get rid of negatives by adding something to both sides of the equation, just as you can get rid of positives by subtracting something from both sides of the equation.

$$3x - 4 = 5$$
$$+4 = +4$$
$$3x = 9$$

You may already see that $x = 3$. But don't forget to write down that last step. Divide both sides of the equation by 3:

$$\frac{3x}{3} = \frac{9}{3}$$
$$x = 3$$

Let's try another one:

$$5x - 13 = 12 - 20x$$

Here's how to crack it

First of all, we want to get all the x values on the same side of the equation:

$$5x - 13 = 12 - 20x$$
$$\underline{+20x \qquad\qquad +20x}$$
$$25x - 13 = 12$$

Now we can get rid of that negative 13:

$$25x - 13 = 12$$
$$\underline{+13 \ +13}$$
$$25x \qquad = 25$$

Now it might be pretty obvious that x is 1, but let's just finish it:

$$25x = 25$$
$$\frac{25x}{25} = \frac{25}{25}$$
$$x = 1$$

Let's try another one:

$$5x + \frac{3}{2} = 7x$$

Here's how to crack it

First multiply both sides by 2 to get rid of the fraction:

$$10x + 3 = 14x$$

Now get both x's on the same side:

$$
\begin{array}{r}
10x + 3 = 14x \\
-10x \quad\quad -10x \\
\hline
3 = 4x
\end{array}
$$

Now finish it up:

$$3 = 4x$$

$$\frac{3}{4} = \frac{4x}{4}$$

$$\frac{3}{4} = x$$

You must always do the same thing to both sides of an equation.

INEQUALITIES

In an equation, one side equals another. In an inequality, one expression does not equal another. The symbol for an equation is an equal sign. Here are the symbols for inequalities:

≠ is not equal to
> is greater than
< is less than
≥ is greater than or equal to
≤ is less than or equal to

You can manipulate any inequality in the same way you can an equation, with one important difference. When you multiply or divide both sides of an inequality by a negative number, the direction of the inequality symbol changes. That is, if $x > y$, then $-x < -y$.

To see what we mean, take a look at a simple inequality:

$$12 - 6x > 0$$

Here's how to crack it

You could manipulate this inequality without ever multiplying or dividing by a negative number. Just add $6x$ to both sides. The sign stays the same. Then divide both sides by positive 6. Again, the sign stays the same.

$$12 - 6x > 0$$
$$\underline{+6x > +6x}$$
$$12 > 6x$$
$$\frac{12}{6} > \frac{6x}{6}$$
$$2 > x$$

But suppose you subtract 12 from both sides at first:

$$12 - 6x > 0$$
$$\underline{-12 \qquad > -12}$$
$$-6x > -12$$
$$\frac{-6x}{-6} < \frac{-12}{-6}$$
$$x < 2$$

Notice that the sign flipped that time. But the answer is the same.

PLUGGING IN

When a problem has variables in the answer choices, PLUG IN!

Many GRE CAT math problems have variables in the answer choices. ETS knows that most people try to do them algebraically. ETS also knows which algebraic mistakes most people will make, and what answers would result from those mistakes. That's how they design the wrong answers to these problems. (Remember distractors?) To avoid trap answers on these problems, the fastest and easiest way to find ETS's answer is by making up numbers and plugging them in. Plugging in makes word problems much less abstract, and much easier to solve. Here's what you do:

1. Pick a number for each variable in the problem and write it on your scratch paper.

2. Solve the problem using your numbers. Write down your numerical answer and circle it; that's your "target answer."

3. Write down the answer choices and plug your numbers in for each one, to see which choice equals the target answer you found in step 2.

Here's an example:

$$3[3a + (5a + 7a)] - (5a + 7a) =$$

- ○ 9a
- ○ 12a
- ○ 15a
- ○ 33a
- ○ 47a

Here's how to crack it

All you have to do is come up with a number for the variable a. How about 2? Write down $a = 2$ on your scratch paper. Now the question says:

$$3\big[3(2)+\big(5(2)+7(2)\big)\big]-\big(5(2)+7(2)\big) =$$

Don't forget about PEMDAS.

$$3[6 + (10 + 14)] - (10 + 14) =$$
$$3[6 + 24] - 24 =$$
$$3(30) - 24 =$$
$$90 - 24 = 66$$

By plugging in, we turned this algebra question into an arithmetic question, and we got 66. Circle the number 66 on your scratch paper, because that's your target answer. Now plug 2 in for the variable in all the answer choices until you get 66. You might see the right answer already, but let's just go through the motions.

- (A) $9(2) = 18$—Nope.
- (B) $12(2) = 24$—Nope.
- (C) $15(2) = 30$—Nope.
- (D) $33(2) = 66$—Bingo!
- (E) $47(2) = 94$—Nope.

Even if you think you can do the algebra, plug in instead. Why? Because if you do the algebra wrong, you won't know it—one of ETS's wrong answers will be there waiting for you. But, if you plug in and you're wrong, you won't get an answer, and you'll know you're wrong, forcing you to try again. Plugging in is foolproof. Algebra isn't.

CAN I JUST PLUG IN ANYTHING?

You can plug in any numbers you like, as long as they're consistent with any restrictions stated in the problem, but it's faster if you use easy numbers. What makes a number easy? That depends on the problem. In most cases, smaller numbers are easier to work with than larger numbers. Usually, it's best to start small, with 3, for example. (Avoid 0 and 1; both 0 and 1 have special properties, which you'll hear more about later.) Do not plug in any numbers that show up a lot in the question or answer choices. Plug in numbers that make the arithmetic easy.

Try this one. Read through the whole question before you start to plug in numbers:

> The price of a certain stock increased 8 points, then decreased 13 points, and then increased 9 points. If the stock price before the changes was x points, which of the following was the stock price, in points, after the changes?
>
> ○ $x - 5$
> ○ $x - 4$
> ○ $x + 4$
> ○ $x + 5$
> ○ $x + 8$

Plug In numbers that will make the math EASY.

Here's how to crack it

Let's use an easy number like 10 for the variable (write down $x = 10$ on your scratch paper!). If the original price was 10, and then it increased 8 points, that's 18. Then it decreased 13 points, so now it's 5 (do everything out on the scratch paper—don't even add or subtract in your head). Then it increased 9 points, so now it's 14. So, it started at 10, and ended at 14. Circle the 14 (our target answer) and plug in 10 for every x in the answer choices. Which one gives you 14?

(A) $10 - 5 = 5$—Nope.

(B) $10 - 4 = 6$—Nope.

(C) $10 + 4 = 14$—Bingo!

(D) $10 + 5 = 15$—Nope.

(E) $10 + 8 = 18$—Nope.

Pretty easy, huh?

GOOD NUMBERS MAKE LIFE EASIER

Always PLUG IN when you see variables in the answer choices!

Small numbers aren't always best. In a problem involving percentages, for example, 10 and 100 are good numbers to use. In a problem involving minutes or seconds, 60 may be the easiest number to plug in. You should look for clues in the problem itself. Here's an example:

At the rate of $\dfrac{f}{3}$ feet per m minutes, how many feet can a bicycle travel in s seconds?

○ $\dfrac{fs}{60m}$

○ $\dfrac{60s}{fm}$

○ $\dfrac{fms}{180}$

○ $\dfrac{fm}{180s}$

○ $\dfrac{fs}{180m}$

Here's how to crack it

Don't forget to write everything down. Let's make $f = 12$ (because it's divisible by 3) and $m = 2$, so the bicycle is going 4 feet per 2 minutes. Since this question involves minutes and seconds, let's use a multiple of 60 for s. We don't want to use numbers that are in the answer choices (such as 60 or 180). What if we made it 120? After all, 120 seconds is the same as 2 minutes, and we already know it's 4 feet per 2 minutes. If s is 120, our target answer is 4. Circle it.

Now to the answers. Remember, $f = 12$, $m = 2$, and $s = 120$, and the target is 4.

(A) $\dfrac{12(120)}{120} = 12$. Nope.

(B) $\dfrac{(60)120}{24} = 300$. Nope.

(C) $\dfrac{(12)(2)(120)}{180} = 16$. Nope.

(D) This will have a really big denominator. Nope.

(E) $\dfrac{(12)(120)}{180(2)} = \dfrac{144}{36} = \dfrac{12}{3} = 4$. Bingo!

See? No algebra, just multiplication and division. Checking all the choices is worth doing. It's fast and easy. If more than one answer choice works with the first numbers you plugged in, eliminate the choices that don't work, and plug in new numbers. Get a new target answer, and plug in your new numbers for the remaining answer choices. Then eliminate the answer choices that don't work with your new numbers.

DON'T LOOK A GIFT HORSE . . .

ETS will sometimes give you a value for one of the variables or terms in an expression and then ask you for the value of the entire expression. Nothing could be easier. Simply plug in the value that ETS gives you and see what you come up with. Here's an example:

> Remember, the answer is on the screen!

If $x = 1$, then

$$\left(2 - \frac{1}{2-x}\right)\left(2 - \frac{1}{3-x}\right)\left(2 - \frac{1}{4-x}\right) =$$

○ $\dfrac{1}{6}$

○ $\dfrac{5}{6}$

○ $\dfrac{5}{2}$

○ $\dfrac{10}{3}$

○ $\dfrac{7}{2}$

Here's how to crack it

Forget about algebra, ETS is actually giving you a number to plug in. So, substitute 1 in for x, and you get this:

$$\left(2 - \frac{1}{2-1}\right)\left(2 - \frac{1}{3-1}\right)\left(2 - \frac{1}{4-1}\right) =$$

$$(2-1)\left(2 - \frac{1}{2}\right)\left(2 - \frac{1}{3}\right) =$$

$$(1)\left(\frac{3}{2}\right)\left(\frac{5}{3}\right) = \frac{5}{2}$$

So, the answer is (C).

You should never, never, never try to solve problems like these by "solving for x" or "solving for y." Plugging in is much easier and faster, and you'll be less likely to make careless mistakes.

"MUST BE" PROBLEMS

These "algebraic reasoning" problems are much easier to solve by plugging in than by "reasoning." On these, you will have to plug in more than once in order to find ETS's answer.

Here's an example:

> If x is a positive integer, for which of the following equations must y be a negative integer?
>
> ○ $xy = 9$
> ○ $x + y = 7$
> ○ $x + 2y = 6$
> ○ $y - x = 4$
> ○ $-x - y = 3$

Try to disprove answer choices on MUST BE problems. Plug In numbers, eliminate answer choices with those numbers, then Plug In different numbers to eliminate any remaining choices.

Here's how to crack it

We need a positive integer for x—how about 10? Plug that into the answer choices to see which one forces y to be negative.

(A) $10y = 9$. Nope. $y = \frac{9}{10}$, which isn't a negative integer. Eliminate this choice.

(B) $10 + y = 7$. Yes. $y = -3$. Keep it.

(C) $10 + 2y = 6$. That's $2y = -4$. $y = -2$, so let's keep it.

(D) $y - 10 = 4$. Nope. $y = 14$. Eliminate it.

(E) $-10 - y = 3$. That means $-y = 13$, or $y = -13$. Yes, keep it.

Okay, we eliminated (A) and (D). Now, because the question says "must be," we need to try another number in the choices we kept after the first round: (B), (C), and (E). Let's try plugging in the number 1:

(B) $1 + y = 7$. So $y = 6$. Eliminate it.

(C) $1 + 2y = 6$. That's $2y = 5$. y isn't an integer. Eliminate it.

(E) $-1 - y = 3$. That's $-y = 4$, or $y = -4$. Bingo.

Notice that on the "second round" of elimination we plugged in a "weird" number that we usually avoid. That's how we found what would always be true. That leads us to . . .

PLUGGING IN ON QUANT COMP

The easiest way to solve most quant comps involving variables is to plug in, just as you would on word problems. But because answer choice (D) is always an option, you always have to make sure it isn't the answer. So...

ALWAYS PLUG IN AT LEAST TWICE IN QUANT COMP

Plugging in on Quant Comp is just like plugging in on "must be" problems. The reason for this is choice (D). On quant comps, it's not enough to determine whether one quantity is sometimes greater than, less than, or equal to the other; you have to determine whether it *always* is. If different numbers lead to different answers, then ETS's answer is choice (D). Practice using this step-by-step procedure:

> On Quant Comp, Plug In "normal numbers," and eliminate two choices. Then Plug In "weird" numbers (zero, one, negatives, fractions, or big numbers) to try to disprove your first answer. If different numbers give you different answers, you've proved that the answer is D.

- Step 1: Write A, B, C, D on your scratch paper.

- Step 2: Plug in "normal" numbers like 2, 3, or 5.

- Step 3: Which column is bigger? Cross out the two choices that you've proved are wrong. Suppose the numbers you plugged in at first made Column A bigger; which answer choices cannot be correct? (B) and (C). Cross them out! (A) and (D) are still possible choices.

- Step 4: Now try to get a different answer! Plug in weird numbers such as 0, 1, negatives, fractions, or really big numbers. If you get a different result, then the answer is (D). If you keep getting the same result, that's your answer.

What makes certain numbers weird? They behave in unexpected ways when added, multiplied, or raised to powers. For example:

- 0 times any number is 0.

- 0^2 is 0.

- 1^2 is 1.

- $\left(\dfrac{1}{2}\right)^2$ is less than $\dfrac{1}{2}$.

- $(-2)(-2)$ is 4.

- a negative number squared is positive.

- really big numbers (100, 1,000) can make a really big difference in your answer.

ZERO KILLS

One of the most important properties of zero is its ability to annihilate other numbers. Any number multiplied by 0 equals 0. This fact gives you an important piece of information. For example, if you are told that $ab = 0$, then you know without a doubt that either a or b or both must be equal to 0. You can plug in zero to make the arithmetic simple on quant comp questions. Keep this in mind.

LET'S DO IT

Okay, let's try a quant comp plugging-in example:

Column A	Column B
	$y > 2$	
$y - 6$	-3

○ the quantity in Column A is always greater
○ the quantity in Column B is greater
○ the quantities are always equal
○ it cannot be determined from the information given

Here's how to crack it

See the variables? This is clearly a plug-in problem. Let's start by plugging in 3 for y. That gives us –3 in both columns. So far the answer is (C). That means you can eliminate choices (A) and (B). But what if we plug in a different number for y? It has to be bigger than 2, so that rules out 0, 1, and negatives. But how about a much bigger number, like 100? That gives us 94 in Column A and –3 in Column B, which gives us (A). Since we got (C) with one number and (A) with another, the answer must be (D). Different numbers gave us different answers.

PLUGGING IN THE ANSWER CHOICES

You don't have to wait for variables to plug in. You get the answer choices, and you know one of them is correct. Why not plug them in? Simply try the number in an answer choice and see if it works. If it works, you have ETS's answer. If it doesn't work, you try another. There are only five choices on regular math problems. One of these choices has to be ETS's answer. You will often find this answer by trying just one or two of the choices; you will never have to try all five.

When plugging in the answer choices, it's usually a good idea to start in the middle and work your way out. As usual, we'll refer to the middle one as choice (C). Why work from the middle? Because GRE CAT answer choices are almost always arranged in order of size. You may be able to tell not only that a particular choice is incorrect but also that it is too big or too small. Sometimes you can eliminate three choices just by trying one! Make sure you write down all the answer choices on your scratch paper so you can cross them out as you go.

Here's an example:

> In a certain hardware store, 3 percent of the lawnmowers needed new labels. If the price per label was $4 and the total cost for new lawnmower labels was $96, how many lawnmowers are in the hardware store?
>
> ○ 1600
> ○ 800
> ○ 240
> ○ 120
> ○ 24

Are you tempted to do algebra? Are there numbers in the answer choices? Plug In the answer choices!

Here's how to crack it

The question is asking us for the number of lawnmowers in the hardware store, so let's plug in 240—answer choice (C). Now go back to the beginning of the question. Three percent of the lawnmowers need new labels, so that's 3% of 240, or 7.2. The price per label is $4 each, which would be 4 multiplied by 7.2, or $28.80. But the question says the total cost for new lawnmower labels is $96, not $28.80.

What we've learned by plugging in the middle choice is that (C) is not the answer, and that 240 is too small a number. Choices (D) or (E) are even smaller, so we can eliminate them. We know we need a bigger number, so let's try choice (B), 800.

Okay, now there are 800 lawnmowers, and 3% of them need new labels. That's 24 labels, and they cost $4 each. What's 4 multiplied by 24? Yes, it's 96. Everything in the question checks out, so (B) is our answer. Note that if (B) didn't work, we would automatically know that the answer is (A)—it would be the only choice left.

It might have been even easier to start with choice (B), or 800, since we needed to take a percentage of the number of lawnmowers, and it's really easy to find percentages of multiples of 100. You don't always have to start with choice (C); you can start with a value near the middle that's easy to work with.

Just make sure you write EVERYTHING down when doing these questions (and indeed, all math questions).

Here's another example:

When you're Plugging In the answer choices, start with choice (C) (or the middle value).

A contest winner received $\frac{1}{4}$ of his winnings in cash, and received four prizes, each worth $\frac{1}{4}$ of the balance. If the cash and one of the prizes were worth a combined total of $35,000, what was the total value of his winnings?

- $70,000
- $75,000
- $80,000
- $95,000
- $140,000

Here's how to crack it

Let's say the answer to the question (the total value of the winnings) is $80,000, or choice (C). Now go back to the beginning of the question. One-fourth of the winnings was in cash, so that's $20,000. The balance would be $60,000, and he got four prizes each worth $\frac{1}{4}$ of $60,000, or $15,000. Now, does the cash ($20,000) plus the value of one of the prizes ($15,000) equal $35,000, as the question requires? Yes, it does. We're done. The answer is (C). Plugging In is a fabulous technique for word problems that can really save you some time on the GRE CAT.

Try this one:

The sum of x distinct integers greater than zero is less than 75. What is the greatest possible value of x?

- 8
- 9
- 10
- 11
- 12

Here's how to crack it

Notice that this time the question is asking for the greatest value of x. The greatest number in the answer choices is 12, choice (E)—so that's where we'll start. Is the sum of 12 distinct integers greater than zero less than 75? Let's see:

$$1 + 2 + 3 + 4 + 5 + 6 + 7 + 8 + 9 + 10 + 11 + 12 = 78$$

So 12 is too big, but by just a little. That means the answer is 11, or (D). Didn't Plugging In make that easy?

FUNCTIONS AND FUNNY-LOOKING SYMBOLS

The GRE CAT contains "function" problems, but they aren't like the functions that you may have learned in high school. GRE functions use funny-looking symbols, such as @, *, and #. Each symbol represents an arithmetic operation or a series of arithmetic operations. All you have to do is follow directions. Here's an example:

Column A   Column B

For any non-negative
integer x, let $x^* = x-1$

$$\frac{15^*}{3^*}$$ $$\left(\frac{15}{3}\right)^*$$

○ the quantity in Column A is
    always greater
○ the quantity in Column B is
    always greater
○ the quantities are always equal
○ it cannot be determined from
    the information given

> With Funny Symbols, follow the directions. Just do it.

Here's how to crack it

Just follow the directions—$15^* = 15 - 1$, or 14, and $3^* = 3 - 1$, or 2. So we get $\frac{14}{2}$, or 7, in Column A. Don't forget PEMDAS for Column B. First, $\frac{15}{3}$ is 5. Then, $5^* = 5 - 1$, or 4. So 7 in Column A and 4 in Column B means the answer is (A). Function questions aren't scary if you follow the directions. Be sure to write everything down on your scratch paper. By the way, these funny-looking symbols aren't always exponents. But you'll always be told what they mean in the question.

PERCENTAGES

You already know that a fraction is another way of representing division and that a decimal is the same thing as a fraction. Well, a percentage is also another way to represent division, and likewise, the same thing as a fraction or a decimal. A percentage is just a way of expressing a fraction whose denominator is 100.

Percent literally means "per 100" or "out of 100" or "divided by 100." If your best friend finds a dollar and gives you 50¢, your friend has given you 50¢ out of 100, or $\frac{50}{100}$ of a dollar, or 50% of a dollar.

You should memorize these percentage-decimal-fraction equivalents. Use these "friendly" fractions and percentages to eliminate answer choices that are way "out of the ballpark":

$$0.01 = \frac{1}{100} = 1\% \qquad\qquad 0.1 = \frac{1}{10} = 10\%$$

$$0.2 = \frac{1}{5} = 20\% \qquad\qquad 0.25 = \frac{1}{4} = 25\%$$

$$0.333... = \frac{1}{3} = 33\frac{1}{3}\% \qquad\qquad 0.4 = \frac{2}{5} = 40\%$$

$$0.5 = \frac{1}{2} = 50\% \qquad\qquad 0.6 = \frac{3}{5} = 60\%$$

$$0.666... = \frac{2}{3} = 66\frac{2}{3}\% \qquad\qquad 0.75 = \frac{3}{4} = 75\%$$

$$0.8 = \frac{4}{5} = 80\% \qquad\qquad 1.0 = \frac{1}{1} = 100\%$$

$$2.0 = \frac{2}{1} = 200\%$$

TRANSLATION

Translation makes figuring out percentages easier.

When you have to find exact percentages, it's much easier if you know how to "translate" word problems. Translating a problem lets you express it as an equation, instead of thinking about words. Here's a "dictionary" that will help:

Word	Equivalent Symbol
percent	/100
is	=
of, times, product	×
what (or any unknown value)	any variable (x, k, b)

Here's an example:

56 is what percent of 80?

- ◯ 66%
- ◯ 70%
- ◯ 75%
- ◯ 80%
- ◯ 142%

Here's how to crack it

To find the exact percentage, let's translate the question and solve for the variable:

$$56 = \frac{x}{100}(80)$$

$$56 = \frac{80x}{100}$$

Don't forget to reduce:

$$56 = \frac{4x}{5}$$

Now multiply both sides of the equation by:

$$\left(\frac{5}{4}\right)\left(\frac{56}{1}\right) = \left(\frac{5}{4}\right)\left(\frac{4x}{5}\right)$$

$$(5)(14) = x$$

$$70 = x$$

> Don't forget to eliminate choices that are out of the ballpark!

That's answer choice (B). Did you notice answer choice (E)? Since 56 is less than 80, the answer would have to be less than 100%, so 142% is way too big, and could have been eliminated from the get-go by ballparking.

Let's try a quant comp example:

Column A   Column B

5 is r percent of 25

s is 25 percent of 60

r s

- ○ the quantity in Column A is always greater
- ○ the quantity in Column B is always greater
- ○ the quantities are always equal
- ○ it cannot be determined from the information given

Here's how to crack it

First, translate the first statement:

$$5 = \frac{r}{100}(25)$$

$$5 = \frac{25r}{100}$$

$$5 = \frac{r}{4}$$

$$(4)(5) = \left(\frac{r}{4}\right)(4)$$

$$20 = r$$

That takes care of Column A. Now translate the second statement:

$$s = \frac{25}{100}(60)$$

$$s = \frac{1}{4}(60)$$

$$s = 15$$

That takes care of Column B. The answer is (A).

CONVERTING FRACTIONS TO PERCENTAGES

Just translate the problem. Then solve for the variable. Here's an example:

Express $\frac{4}{5}$ as a percentage.

Here's how to crack it

$\frac{4}{5}$ is what percent?

$$\frac{4}{5} = \frac{x}{100}$$

$$\frac{400}{5} = x$$

$$80 = x$$

So $\frac{4}{5}$ is the same as 80%.

CONVERTING DECIMALS TO PERCENTAGES

Just move the decimal point two places to the right. This turns 0.8 into 80%, 0.25 into 25%, 0.5 into 50%, and 1 into 100%.

PERCENTAGE INCREASE/DECREASE

To find a percentage increase or decrease, first find the amount of increase or decrease, then ask yourself: "The amount of change is what percent of the original number?" Here's the formula:

Amount change $= \dfrac{x}{100} \times$ original number

For example, if you had to find the percent decrease from 4 to 3, first figure out what the actual decrease is. The decrease from 4 to 3 is 1. So, $1 = \dfrac{x}{100}$ (4), since 4 is the original number. Now solve for x:

$$1 = \frac{4x}{100}$$
$$1 = \frac{x}{25}$$
$$25 = x$$

The percent decrease from 4 to 3 is 25%.

CHARTS

You'll probably be asked to solve a few percent problems about a chart. Every GRE CAT math section has a few questions based on a chart or graph (or on a group of charts or graphs). The most important thing that chart questions test is your ability to remember the difference between real-life charts and ETS charts.

Friends give you charts to display the information they want you to see, and to make that information easier to understand. ETS constructs charts to hide the information you need to know, and to make that information hard to understand.

The chart problems just recycle the basic arithmetic concepts we've already covered: fractions, percentages, and so on. Use the techniques we've discussed for each type of question. But there are two techniques that are especially important to use when doing chart questions.

> On Charts, look for information ETS is trying to hide.

Don't Start With the Questions; Start With the Charts

Take a minute to look for and write on your scratch paper:

> **Information in titles:** If one chart is about Country A and the other is about Country B, write a big "A" on your scratch paper to represent Country A's chart and a big "B" to represent Country B's chart.

> **Asterisks, footnotes, parentheses, and small print:** Make sure you read these carefully and note the information from them on your scratch paper; they're almost always added to hide crucial information.

Funny units: Pay special attention when a title says "in thousands" or "in millions." You can usually ignore the units when you do the calculations, but you have to remember them to get the right answer.

APPROXIMATE, ESTIMATE, AND BALLPARK

You probably don't estimate enough! Like some of our other techniques, you have to train yourself to do it. You should estimate, not calculate exactly:

- whenever you see the word "approximately" in a question.
- whenever the answer choices are far apart in value.
- whenever you start to answer a question and you justifiably say to yourself, "This is going to take a lot of calculation!" Since you can't use a calculator on this test, you'll never be asked "calculator" math questions.

Review those "friendly" percentages and their fractions to use as reference points. For example, 34% is a little more than $\frac{1}{3}$.

Try this:

What is approximately 9.6% of 21.4?

Here's how to crack it

Use 10% as a friendlier percentage and 20 as a friendlier number. One-tenth of 20 is 2 (it says "approximately"—who are you to argue?). That's all you need to do to answer most chart questions.

CHART PROBLEMS

Make sure you've read everything carefully, and take notes before you try the first question:

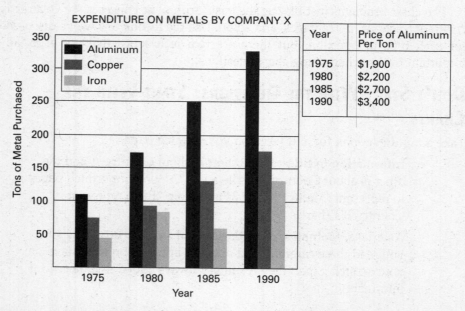

EXPENDITURE ON METALS BY COMPANY X

Year	Price of Aluminum Per Ton
1975	$1,900
1980	$2,200
1985	$2,700
1990	$3,400

Note: Graphs drawn to scale.

Approximately how many tons of aluminum and copper combined were purchased in 1985?

- ○ 125
- ○ 255
- ○ 325
- ○ 375
- ○ 515

How much did Company X spend on aluminum in 1980?

- ○ $675,000
- ○ $385,000
- ○ $333,000
- ○ $165,000
- ○ $139,000

Approximately what was the percent increase in the price of aluminum from 1975 to 1985?

- ○ 8%
- ○ 16%
- ○ 23%
- ○ 30%
- ○ 42%

Always write A B C D E on your scratch paper to represent the answer choices (or A B C D if it's quant comp)

Okay, first question . . .

Here's how to crack it

First we have to decide which chart to use. We need to find out how many tons were purchased, so that would be the big chart. In 1985, the bnfSk bar (which indicates aluminum) is at 250, and the gray bar (which indicates copper) is at approximately 125. Add those up and you get the number of tons of aluminum and copper combined that were purchased in 1985: 250 + 125 = 375. That's answer choice (D). Notice that the question says "approximately," because the numbers in the answer choices are pretty far apart.

Next question . . .

Here's how to crack it

We'll need both charts for this question, because we need to find the number of tons of aluminum purchased in 1980 and multiply it by the price per ton of aluminum in 1980 in order to figure out how much was spent on aluminum in 1980. The bar graph tells us that 175 tons of aluminum were purchased in 1980, and the little chart tells us that aluminum was $2,200 per ton in 1980. 175 × $2,200 = $385,000. That's answer choice (B).

Last question . . .

Here's how to crack it

Remember that percent increase formula?

$$\text{Amount change} = \frac{x}{100} \times \text{original number}$$

We'll need the little chart for this one. In 1975, the price of aluminum was $1,900 per ton. In 1985, the price of aluminum was $2,700 per ton. Now use the formula. The amount of change is the difference between those two numbers:

$$2,700 - 1,900 = 800.$$

So, $800 = \frac{x}{100} \times$ the starting point, or $1,900. Let's solve for the variable:

$$800 = \left(\frac{x}{100}\right)(1,900)$$

$$800 = \frac{1,900x}{100}$$

$$800 = 19x$$

$$\frac{800}{19} = \frac{(19x)}{19}$$

$$\frac{800}{19} = x$$

At this point, you could divide 800 by 19. But the question tells us to approximate, and that's always easier and more error-proof, so let's do that. What's 800 divided by 20? It's 40. Which answer choice is closest to 40? Answer choice (E), which is ETS's answer.

AVERAGES

Averages shouldn't look foreign to you; they're used in baseball statistics and GPAs.

The average (arithmetic mean) of a set of numbers is the sum, or total value, of all the numbers divided by the number of numbers in the set. The average of the set {1, 2, 3, 4, 5} is the total of the numbers (1 + 2 + 3 + 4 + 5, or 15) divided by the number of numbers in the set (which is 5). Dividing 15 by 5 gives us 3, so 3 is the average of the set.

ETS always refers to an average as an "average (arithmetic mean)." This confusing parenthetical remark is meant to keep you from being confused by other kinds of averages, such as medians and modes. You'll be less confused if you simply ignore the parenthetical remark and know that average means total divided by number of elements. We'll tell you about medians and modes later.

THINK TOTAL

Don't try to solve average problems all at once. Do them piece by piece. The critical formula to keep in mind is this:

$$\text{Average} = \frac{\text{the sum of the numbers being averaged}}{\text{the number of elements}}$$

You are always going to need the sum of the numbers being averaged: the total amount, the total height, the total weight, the total of the scores, the total distance. Averaging questions are always really about totals. In fact, an average is just another way of expressing a total; an average is the total divided by the number of elements. In averaging problems, you should always find the total first, before you do anything else.

For Average problems (arithmetic mean), think TOTAL.

Try this one:

Column A	Column B
the average	the average
(arithmetic mean)	(arithmetic mean)
of 7, 3, 4, and 2	of $2a + 5$, $4a$,
	and $7 - 6a$

- ○ the quantity in Column A is always greater
- ○ the quantity in Column B is always greater
- ○ the quantities are always equal
- ○ it cannot be determined from the information given

Here's how to crack it

Let's deal with Column A first. The average of 7, 3, 4, and 2 would be $7 + 3 + 4 + 2$, or 16, divided by 4, which gives us 4. Now let's deal with Column B. Let's add:

$$2a + 5 + 4a + 7 - 6a =$$
$$2a + 4a - 6a + 5 + 7 =$$
$$5 + 7 = 12$$

Don't forget that we have to divide the total, 12, by the number of things, which was 3. That's 4. So the answer is (C).

By the way, could you have plugged in for Column B? Sure, let's try it using 2:

$$2a + 5 + 4a + 7 - 6a =$$
$$2(2) + 5 + 4(2) + 7 - 6(2) =$$
$$4 + 5 + 8 + 7 - 12 =$$
$$9 + 15 - 12 =$$
$$24 - 12 = 12$$

Same thing, right?

UP AND DOWN

Averages are very predictable. You should make sure you know automatically what happens to them in certain situations. For example, suppose that you take three tests and earn an average score of 90. Now you take a fourth test. What do you know?

If the average goes up as a result of the fourth score, then you know that the fourth score was higher than 90. If the average stays the same as a result of the fourth score, then you know that the fourth score was exactly 90. If the average goes down as a result of the fourth score, then you know that the fourth score was less than 90.

MEDIAN AND MODE

The median is the middle value in a set of numbers; above and below it lie an equal number of values. For example, in the set {1, 2, 3, 4, 5, 6, 7} the median is 4, because it's the middle number (and there is an odd number of numbers in the set). If the set were {1, 2, 3, 4, 5, 6} the median would be the average of 3 and 4, or 3.5, because there is an even amount of numbers. Just think "median = middle."

The mode is the number or range of numbers in a set that occurs the most frequently. For example, in the set {2, 3, 4, 5, 3, 8, 6, 9, 3, 9, 3} the mode is 3, because 3 shows up the most. Just think "mode = most."

STANDARD DEVIATION

On a hard question you might be asked about standard deviation. The standard deviation of a set is a measure of the set's variation from its mean. You'll rarely, if ever, have to actually calculate it, so just remember this: The bigger the standard deviation, the more widely dispersed the values are. The smaller the standard deviation, the more closely grouped the values in a set are around the mean. Here's an example:

Column A	Column B
The standard deviation of the sample numbers 4, 4, and 4	The standard deviation of the sample numbers 6, 0, and 6

○ the quantity in Column A is always greater
○ the quantity in Column B is always greater
○ the quantities are always equal
○ it cannot be determined from the information given

Since the numbers in Column B, 6, 0, and 6, are more widely dispersed than the numbers in Column A, 4, 4, and 4, the standard deviation in Column B is bigger than that in Column A.

RATIOS AND PROPORTIONS

Ratios, like fractions, percentages, and decimals, are just another way of representing division. Don't let them make you nervous.

EVERY FRACTION IS A RATIO, AND VICE VERSA

A fraction is a ratio between its numerator and its denominator. Every ratio can be expressed as a fraction. A ratio of 1:2 means that there can be a total of three things (or a multiple of three), and the fraction $\frac{1}{2}$ means "1 out of 2".

On the GRE CAT, you may see ratios expressed in several different ways:

- $x:y$
- the ratio of x to y
- x is to y

TREAT A RATIO LIKE A FRACTION

Anything you can do to a fraction you can also do to a ratio. You can cross-multiply, find common denominators, reduce, and so on.

COUNT THE PARTS

If you have 3 coins in your pocket and the ratio of pennies to nickels is 2:1, how many pennies and nickels are there? Two pennies and 1 nickel, right?

If you have 24 coins in your pocket and the ratio of pennies to nickels is 2:1, how many pennies and nickels are there? That's a little trickier. You have 16 pennies and 8 nickels. How did we find that answer? We counted "parts."

The ratio 2:1 contains 3 parts—there are 2 pennies for every 1 nickel, making 3 parts altogether. To find out how many of our 24 coins are pennies, we simply divide 24 by the number of parts (3) and then multiply the result by each part of the ratio. Dividing 24 by 3 yields 8—that is, each of the 3 parts in our ratio consists of 8 coins. Two of the parts are pennies; at 8 coins per part, that makes 16 pennies. One of the parts is nickels; that makes 8 nickels.

Here's another way to understand ratios. It's called the ratio box. Again, the question is, if you have 24 coins in your pocket and the ratio of pennies to nickels is 2:1, how many pennies and nickels are there? This is what the ratio box would look like for this question, with all of the information we're given already filled in:

	pennies	nickels	Total
ratio	2	1	3
multiply by			
real			24

A ratio box can help you organize your ratio information.

"Real" means what we really have, not in the conceptual world of ratios, but in real life. Again, the ratio total (the number you get when you add up the number of parts in the ratio) is 3. The real total number of coins is 24. How do we get from 3 to 24? We multiply by 8. That means our "multiply by" number is 8. This is what the ratio box would look like now:

	pennies	nickels	Total
ratio	2	1	3
multiply by	8	8	8
real			24

Now let's finish filling in the box by multiplying everything else out:

	pennies	nickels	Total
ratio	2	1	3
multiply by	8	8	8
real	16	8	24

Let's try a GRE CAT example:

Flour, eggs, yeast, and salt are mixed by weight in the ratio of 11 : 9 : 3 : 2, respectively. How many pounds of yeast are there in 20 pounds of the mixture?

○ $1\frac{3}{5}$

○ $1\frac{4}{5}$

○ 2

○ $2\frac{2}{5}$

○ $8\frac{4}{5}$

Here's how to crack it

Let's make a ratio box and fill in what we know:

	flour	eggs	yeast	salt	Total
ratio	11	9	3	2	
multiply by					
real					20

First, add up all of the numbers in the ratio to get the ratio total:

	flour	eggs	yeast	salt	Total
ratio	11	9	3	2	25
multiply by					
real					20

Now, what do we multiply 25 by to get 20?

$$25x = 20$$
$$\frac{25x}{25} = \frac{20}{25}$$
$$x = \frac{20}{25}$$
$$x = \frac{4}{5}$$

So $\frac{4}{5}$ is our "multiply by" number. Let's fill it in:

	flour	eggs	yeast	salt	Total
ratio	11	9	3	2	25
multiply by	$\frac{4}{5}$	$\frac{4}{5}$	$\frac{4}{5}$	$\frac{4}{5}$	$\frac{4}{5}$
real					20

Okay, the question is asking for the amount of yeast, so we don't have to worry about the other ingredients. Just look at the yeast column. All we have to do is multiply 3 by $\frac{4}{5}$ and we have our answer $3 \times \frac{4}{5} = \frac{12}{5}$, or $2\frac{2}{5}$. That's answer choice (D).

PROPORTIONS

The GRE often contains problems in which you are given two proportional, or equal, ratios from which one piece of information is missing. These questions take a given relationship, or ratio, and project it onto a larger or smaller scale. Here's an example:

> If the cost of a one-hour telephone call is $7.20, what would be the cost of a ten-minute telephone call at the same rate?
>
> ○ $7.10
> ○ $3.60
> ○ $1.80
> ○ $1.20
> ○ $ .72

The key to proportions is setting them up correctly.

Here's how to crack it

The most important thing when doing a proportion problem is making sure you set it up correctly. Let's express the ratios here as dollars over minutes, since we're being asked to find the cost of a 10-minute call. That means that we have to convert the 1 hour to 60 minutes (otherwise it wouldn't be a proportion).

$$\frac{\$}{\min} = \frac{\$7.20}{60} = \frac{x}{10}$$

Now cross multiply:

$$60x = (7.2)(10)$$
$$60x = 72$$
$$\frac{60x}{60} = \frac{72}{60}$$
$$x = \frac{6}{5}$$

Now we have to convert $\frac{6}{5}$ to a decimal. But first we can ballpark and eliminate some choices. We know $\frac{6}{5}$ is a little more than 1, so that eliminates choices (A), (B), and (E). Now let's finish it off: $6 \div 5 = 1.2$, so ETS's answer is (D).

MORE MANIPULATING EQUATIONS

F.O.I.L.

When you see two sets of parentheses, all you have to do is remember to multiply every term in the first set of parentheses by every term in the second set of parentheses. Use F.O.I.L. to remember the method. F.O.I.L. stands for First, Outer, Inner, Last—the four steps of multiplication. Here's an example:

This also works in the opposite direction. For example, if you were given $x^2 + 7x + 12 = 0$, you could solve it by breaking it down as follows:

$$(x +)(x +) = 0$$

We know to use "plus" signs because the 7 and the 12 are both positive. Now we have to think of two numbers that when added together, give us 7, and when multiplied together, give us 12. Yep, they're 4 and 3:

$$(x + 4)(x + 3) = 0$$

Note that this will have two solutions for x. Either one of the equations can equal zero for the whole thing to equal 0. So, x can either be –4 or –3.

Quadratic Equations

There are three expressions of quadratic equations that can appear on the GRE CAT. You should know them cold, in both their factored and unfactored forms. Here they are:

Expression 1:

Factored form: $x^2 - y^2$ (the difference between two squares)

Unfactored form: $(x + y)(x - y)$

Expression 2:

Factored form: $(x + y)^2$

Unfactored form: $x^2 + 2xy + y^2$

Expression 3:

Factored form: $(x - y)^2$

Unfactored form: $x^2 - 2xy + y^2$

Let's see how this would look on the GRE CAT:

If x and y are positive integers, and if $x^2 + 2xy + y^2 = 25$, then $(x + y)^3 =$

- ◯ 5
- ◯ 15
- ◯ 50
- ◯ 75
- ◯ 125

Here's how to crack it

This is why you have to memorize those quadratic equations. The equation in this question is Expression 2 from above: $x^2 + 2xy + y^2 = (x + y)^2$. The question tells us that $x^2 + 2xy + y^2$ is equal to 25, which means that $(x + y)^2$ is also equal to 25. Think of $x + y$ as one unit that, when squared, is equal to 25. Since this question specified that x and y are positive integers, what positive integer squared equals 25? Right, 5. So $x + y = 5$. The question is asking for $(x + y)^3$. In other words, what's 5 cubed, or $5 \times 5 \times 5$? It's 125. That's answer choice (E).

BUT WHENEVER YOU SEE VARIABLES . . .

Don't forget to plug in! You will save yourself a lot of trouble if you just plug in numbers for the variables in complicated algebraic expressions. Here's an example of a complicated algebraic expression:

$$(4x^2 + 4x + 2) + (3 - 7x) - (5 - 3x) =$$

Let's plug in 2 for the x's in the expression.

$$(4 \times 2^2 + 4 \times 2 + 2) + (3 - 7 \times 2) - (5 - 3 \times 2) =$$
$$16 + 8 + 2 + 3 - 14 - 5 + 6 = 16$$

Then you would plug in 2 for x in all the answer choices, and look for our target answer, 16.

You MUST Plug In twice on quant comp!

SIMULTANEOUS EQUATIONS

ETS will sometimes give you two equations and ask you to use them to find the value of a given expression. Don't worry, you don't need any math-class algebra; in most cases all you have to do to find ETS's answer is to add or subtract the two equations.

Here's an example:

If $5x + 4y = 6$ and $4x + 3y = 5$, then $x + y = ?$

Here's how to crack it

All you have to do is add together or subtract one from the other. Here's what we get when we add them:

$$\begin{array}{r} 5x + 4y = 6 \\ + \ 4x + 3y = 5 \\ \hline 9x + 7y = 11 \end{array}$$

A dead end. So let's try subtraction:

$$\begin{array}{r} 5x + 4y = 6 \\ - \ 4x + 3y = 5 \\ \hline x + \ y = 1 \end{array}$$

Bingo. The value of the expression $(x + y)$ is exactly what we're looking for. On the GRE CAT, you may see the two equations written horizontally. Just rewrite the two equations, putting one on top of the other, then simply add or subtract them.

12

Figures

The good news is that you don't need to know much about actual geometry to do well on the GRE CAT. We've boiled geometry down to the handful of bits and pieces that ETS actually tests.

DEGREES, LINES, AND ANGLES

You need to know that:

1. A line (which can be thought of as a perfectly flat angle) is a 180-degree angle.

2. When two lines intersect, four angles are formed; the sum of the angles is 360 degrees.

3. When two lines are perpendicular to each other, their intersection forms four 90-degree angles. Here is the symbol ETS uses to indicate a perpendicular angle: ⊥

4. Ninety-degree angles are also called right angles. A right angle on the GRE CAT is identified by a little box at the intersection of the angle's arms:

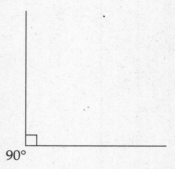

90°

5. A triangle contains 180 degrees.

6. Any four-sided figure contains 360 degrees.

7. A circle contains 360 degrees.

8. Any line that extends from the center of the circle to the edge of the circle is called a *radius* (plural is *radii*).

VERTICAL ANGLES

Vertical angles are the angles across from each other that are formed by the intersection of lines. Vertical angles are equal. In the drawing below, angle *x* is equal to angle *y* and angle *a* is equal to angle *b*.

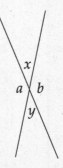

PARALLEL LINES

Don't worry about remembering what certain angles are called. Just remember: when two parallel lines are cut by a third line, only two angles are formed, big angles and small angles. All the big angles are equal. All the small angles are equal. The sum of *any* big and *any* small angle is always 180 degrees. Here's an example:

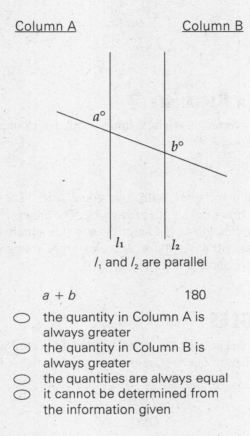

Column A   Column B

l_1 and l_2 are parallel

Column A	Column B
$a + b$	180

○ the quantity in Column A is always greater
○ the quantity in Column B is always greater
○ the quantities are always equal
○ it cannot be determined from the information given

ALWAYS write down A, B, C, D for quant comps.

Here's how to crack it

Notice that you are told that the lines are parallel. You need to know that; otherwise, you can't assume that they are just because they look like they are. As you just learned, only two angles are formed when two parallel lines are cut by a third line, a big angle (greater than 90 degrees) and a small one (smaller than 90 degrees). Look at angle *a*. Looks smaller than 90, right? Now look at angle *b*. Looks bigger than 90, right? So *a* + *b* would have to add up to 180. The answer is (C).

FOUR-SIDED FIGURES

Any figure with four sides has 360 degrees. That includes rectangles, squares, and parallelograms (a four-sided figure made out of two sets of parallel lines whose area can be found with the formula $A = bh$, where *h* is the height perpendicular to the base).

PERIMETER OF A RECTANGLE

The perimeter of a rectangle is just the sum of the lengths of the four sides.

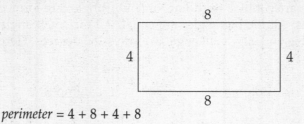

perimeter = 4 + 8 + 4 + 8

AREA OF A RECTANGLE

The area of a rectangle is length times width. For example, the area of the rectangle above is 32 (or 8 × 4).

SQUARES

A square is a rectangle with four equal sides. The perimeter of a square is, therefore, 4 times the length of any side. The area is the length of any side times itself, or in other words, the length of any side squared. The diagonal of a square splits it into two 45:45:90, or isosceles, right triangles. What was that? Don't worry, you're about to find out . . .

TRIANGLES

The three angles of a triangle ALWAYS add up to 180 degrees.

Every triangle contains three angles that add up to 180 degrees. You must know this. It applies to every triangle, no matter what it looks like. Here are some examples:

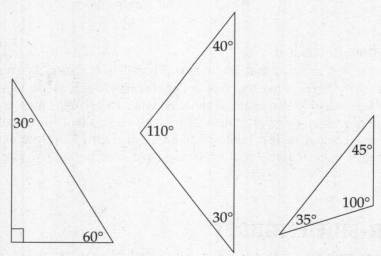

EQUILATERAL TRIANGLES

An equilateral triangle is one in which all three sides are equal in length. Because the sides are all equal, the angles are all equal, too. If they're all equal, how many degrees is each? We hope you said 60 degrees, because 180 divided by 3 is 60.

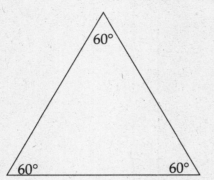

ISOSCELES TRIANGLES

An isosceles triangle is a triangle in which two of the three sides are equal in length. This means that two of the angles are also equal, and that the third angle is not (otherwise it would be equilateral, right?).

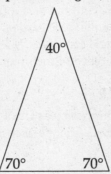

If you know the degree measure of any angle in an isosceles triangle, you usually also know the degree of measures of the other two. For example, if one of the two equal angles measures 30 degrees, then the other one does, too. Two 30-degree angles add up to 60 degrees. Since any triangle contains 180 degrees altogether, the third angle—the only one left—must measure 120 degrees.

RIGHT TRIANGLES

You CAN improve your scores!

A right triangle is one in which one of the angles is a right angle—a 90-degree angle. The longest side of a right triangle—the side opposite the 90-degree angle—is called the hypotenuse. On the GRE CAT, a right triangle will always have a little box in the 90-degree corner, like so:

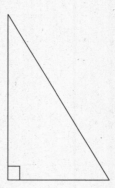

ANGLE/SIDE RELATIONSHIPS IN TRIANGLES

In any triangle, the longest side is opposite the largest interior angle; the shortest side is opposite the smallest interior angle. That's why the hypotenuse of a right triangle is its longest side—there couldn't be another angle in the triangle bigger than 90 degrees. Furthermore, equal sides are opposite equal angles.

Also, the third side of a triangle can never be longer than the sum of the other two sides, or less than the difference of the other two sides.

PERIMETER OF A TRIANGLE

The perimeter of a triangle is simply a measure of the distance around it. All you have to do to find the perimeter of a triangle is to add up the lengths of the sides.

AREA OF A TRIANGLE

The area of any triangle is the height (or "altitude") multiplied by the base, divided by 2. (That's $A = \frac{1}{2} bh$.) After all, isn't a triangle really half of a rectangle or square? The altitude is defined as a perpendicular line to the base:

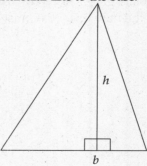

This formula works on any triangle:

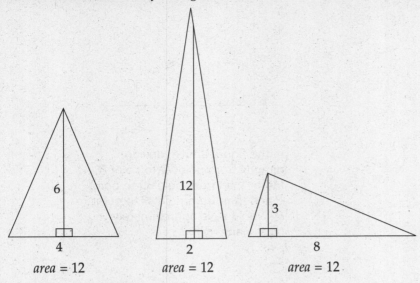

$area = 12$ $area = 12$ $area = 12$

PYTHAGOREAN THEOREM

The Pythagorean Theorem applies only to right triangles. The theorem states that in a right triangle, the square of the length of the hypotenuse (the longest side, remember?) equals the sum of the squares of the lengths of the two other sides. In other words, $c^2 = a^2 + b^2$, where c is the length of the hypotenuse:

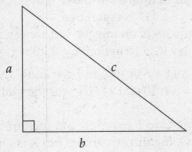

    Problems on the GRE CAT often involve right triangles whose sides measure 3, 4, and 5, or multiples of those numbers. Why is this? Because a 3-4-5 right triangle is the smallest one in which measures of the sides are all integers. Does $3^2 + 4^2 = 5^2$? It sure does. Here are three examples of right triangles based on the basic 3-4-5 right triangle:

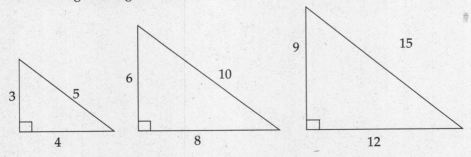

Let's try an example:

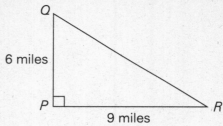

In the figure above, driving directly from point Q to point R, rather than from point Q to point P and then from point P to point R, would save approximately how many miles?

○ 0
○ 1
○ 2
○ 3
○ 4

Here's how to crack it

Okay, we've got a right triangle here, with QR as the hypotenuse, or c. Let's use the Pythagorean Theorem to figure out the length of QR. That's $6^2 + 9^2 = c^2$. In other words, $36 + 81 = c^2$. So 117 is equal to c^2.

Now, 117 is not the square of an integer, but we can approximate the square root of 117. How? Well, try to zero in on it by thinking of easy nearby numbers. For example, we know that 10^2 is 100, and we know that 11^2 is 121. So, $\sqrt{117}$ must be somewhere between 10 and 11. The question tells us to approximate, so we did.

Now, if we drove from Q to P (6 miles) and then from P to R (9 miles), we'd have traveled 15 miles. Going directly from Q to R is almost 11 miles. So, we'd be saving approximately 4 miles. That's answer choice (E).

The Pythagorean Theorem will sometimes be the key to solving problems involving squares or rectangles. For example, every rectangle or square can be divided into two right triangles. This means that if you know the length and width of any rectangle or square, you also know the length of the diagonal—it's the shared hypotenuse of the hidden right triangles. Here's an example:

Write everything down on scratch paper! Don't do anything in your head!

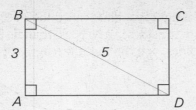

In the rectangle above, what is the area of triangle *ABD*?

- ○ 6
- ○ 7.5
- ○ 10
- ○ 12
- ○ 15

Here's how to crack it

We know this is a rectangle, which means triangle *ABD* is a right triangle. Not only that, but it's a 3-4-5 right triangle (with a side of 3 and a hypotenuse of 5, it must be). That means side *AD* is 4. So, the area of triangle *ABD* is $\frac{1}{2}$ the base (3) times the height (4). That's $\frac{1}{2}$ of 12, otherwise known as 6. The answer is (A).

TWO SPECIAL RIGHT TRIANGLES

There are two special right triangles you may see on the GRE CAT. The first is the **45:45:90**. This is also called an **isosceles right triangle**. In such a triangle, the two non-hypotenuse sides are equal. If the length of each short leg is *x*, then the length of the hypotenuse is $x\sqrt{2}$. Here's an example:

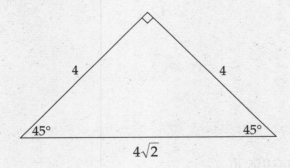

The second special right triangle is called the **30:60:90** right triangle. The ratio between the lengths of the sides in a 30:60:90 triangle is constant. If you know the length of any of the sides, you can find the lengths of the others. Here's the ratio of the sides:

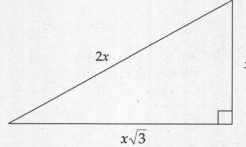

That is, if the shortest side is length x, then the hypotenuse is $2x$, and the remaining side is $x\sqrt{3}$.

Use that paper!

Let's try an example involving a special right triangle:

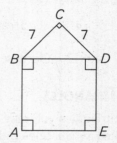

In the figure above, what is the area of square *ABDE*?

- ○ $28\sqrt{2}$
- ○ 49
- ○ $49\sqrt{2}$
- ○ 98
- ○ $98\sqrt{2}$

Here's how to crack it

In order to figure out the area of square *ABDE*, we need to know the length of one of its sides. We get the length of *BD* by using the isosceles right triangle attached to it. *BD* is the hypotenuse, which means its length is $7\sqrt{2}$. To get the area of the square we have to square the length of the side we know, or $\left(7\sqrt{2}\right)\left(7\sqrt{2}\right) = (49)(2) = 98$. That's answer choice (D).

CIRCLES

THE WORLD OF PI

You may remember being taught in math class that the value of pi (π) is 3.14, or even 3.14159. On the GRE CAT, π = 3+ is a close enough approximation. You don't need to be any more precise than that in order to find ETS's answer. There will probably be questions on your GRE that you will be able to solve simply by plugging in 3 for each π among the answer choices and comparing the results. Just remember that π is a little bigger than 3.

Keep in mind the relationship that π expresses. Pi is the ratio between the circumference of a circle and its diameter. When we say that π is a little bigger than 3, we're saying that every circle is about three times as far around as it is across.

Pi has been calculated to hundreds of decimal places, but don't worry, you only need to know that it's three-ish.

RADII AND DIAMETERS

The *radius* of a circle is any line that extends from the center of a circle to the edge of the circle. If the line extends from one edge of a circle to the other, and goes through the circle's center, it's the circle's *diameter*. Therefore, the diameter is twice as long as the radius.

CIRCUMFERENCE OF A CIRCLE

The circumference of a circle is like the perimeter of a triangle: It's the distance around the outside. The formula for finding the circumference of a circle is 2 times π times the radius, or π times the diameter:

$$\text{circumference} = 2\pi r \text{ or } \pi d$$

If the diameter of a circle is 4, then its circumference is 4π, or roughly 12+. If the circumference of a circle is 10, then its diameter is 10π, or a little more than 30.

An *arc* is a section of the outside, or circumference of a circle. An angle formed by two radii is called a central angle (it comes out to the edge from the center of the circle). There are 360 degrees in a circle, so if there is an arc formed by, say, a 60-degree central angle, and 60 is $\frac{1}{6}$ of 360, then the arc formed by this 60-degree central angle will be $\frac{1}{6}$ of the circumference of the circle.

AREA OF A CIRCLE

The area of a circle is pi times the square of the radius:

$$area = \pi r^2$$

Let's try an example involving circles:

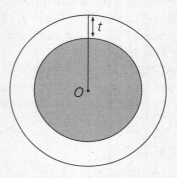

In the wheel above, with center O, the area of the entire wheel is 169π. If the area of the shaded hubcap is 144π, then $t =$

○ 1
○ 2
○ 3
○ 5
○ 12.5

Write everything down on scratch paper! Don't do anything in your head!

Here's how to crack it

We have to figure out what t is, and it's going to be the length of the radius of the entire wheel minus the length of the radius of the hubcap. If the area of the entire wheel is 169π, the radius is $\sqrt{169}$, or 13. If the area of the hubcap is 144π, the radius is $\sqrt{144}$, or 12. $13 - 12 = 1$, or answer choice (A).

Let's try another one:

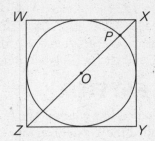

In the figure above, a circle with the center O is inscribed in square $WXYZ$. If the circle has radius 3, then $PZ =$

○ 6

○ $3\sqrt{2}$

○ $6 + \sqrt{2}$

○ $3 + \sqrt{3}$

○ $3\sqrt{2} + 3$

Ballparking answers will help you eliminate choices.

Here's how to crack it

"Inscribed" means the edges are touching. The radius of the circle is 3, which means PO is 3. If Z were at the other end of the diameter from P, this problem would be easy and the answer would be 6, right? But Z is beyond the edge of the circle, which means that PZ is a little more than 6. Let's stop there for a minute and glance at the answer choices. We can eliminate anything "out of the ballpark"—in other words, any answer choice that's less than 6, equal to 6 itself, or a lot more than 6. Remember when we told you to memorize a few of those square roots? Let's use them:

(A) Exactly 6? Nope.

(B) That's 1.4 × 3, which is 4.2. Too small.

(C) That's 6 + 1.4, or 7.4. Not bad. Let's leave that one in.

(D) That's 3 + 1.7, or 4.7. Too small.

(E) That's (3 × 1.4) + 3, which is 4.2 + 3, or 7.2. Not bad. Let's leave that one in too.

So, we eliminated three choices with ballparking. We're left with choices (C) and (E). You could take a guess here if you had to, but let's do a little more geometry to find ETS's answer.

Because this circle is inscribed in the square, the diameter of the circle is the same as a side of the square. Draw in a diameter parallel to ZY to prove it to yourself. We already know that the diameter of the circle is 6, so that means that ZY, and indeed all the sides of the square, are also 6. Now, if ZY is 6, and XY is 6, what's XZ, the diagonal of the square? Well, XZ is also the hypotenuse of the isosceles right triangle XYZ. The hypotenuse of a right triangle with two sides of 6 is $6 \times \sqrt{2}$. That's approximately 6 × 1.4, or 8.4.

The question is asking for PZ, which is a little less than XZ. It's somewhere between 6 and 8.4. The pieces that aren't part of the diameter of the circle are equal to 8.4 – 6, or 2.4. Divide that in half to get 1.2, which is the distance from the edge of the circle to Z. That means that PZ is 6 + 1.2, or 7.2. Check your remaining answers: Choice (C) is 7.4, and choice (E) is 7.2. Bingo! The answer is (E).

THE COORDINATE SYSTEM

A coordinate system is shaped like a cross. The horizontal line is called the **X-axis**; the vertical line is called the **Y-axis**. The four areas formed by the intersection of these axes are called **quadrants**. The point where the axes intersect is called the **origin**. This is what it looks like:

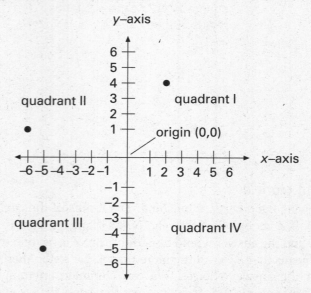

To express any point in the coordinate system, first give the horizontal value, then the vertical value, or (x, y). In the diagram above, the marked point above and to the right of the origin can be described by the coordinates (2, 4). That is, the point is two spaces to the right of the origin and four spaces above the origin. The point above and to the left of the origin can be described by the coordinates (–6, 1). That is, it is six spaces to the left and one space above the origin. What are the coordinates of the point to the left of and below the origin? Right, it's (–5, –5). Here's a GRE CAT example:

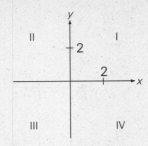

Points $(x, 5)$ and $(-6, y)$, not
shown in the figure above, are in
quadrants I and III, respectively.
If $xy \neq 0$, in which quadrant is
point (x, y)?

- ○ IV
- ○ III
- ○ II
- ○ I
- ○ It cannot be determined from
  the information given

Here's how to crack it

If point $(x, 5)$ is in quadrant I, that means x is positive. If point y is in quadrant III, that means y is negative. The quadrant that would contain a positive x and a negative y is quadrant IV. That's answer choice (A).

SLOPE

Trickier questions involving the coordinate system might give you the equation of a line on the grid, which will involve something called the slope. The equation of a line is:

$$y = mx + b$$

That's where the x and the y are points on the line, b stands for the **y-intercept**, or the point at which the line crosses the y-axis, and m is the **slope** of the line, or the change in y divided by the change in x. Sometimes on the GRE, the m is an a, as in $y = ax + b$. Let's see this in action:

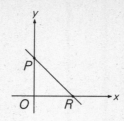

The line $y = -\dfrac{8}{7}x + 1$ is graphed on the rectangular coordinate axes.

Column A	Column B
OR	OP

○ the quantity in Column A is always greater
○ the quantity in Column B is always greater
○ the quantities are always equal
○ it cannot be determined from the information given

Here's how to crack it

The b in this case is 1. That means the line crosses the y-axis at 1. So the coordinates of point P are (0, 1). Now we have to figure out what the coordinates of point R are. We know the y coordinate is 0, so let's stick that into the equation (the slope and the y-intercept are constant, meaning they don't change):

$$y = mx + b$$

$$0 = -\frac{8}{7}x + 1$$

Now let's solve for x:

$$0 = -\frac{8}{7}x + 1$$

$$0 - 1 = -\frac{8}{7}x + 1 - 1$$

$$\overline{\qquad\qquad\qquad\qquad}$$

$$-1 = -\frac{8}{7}x$$

$$\left(-\frac{7}{8}\right)(-1) = \left(-\frac{7}{8}\right)\left(-\frac{8}{7}\right)x$$

$$\frac{7}{8} = x$$

So the coordinates of point R are ($\frac{7}{8}$, 0). That means *OR*, in Column A, is equal to $\frac{7}{8}$, and *OP*, in Column B, is equal to 1. The answer is (B).

VOLUME

You can get the volume of a three-dimensional figure by multiplying the area of a two-dimensional figure by height (or depth). For example, to find the volume of a rectangular solid, you take the area of a rectangle and multiply by the depth. The formula is *lwh* (length times width times height). To find the volume of a circular cylinder, take the area of a circle and multiply by the height. The formula is πr^2 times the height (or $\pi r^2 h$).

SURFACE AREA

The surface area of a rectangular box is equal to the sum of the areas of all of its sides. In other words, if you had a box whose dimensions were 2 by 3 by 4, there would be two sides that are 2 by 3 (area of 6), two sides that are 3 by 4 (area of 12), and two sides that are 2 by 4 (area of 8). So, the surface area would be 6 + 6 + 12 + 12 + 8 + 8, which is 52.

PLUG IN ON GEOMETRY PROBLEMS

Remember, *whenever* you see variables in the answer choices, plug in. On geometry problems, you can plug in values for angles or lengths as long as the values you plug in don't contradict either the wording of the problem or the laws of geometry (you can't let the interior angles of a triangle add up to anything but 180, for instance).

Here's an example:

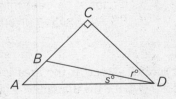

In the drawing above, if *AC* = *CD*, then *r* =

○ 45 − *s*
○ 90 − *s*
○ *s*
○ 45 + *s*
○ 60 + *s*

For quant comp geometry, draw, eliminate, and REDRAW; it's like plugging in twice.

Here's how to crack it

See the variables in the answer choices? Let's plug in. First of all, we're told that *AC* and *CD* are equal, which means that *ACD* is an isosceles right triangle. So angles *A* and *D* both have to be 45 degrees. Now it's plugging-in time. The smaller angles, *r* and *s*, have to add up to 45 degrees, so let's make *r* = 40 degrees and *s* = 5 degrees. The question is asking for the value of *r*, which is 40, so that's our target answer choice. Now eliminate answer choices by plugging in 5 for *s*:

(A) 45 − 5 = 40. Bingo! Check the other choices to be sure.

(B) 90 − 5 = 85. Nope.

(C) 5. Nope.

(D) 45 + 5 = 50. Eliminate.

(E) 60 + 5 = 65. No way.

By the way, we knew that the correct answer couldn't be greater than 45 degrees, since that's the measure of the entire angle D, so you could have eliminated choices (D) and (E) right away.

Remember, plug in whenever you see variables!

DRAW IT YOURSELF

When ETS doesn't include a drawing with a geometry problem, it usually means that the drawing, if supplied, would make ETS's answer obvious. In that case, you should just draw it yourself. Here's an example:

Column A	Column B
The diameter of a circle with area 49π	14

- the quantity in Column A is always greater
- the quantity in Column B is always greater
- the quantities are always equal
- it cannot be determined from the information given

Here's how to crack it

Draw that circle on your scratch paper! If the area is 49π, what's the radius? Right, 7. And if the radius is 7, what's the diameter? Right, 14. The answer is (C). Isn't it helpful to see the picture?

REDRAW

On tricky quant comp questions, you may need to draw the figure once, eliminate two answer choices, and then redraw the figure to try to disprove your first answer, in order to see if the answer is (D). Here's an example:

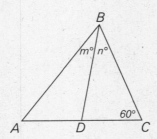

D is the midpoint of AC.

Column A	Column B
m	n

○ the quantity in Column A is always
   greater
○ the quantity in Column B is always
   greater
○ the quantities are always equal
○ it cannot be determined from the information given

Do we really know that this triangle looks like this? Nope. We know that the lengths of AD and DC are equal; from this figure, it looks like angles m and n are also equal. Since they could be, we can eliminate choices (A) and (B). But let's redraw the figure to try to disprove our first answer. Let's make the triangle a right triangle, since right triangles are very familiar.

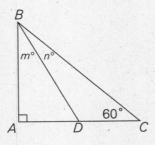

Remember that D is still the midpoint of side AC. But we can now see that the triangle with the 60-degree angle C also includes angle BDC, which is greater than 90 degrees. Let's plug in to be sure that angle n is smaller than angle m. Let's plug in 110 degrees for angle BDC, so angle n would have to be 10 degrees. If angle BDC is 110, then the angle next to it would have to be 70 degrees, and angle m would be 20 degrees. By redrawing the figure, the value of m is greater than the value of n, which eliminates choice (C). The correct answer choice must be (D).

PART ◆ IV

How to Crack the Analytic Section

13

The Geography of the Analytic Section

The analytic section has two types of questions, which we call *games* (ETS claims these test "analytical reasoning") and *arguments* (which supposedly measure "logical reasoning"). This is how it breaks down:

The section is 60 minutes long, with 35 questions.

- There are 21 to 25 games questions on 5 to 7 games.
- There are 10 to 14 arguments. The section usually starts with an argument.

WHAT IS THIS STUFF?

Work slowly and carefully on the Analytic section. Write everything down on your scratch paper!

This is one section that contains material you've never seen before (unless, perhaps, you've already taken the Law School Admissions Test, or LSAT). But that's good. The methods are something you must learn anew, not something to rummage around in your brain and remember, like math. And this is good news because you haven't had time to talk yourself into "not being able" to do it; we're starting from scratch. And you must always remember that, like everything else on the GRE CAT, *your intelligence is not being tested*. Your ability to do this is not directly, or even indirectly, connected to how smart you are. The GRE only measures how well you do on the GRE.

Arguments and games give you a very narrow playing field. In a game, your job is to organize information based on the facts given. In arguments, you have to answer questions without getting caught up in the subject matter, and without bringing in any issues that are outside the narrow parameters of the argument itself. In both cases, all you know is what's printed on the screen, and that's what you work with.

SCRATCH PAPER

You may be tempted to try to solve analytic questions "in your head." You may think that writing things down on your scratch paper is a waste of time. Wrong. Many of the analytic techniques require the effective use of your scratch paper. Always write everything down. You can't afford to make careless mistakes. Don't take silly "mental" shortcuts.

Now, let the Games and Arguments begin. . .

14

Arguments

WHAT YOU WILL SEE

The analytic section of your GRE CAT will contain 10 to 14 arguments. The section usually starts with at least one.

ETS's Directions

Here are the directions for the analytical section as they will appear on your GRE CAT. ETS intends these directions to apply to both games and arguments.

> Directions: Each question or group of questions is based on a passage or set of conditions. In answering some of the questions, it may be useful to draw a rough diagram. For each question, select the best answer choice given.

Our Own Directions for Arguments

Our directions will give you a much clearer idea of what you're supposed to do on the test. Here they are:

> Directions: Each GRE argument consists of a brief argument followed by a question. The question following each argument is intended to test your ability to break down an argument into its parts, and determine how those parts are related to each other.

The Parts of an Argument

You don't need to know anything about logic, but you do need to know a few simple terms to follow the rest of this chapter. Here's what you need to know:

- **Conclusion:** A conclusion is a claim, the main point of an argument.

- **Premise:** A premise is a stated reason or a piece of evidence that supports the conclusion.

- **Assumption:** An assumption is an *unstated* premise that supports the conclusion.

These are not like arguments you have with your brother!

Our Step-By-Step Strategy for All Arguments Questions

1. **Read the question first.** The question tells you what to look for in the argument, and how to approach it.

2. **Read the entire argument.** Read the argument carefully, for full understanding. This isn't like Reading Comprehension! You really have to carefully follow the logic of the argument. Then find the conclusion.

3. Reread the question and **try to answer it in your own words**, before you go to the answer choices. Of course, the answer that you come up with will depend on the question you're answering. But always take the time to refamiliarize yourself with the intent of the question, and get a rough idea of what you're looking for, before you consider the choices. This will prevent careless mistakes, such as choosing an answer that weakens an argument when the question asks you to strengthen it.

4. Use the **Process of Elimination** to eliminate wrong answer choices.

READ THE QUESTION FIRST!

You need to read the question first in order to get an idea of what you're dealing with. Since there are only a handful of different argument questions, you just want to decide what the question's asking before you read the argument. You shouldn't read the choices. Just read the question to see what you're looking for.

On Arguments, always read the QUESTION first.

HOW TO READ ARGUMENTS

You should read arguments closely. As you read, you should always look for the conclusion. Ask yourself, "What's the main point?" The point of the argument is the conclusion. Let's try a simple example.

> "My computer isn't working. I will need to use a computer in graduate school. Therefore, I should get a new computer."

What's the main point? "I should get a new computer." Did you notice that the conclusion was preceded by the word **therefore**? Words like **therefore** are grammatical indications that a conclusion is about to be made. The conclusion often comes after words such as:

- therefore
- so
- thus
- hence

- then
- consequently
- as a result

To find the conclusion of an argument, look for statements that make *judgments*, *recommendations*, and *predictions*.

A judgment is a statement that something is better or worse than something else. A recommendation is a statement that some course of action should be taken (see the argument above: " . . . I should get a new computer"). A prediction, of course, predicts the future.

Use the "Why Test"

Remember that the conclusion is *supported by* the other statements in the argument. The "Why Test" is a way to check that the statement you chose as the conclusion is supported by the other statements. State what you think is the conclusion, then say, "Why?" The other statements should provide the reasons why.

Try using the "Why Test" on the earlier example:

Conclusion: "I should get a new computer."

Why? "My computer isn't working. I will need to use a computer in graduate school."

You can see how the other statements support the conclusion. Notice that if we had mistakenly chosen the wrong statement as the conclusion, the other sentences would not have supported it.

Conclusion: "My computer isn't working."

Note the CONCLUSION for every argument. Use the Why Test to make sure you've got the right conclusion.

Why? "I will need to use a computer in graduate school. I should get a new computer."

What? It just doesn't make sense this way. The other statements don't support this conclusion. This way you'd know that you chose the wrong statement as the conclusion.

Premises

Premises are the parts of the argument that support the conclusion. The premises answer the question, "Why?" They are reasons that back up the claim made in the conclusion. Most of the time premises are facts, but they can also be assertions that are just given as evidence for the claim in the conclusion. A conclusion gets support; premises provide support.

Certain words are used to introduce the premises of an argument:

- because
- since
- if

- given that
- in view of
- assume

Drill

Find the conclusions for the following arguments. Be sure to use the Why Test to check that you have the right conclusion.

1. A diet that is low in saturated fats reduces the risk of heart disease. Vegetables are low in saturated fats. Therefore, you should eat vegetables regularly to reduce your risk of heart disease.

   Conclusion: _____

   Why? _____

2. Making seat belt use mandatory will reduce automobile fatali-ties. State X has one of the lowest automobile fatality rates in the country, and seat-belt use is required by law there.

   Conclusion: _____

   Why? _____

3. Traditional economic theory assumes that demand for a prod-uct will increase when the price of that product decreases, and that among products of equal quality, consumers will always choose to purchase the product at the lowest possible price. However, consumer demand for such products as apparel and sunglasses has been greater for higher-priced "designer" brands than it has been for lower-priced brands of comparable quality.

   Conclusion: _____

   Why? _____

Here's how to crack it

1. *Conclusion:* Therefore, you should eat vegetables regularly to reduce your risk of heart disease.

   Why? A diet that is low in saturated fats reduces the risk of heart disease. Vegetables are low in saturated fats. (Notice that the conclusion of this argument is a directive—it tells you what you should do.)

2. *Conclusion:* Making seat-belt use mandatory will reduce auto-mobile fatalities.

   Why? State X has one of the lowest automobile fatality rates in the country, and seat-belt use is required by law there. (Notice that, in this example, the conclusion is given first, followed by the premises. Whether a statement is the conclusion of an argument depends on the *logic* of the argument, not on the location of the statement.)

3. *Conclusion:* The traditional assumption of economic theory—that demand for a product will increase when the price of that product decreases, and that among products of equal quality, consumers will always choose to purchase the product at the lowest possible price—may be wrong.

   Why? Because consumer demand for such products as apparel and sunglasses has been greater for higher-priced "designer" brands than it has been for lower-priced brands of comparable quality. (Notice that the conclusion in this example was not directly stated in the argument!)

CONCLUSION QUESTIONS

Conclusion questions, which are pretty rare, ask you to identify the conclusion of an argument. These questions can be worded in several different ways:

> The main point of the passage is that . . .

> Which of the following best states the author's conclusion in the passage above?

> Which of the following conclusions can be most properly drawn from the data above?

Don't forget to jot down the conclusion.

> Which of the following statements about _____ is best supported by the statements above?

> Which of the following best states the author's main point?

All of these questions are merely asking you to identify the conclusion of the argument. Always use our step-by-step method:

1. **Read the question.**
2. **Read the argument, find the conclusion, and mark it.** Use the Why Test to check.
3. **Answer the question in your own words.**
4. **Use POE.**

Scope

The most important consideration when using POE is whether an answer choice goes outside the scope of the argument. "Scope" is the narrow world of the argument. The scope is restricted by the conclusion and premises as stated in the passage.

If an answer choice goes beyond the issues of the argument, then it's outside the scope—eliminate it! If you have to make a case for the answer choice ("Well, if you look at it this way . . .") then it's outside the scope. Remember that all you know about the topic is what you've been told in the passage! Never consider whatever outside knowledge or opinions you may have of the issues in the argument.

Extreme Wording

The best answer to a conclusion question will use indisputable, rather than extreme, language. Indisputable (soft) answer choices tend to use words like *can*, *may*, *might*, *often*, *some*, and so forth. Extreme answer choices tend to use words like *all*, *always*, *totally*, *must*, *no*, and *only*, or *the best*, *the first*. When two answer choices seem very similar, look for these differences in wording. Eliminate answer choices that use extreme language.

Use More Than One Round of Elimination

The first time you go through the answer choices, you should eliminate those answers that you know for sure are out of the scope. If you're not sure what an answer choice means, don't eliminate it at first. But when you're down to two or three choices on the second round of elimination, you'll have to look more closely at the choices left. Focus on what makes an answer *wrong*. You don't have to understand why the best answer is right, only why the other four choices can't be right. So compare the choices you have left, word for word, looking for a reason to eliminate one.

> Eliminate answer choices that are OUT OF THE SCOPE of the argument.

Not Sure?

If you don't understand an answer choice, don't eliminate it! Treat an argument answer choice that you don't understand in the same way that you would a word that you can't define in a Verbal answer choice. It could be the best answer! Focus on what's *wrong* with the answer choices that you *do* understand.

Try this example:

Since the winners of professional golf tournaments are receiving larger cash prizes than ever before, many people are encouraging young people to aim for careers as professional golfers. Analogously, a few years ago children were urged to play basketball, during the enormous upsurge in the popularity of professional basketball. Today, however, it is obvious that there are opportunities for only a tiny fraction of talented basketball players at the professional level of the game.

The point of the analogy above is that

○ professional basketball players are also increasingly likely to play golf.

○ professional golfers are becoming more popular than professional basketball players.

○ in the future there will be more opportunities for talented players in professional basketball.

○ there will probably be very few opportunities for many talented golfers.

○ professional basketball players and professional golfers will soon be competing with each other for the same prize money.

Here's how to crack it

On Arguments, always read the QUESTION first.

The conclusion of this argument is not directly stated. In your own words, the conclusion would be something like "There probably won't be very many opportunities to play golf professionally." Why? Because "there are opportunities for only a tiny fraction of talented basketball players at the professional level." Then use POE.

(A) This may be true in real life, but this statement is not supported by the passage. Whether pro basketball players also play golf is outside the scope of this argument.

(B) This choice is also outside the scope of the argument. The passage doesn't compare the popularity of golf with the popularity of basketball.

(C) This also goes *against* information in the passage. The conclusion must be supported by statements in the passage.

(D) This is very close to the conclusion that we put in our own words. Let's keep it.

(E) This is even worse than choice (A). Notice that it also has extreme language, "*the same* prize money."

The best answer is choice (D).

INFERENCE QUESTIONS

Arguments on the GRE often ask you to make inferences. "Inference" has a unique meaning on the GRE; it means something that *must be true* based on the information in the argument. Here are some examples of the ways in which these questions can be worded:

> Which of the following inferences is best supported by the statement made above?

> If the statements above are true, which of the following must also be true?

> Which of the following is implied in the passage above?

> Which of the following conclusions can most properly be drawn if the statements above are true?

Note that some of these questions appear to be conclusion questions, and may not even use the word *infer*. In general, to spot inference questions, look for words such as:

- infer
- most reasonably
- imply
- must also be true
- implicit

An Inference is something KNOWN to be true.

What's the Difference Between a Conclusion and an Inference?

Sometimes there is no difference. When the conclusion to an argument is not explicitly stated in the passage, it is something you could infer. In other cases, inferences have nothing to do with the main point of an argument. You can make inferences from the facts that are stated as premises.

All inference questions ask you to find something that is *known* to be true from information presented in the argument.

How to Approach Inference Questions

1. **Read the question.**
2. **Read the argument and find the conclusion if there is one.** (Use the Why Test to check.) Many inference passages are just a series of facts that don't lead to a single conclusion.
3. **Answer the question in your own words.** (Note: On most inference questions, there are so many possible inferences you could make that it's best to proceed directly to the next step.)
4. **Use POE.**

Eliminating Answer Choices on Inference Questions

Immediately eliminate any answer choices that are obviously outside the scope of the argument. You're looking for something that comes very close to what was stated in the passage, but that was not stated explicitly as such.

Then, as you consider the remaining choices, ask yourself, "Is this *known* to be true, according to the passage?" In other words, "Do I know this?" If you can't find the exact place in the passage that proves the answer choice is true, then eliminate that choice.

Not sure? If you don't understand an answer choice—don't eliminate it! Focus on what could be wrong with the answer choices that you do understand.

Try this one:

The greater the number of autonomous departments in a government, the more essential is a high level of cooperation. This is because increased numbers of autonomous departments demand a larger number of specialized policy makers, which leads to a greater burden on administrators and, possibly, to a greater number of difficulties in setting a general policy.

There are always greater numbers of autonomous departments in democratic governments than in centralized governments.

Which of the following statements must be true if all of the statements above are true?

Check all five answer choices.

- ○ Difficulties in setting general policy occur more often in centralized governments than in democratic governments.
- ○ There are more specialized policy makers in centralized governments than in democratic governments.
- ○ A high level of cooperation is more essential in democratic governments than in centralized governments.
- ○ An administrator's job is easier in a democratic government than in a centralized government
- ○ Autonomous departments operate with greater efficiency in democratic governments than in centralized governments.

Here's how to crack it

The conclusion in this argument is: "The greater the number of autonomous departments in a government, the more essential is a high level of cooperation." Why? Because "increased numbers of autonomous departments demand a larger number of specialized policy makers, which leads . . . to a greater number of difficulties in setting a general policy." Phew!

Notice that the passage also states that "there are always greater numbers of autonomous departments in democratic governments than in centralized governments." How would this statement be connected to the argument above? You could say that "cooperation is more essential in democratic governments than in centralized ones." This connection is probably the best inference you can make. Let's use POE.

(A) This is not known to be true from the information in the passage. In fact, it contradicts what we know to be true. Eliminate.

(B) This also goes against the information in the passage. There are more specialized policy makers when there are more autonomous departments, and there are more autonomous departments in democratic governments. Eliminate this choice.

POE is your new religion.

(C) This looks good. It is definitely known to be true according to the statements in the passage.

(D) This choice also contradicts information in the passage. The passage states that there is a greater burden on administrators when there is a greater number of autonomous departments, and there are more autonomous departments in democratic governments than in centralized ones.

(E) "Operate with greater efficiency"? Do we know anything about efficiency from the passage? No. This choice is out of scope. Eliminate it.

The answer is (C).

ASSUMPTION QUESTIONS

These questions can be worded in several ways:

> Which of the following is an assumption that, if true, would support the conclusion in the passage above?

> Which of the following most accurately states a hidden assumption that the author must make in order to advance the argument above?

> The author depends upon which of
> the following to draw his/her
> conclusion?

> In arguing his/her conclusion the
> author relies on . . .

Notice that some of these questions don't even use the word assumption. Just remember that an assumption is something that the author's conclusion "depends on" or "relies on."

WHAT'S AN ASSUMPTION?

An assumption is an unstated premise that supports the author's conclusion. It's the connection between the stated premises and the conclusion. Let's consider a simple example:

> The university president announced: "The cheating problem has been solved. The university will immediately expel any student caught cheating."

What's the conclusion? "The cheating problem has been solved." Why? Because "The university will immediately expel any student caught cheating." What's being assumed? The university president is assuming that the threat of immediate expulsion is sufficient to solve the cheating problem. The assumption is the missing link in the argument that connects the premises to the conclusion.

HOW TO APPROACH ASSUMPTION QUESTIONS

1. **Read the question.**
2. **Read the argument** and use the Why Test to **find the conclusion** and the premises.
3. **Answer the question in your own words.** Look for a gap between the premises and conclusion. Before you go to the answer choices, try to get a sense of what assumption is necessary to fill that gap.
4. **Use the Process of Elimination.**

ELIMINATING ANSWER CHOICES ON ASSUMPTION QUESTIONS

Since an assumption is an unstated connection between the stated premises and the conclusion, you can eliminate any answer choice that goes beyond the explicit scope of the passage.

An assumption must support the conclusion that was stated in the argument. You can adapt the Why Test to check whether the answer choice supports the conclusion. State the conclusion, then ask "Why?" If an answer choice tells you why the conclusion is true, then it's an assumption that supports the conclusion.

Beware of extreme language in the answer choices of assumption questions. If an answer choice is extreme, it would most likely be a different conclusion

An assumption must support the conclusion.

from the one stated in the argument. In other words, if it would have to be supported by *other* statements, it would not support the conclusion stated in the passage.

Not sure? If you don't understand an answer choice, don't eliminate it! Focus on what could be wrong with the answer choices that you do understand.

The sampling assumption

I heard that the professor give a great lecture today, so I'm sure that her course next semester will be great.

Conclusion: _____

Why? (premises) _____

What is being assumed? _____

The conclusion is that the professor's course next semester will be great. Why? Because her lecture today was great. What's being assumed? The assumption is that the professor's lecture today is representative of the quality of the professor's course.

To spot a sampling argument, look for a conclusion that generalizes from a small sample of evidence. Sampling arguments assume that the sample is representative (not biased).

The analogy assumption

I've been able to ski expert "black diamond" ski trails at ski areas in Colorado, so I will probably be able to ski the "black diamond" ski trails at New Hampshire ski areas.

Conclusion: _____

Why? _____

Assumption: _____

What's the conclusion? "I will probably be able to ski the 'black diamond' ski trails at New Hampshire ski areas." Why? Because "I've been able to ski expert 'black diamond' ski trails at ski areas in Colorado." What's being assumed? The assumption is that the expert ski trails at New Hampshire ski areas will be similar to the expert ski trails in Colorado.

To spot arguments by analogy, look for comparisons. Arguments by analogy assume that the things being compared are, in fact, similar.

The causal assumption

Whenever I eat spicy foods for dinner, I have indigestion all night. Therefore, eating spicy foods causes my indigestion.

Conclusion: _____

Why? _____

Assumption: _____

What's the conclusion? That "eating spicy foods causes my indigestion." Why? Because "whenever I eat spicy foods for dinner, I have indigestion all night." What's being assumed? Causal arguments on the GRE take a strict view of causality. If you argue that eating spicy foods causes your indigestion, one assumption is that if you *don't* eat spicy foods, you *won't* have indigestion. Also, strictly speaking, if you claim that eating spicy foods causes indigestion, you're also assuming that nothing else is causing the problem.

To spot causal arguments, look for indicator words like "causes," "responsible for," and "due to."

Causal arguments always assume that

1. if you remove the cause, that will remove the effect, and

2. that there is no alternative cause.

Now try this one:

> Strep throat is an inflammatory condition caused by certain bacteria. Many of the individuals afflicted with strep throat have repeatedly recurring symptoms. It is clear that, for each of these people, the initial case of strep throat was never entirely cured.
>
> This argument about individuals who have recurring strep throat symptoms makes which of the following assumptions?
>
> ○ Those individuals can never be completely cured of strep throat once it is initially contracted.
> ○ Those individuals do not understand the causes of strep throat.
> ○ Those individuals did not seek medical attention when they initially contracted strep throat.
> ○ Those individuals have not been repeatedly reinfected with strep throat.
> ○ Those individuals did not take precautionary measures to avoid contracting strep throat.

If it's out of scope, eliminate it!

Here's how to crack it

What's the conclusion? For many people, "the initial case of strep throat was never entirely cured." Why? Because "many individuals afflicted with strep throat have repeatedly recurring symptoms." What's being assumed? Did you notice that this is a causal argument? So the assumption is that the fact that the original case of strep throat was never completely cured, and nothing else, is the only cause of the recurring symptoms. Now let's use POE:

(A) This choice goes beyond the scope of the argument and uses really extreme language. Whether these people can ever be completely cured of strep throat goes way too far. Eliminate this choice.

(B) Whether the individuals "understand" the causes of strep throat is outside the scope of this argument. Eliminate.

(C) Whether the people received medical treatment is also irrelevant. The issue is what causes their recurring symptoms.

(D) This choice rules out an alternative cause for the recurring symptoms, and supports the conclusion of the argument. Let's keep it and check choice (E).

(E) Whether these people took "precautionary measures to avoid contracting strep throat" is outside the scope of the argument, since the whole argument is about what happened *after* the people had contracted strep throat.

The best answer is choice (D).

"STRENGTHEN" AND "WEAKEN" QUESTIONS

Now that you can recognize common assumptions, know this: To strengthen an argument, you support the assumption; to weaken an argument, you attack the assumption. Strengthen questions ask you to find the answer choice that provides the best evidence to make the argument stronger. Weaken questions ask you to find the answer choice that provides the best evidence to weaken the argument.

Here are some examples of the ways in which these questions are worded:

Strengthening:

Which of the following, if true, would most strengthen the conclusion drawn in the passage above?

The argument as it is presented in the passage above would be most strengthened if which of the following were true?

The conclusion would be more properly drawn if it were made clear that . . .

> Weaker language works for conclusion questions, but stronger language works for strengthen/weaken questions.

Weakening:

Which of the following, if true, most seriously weakens the conclusion drawn above?

Which of the following, if true, would provide the strongest evidence against the above?

Which of the following, if true, casts the most serious doubt on the conclusion drawn above?

How to Approach Strengthen and Weaken Questions

1. **Read the question first.**

2. **Read the argument, find the conclusion, and identify the premises.**
   Use the Why Test.

3. **Answer the question in your own words.** Uncover assumptions specific to the argument. Ask yourself if the argument makes any of the causal, sampling, or analogy assumptions. Look for an answer choice that, if true, would support or attack the assumptions of the argument.

4. **Use POE.**

- First eliminate answer choices that are way outside the scope of the argument.

- If you're not sure, don't eliminate.

- For weakening and strengthening questions, *don't eliminate answers that use extreme language*. Remember that you're looking for the choice that *most* weakens or strengthens the argument.

- When you're down to two answer choices on strengthening and weakening questions, go with the answer choice that uses stronger language. Stronger wording makes that choice a better support for or a better attack on the argument.

To strengthen an argument, don't simply restate the conclusion, support it by adding a missing premise or by making an assumption explicit. **To strengthen, find the assumption in the argument and support it.**

Always cross off wrong answer choices on your scratch paper.

Here's an example:

Critics have recently called into question the authenticity of a painting, long believed to be the work of a famous artist, which they believe may have been executed by one of the artist's assistants. In order to determine the painting's authenticity, its visual patterns were compared to those in five works known to have been painted by the artist. Many patterns were examined, including composition and the prominence and width of brush strokes. The patterns displayed by the work in question were very similar to those in the five genuine works, thereby establishing the authenticity of the sixth painting.

Which of the following, if true, gives the strongest support to the conclusion above?

○ The visual patterns displayed by different painters are not likely to be similar.

○ Painters from different schools sometimes use the same composition and patterns of brush strokes, but do so to achieve different effects.

○ Many painters endeavor to change their visual patterns with each painting, so as not to grow stale.

○ The stock of visual patterns from which all painters draw is surprisingly limited, thereby insuring some overlap among the patterns displayed by different artists.

○ Composition is not a reliable indicator of a painting's authenticity.

Here's how to crack it

Use that paper!

What's the conclusion? It's that the sixth painting is authentic. Why? Because its visual patterns were compared to those in five works known to have been painted by the artist, and the patterns in the work in question were very similar to those in the five genuine works. What's the assumption? It's an argument by analogy; it's assuming that if the visual patterns in artworks are similar, then they are works by the same artist. Let's go to the answer choices. We're looking for a choice that strengthens the analogy.

(A) This looks good. Let's make sure that the other choices are wrong.

(B) If different painters use the same patterns, that undermines the conclusion of the argument. Since we're trying to strengthen this argument, eliminate this choice.

(C) If painters change their visual patterns with each painting, that undermines the comparison in the argument and weakens the conclusion. Eliminate.

(D) Once again, if different painters use the same patterns, that weakens. Get rid of this choice too.

(E) Since composition was one of the points of comparison used in the argument, if composition is not a reliable indicator of a painting's authenticity, that would weaken the conclusion. Remember, this is a strengthen question! The best answer is choice (A).

To weaken an argument, don't attack the conclusion directly. Attack a premise or an assumption on which the conclusion is based.

Try this one:

> Medical researchers have recently suggested that candidates for heart bypass surgery actually achieve similar benefit by adopting a regimen of increased exercise and dietary changes, if maintained for a ten-year period. Although bypass surgery is now considered a relatively routine procedure, it still puts the patient at risk for heart failure during, or immediately following, the operation. Therefore, the performance of bypass surgery should be ceased.

Don't forget to jot down the conclusion.

> Which of the following, if true, casts the most serious doubt on the conclusion drawn above?
>
> ○ Patients undergoing bypass surgery can suffer aneurysms, stroke, or other potentially life-threatening afflictions.
> ○ Almost all candidates for bypass surgery are at a significant risk of suffering a heart attack within five years.
> ○ Although patients who undergo bypass surgery are often at risk for suffering heart attacks during or after the operation, most patients survive the procedure.
> ○ Since the occurrence of heart attacks during and immediately following bypass surgery is rare, the benefits of the surgery outweigh its liabilities.
> ○ A regimen of exercise and dietary changes can be undertaken at little cost, whereas bypass surgery is an expensive procedure.

Here's how to crack it

What's the conclusion? It's that "the performance of bypass surgery should be ceased." Wow, that's pretty radical! Why? Because "candidates for heart bypass surgery actually achieve similar benefit by adopting a regimen of increased exercise and dietary changes," and because bypass surgery "puts the patient at risk for heart failure during, or immediately following, the operation." What's being assumed?

You can think of this as another argument by analogy. It's assuming that changes in diet and exercise will have similar benefits to bypass surgery, without the risks of surgery. It's also assuming that there are no benefits to surgery that would be missing from the diet/exercise treatment, and that there is no downside to the diet/exercise regimen comparable to the risks of surgery. So to weaken the argument, look for some choice that gives evidence that surgery is better or that the diet/exercise program has problems.

(A) This choice gives evidence of even more problems with bypass surgery, so it strengthens the conclusion. We're trying to weaken, so eliminate this choice.

(B) So what? Does this give evidence that either bypass surgery or the diet/exercise program is better? It really doesn't have any impact on the conclusion, so eliminate it.

(C) This might be evidence that bypass surgery isn't so bad, so let's keep this choice and consider the rest of the choices.

(D) This also seems to indicate that bypass surgery isn't so bad. Let's keep it on the first round.

(E) Cost, in the financial sense, is definitely outside the scope of this argument. So eliminate this choice.

If it's out of scope, eliminate it!

Between choices (C) and (D), which weakens the argument *more*? What would the author of the argument say in response to each of these choices? The author could respond to choice (C) by saying, "The whole point of switching to the diet/exercise program is to prevent heart attacks, not to survive them." But if choice (D) is true, the author really can't respond, because it attacks the assumption about the greater risks of bypass surgery. Choice (D) is a stronger attack on the argument, so it's the best answer choice.

RESOLVE-THE-PARADOX QUESTIONS

These questions present you with a **paradox**, (a seeming contradiction in the argument), and ask you to resolve it or explain how that contradiction could exist. Here are some examples of the ways in which these questions are worded:

> Which of the following, if true, would help to resolve the apparent paradox presented above?

> Which of the following, if true, contributes most to an explanation of the apparent discrepancy described above?

How to Approach Resolve-the-Paradox Questions

1. **Read the question first.**
2. **Read the argument** and find the apparent paradox, discrepancy, or contradiction.

3. State the apparent paradox, discrepancy, or contradiction **in your own words**.

4. **Use POE.** The best answer will explain how both sides of the paradox, discrepancy, or contradiction can be true. Eliminate answers that are out of scope, or that only address one side of the paradox.

Here's an example:

Last winter in a certain national forest one-sixth of the black bear population was unable to find appropriate dens for hibernation. This is somewhat curious given the fact that during the same period, the summer animals that had inhabited the dens during the autumn months had migrated. Many of the dens were large enough to accommodate the bears and were well insulated against the harsh winter weather.

Which of the following statements, if true, would best explain why the black bears were unable to find appropriate places to hibernate when there were ample dens available?

○ Most of the dens which were left vacant were in the higher parts of the forest region and were therefore inaccessible to the bears who inhabit the lower region.

○ During the winter, a few black bears continue to live in dens which they inhabited during the autumn months.

○ Many of the dens are not conducive to the rearing of small cubs.

○ A very few of the black bears migrate to a nearby animal preserve during the winter and therefore do not need to find dens within the national forest.

○ The number of forest rangers who help the black bears to find dens for hibernation has been cut drastically in the last year.

Here's how to crack it

First, check out that question. We have to explain a seeming contradiction, that the bears couldn't find places to hibernate even though there were dens around. Seems like we have to figure out something wrong with the existing dens, something that would prevent the bears from using them. Do we even know what kind of animals were in these dens before they migrated? Or where the dens were?

Let's check out the answer choices:

(A) That means the bears couldn't get to these dens. That would explain how there could be a lot of existing dens, but not a lot of bears able to find them.

(B) But we're concerned with the bears who were looking to hibernate, not the ones who were already living in dens.

(C) Cub rearing is out of the scope.

(D) But what about the ones who don't go to the animal preserve, the ones who are looking for appropriate places to hibernate?

(E) But there still might be enough. We don't know how many rangers there were before or after the cut.

The best answer is (A).

REASONING QUESTIONS

On Arguments, always read the QUESTION first.

Reasoning questions ask you to describe how the argument was made, not necessarily what it says. Here are some examples of the ways in which these questions are worded:

> The author's point is made chiefly by . . .
>
> A major flaw in the argument above is that it . . .
>
> B's attempt to counter A's claim is best described by which of the following?
>
> Bobby's response has which of the following relationships to Danny's argument?

HOW TO APPROACH REASONING QUESTIONS

1. **Read the question first.**

2. **Read the argument and find the conclusion.** Use the Why Test.

3. **State the reasoning in your own words.** Describe how the author gets from the premises to the conclusion.

4. **Use POE.** The best answer will describe the reasoning used in the argument. Eliminate answer choices that don't match the reasoning used in the argument.

Here's an example:

Aramayo: Our federal government seems to function most efficiently when decision-making responsibilities are handled by only a few individuals. Therefore, our government should consolidate its leadership and move away from a decentralized representative democracy.

Tello: But moving our government in this direction could violate our constitutional mission to provide government "of, for, and by the people."

Which of the following statements describes Tello's response to Aramayo?

○ Tello contradicts the reasoning used by Aramayo.
○ Tello uncovers an assumption used in Aramayo's reasoning.
○ Tello brings up a possible negative consequence of accepting Aramayo's argument.
○ Tello reveals the circular reasoning used by Aramayo.
○ Tello shows that Aramayo generalizes a very special situation.

You CAN improve your scores!

Here's how to crack it

First let's be clear on what these two are saying. Aramayo's point (see that lovely "therefore"?) is that the government should consolidate its leadership and be more centralized. Tello's point is that this might be unconstitutional. The question asks for a description of Tello's response. Let's describe it. What Tello did was point out something bad that could result from Aramayo's idea. Let's check out the answers:

(A) Is there any contradiction in Tello's response? Nope. This doesn't match the argument.

(B) What assumption? Tello brings up something new.

(C) Exactly. The fact that this plan might be unconstitutional is definitely a negative consequence.

(D) Is Aramayo using circular reasoning? In other words, is the premise, that the government is more efficient with fewer people in control, the same as the conclusion, that from now on the government should try to be more centralized? No, that's not circular.

(E) What very special situation? There is no very special situation mentioned.

The best answer is (C).

UNDERLINED PORTION QUESTIONS

Sometimes an argument will have parts of it underlined, and you'll be asked to determine the purpose of these statements. Don't let it throw you; your new-found ability to take an argument apart is all you need. Let's look at one:

Learn to take apart an argument.

Although I just had service performed on my car's engine, it is still not running well. During the service, the timing belt was replaced, and the fuel filter was checked and found to be sound. <u>So the problem with the engine cannot be the timing belt or the fuel filter</u>. Most cars of the same model and year as mine have experienced either timing belt slippage or water pump failure. <u>Therefore, the problem with my engine must be a failing water pump</u>.

The two underlined statements serve which of the following functions?

(A) The first statement provides context for the argument, and the second statement serves as a premise supporting the main conclusion.

(B) The first statement is a premise that supports an intermediate conclusion, and the second statement is the main conclusion of the argument.

(C) The first statement is an intermediate conclusion that is refuted by the main conclusion, and the second statement is the main conclusion of the argument.

(D) The first statement is an intermediate conclusion that supports the main conclusion, and the second statement is the main conclusion of the argument.

(E) The first statement is the main conclusion of the argument, and the second statement is an intermediate conclusion that supports the main conclusion.

Here's how to crack it

Process of Elimination will serve you well on these questions. We can quickly identify the second underlined statement as the main conclusion of the argument, which eliminates choices (A) and (E). Now go through the answer choices that are left and ask "Is this actually the case?" For choice (B), is it the case that the first statement is a premise in support of an intermediate conclusion? That first underlined statement looks like an opinion, not a fact, and therefore not a premise. Eliminate it. For (C), is it the case that the first statement is refuted by the main conclusion? No, it's not refuted, so eliminate (C). Choice (D) looks good, because the first statement looks like a conclusion of some sort, and it definitely supports the main conclusion. (D) is the best answer.

QUESTIONS IN THE ANSWER CHOICES?

Though it's generally considered bad form to answer a question with a question, sometimes ETS makes its Argument answer choices into questions. Take a look:

No matter what type of Argument you're doing, always identify the Conclusion.

Johnstone contended that employee-owned companies would invariably be less productive than privately owned enterprises. Each individual, recognizing that his fellow employees would be working harder out of a sense of proprietorship, would be tempted to lighten his own workload. If each person follows this reasoning, overall productivity would greatly decrease. However, a study comparing 15 companies that had recently become employee-owned and 34 privately owned companies revealed significantly better performances from the employee-owned companies.

The answer to which of the following questions would be most useful in evaluating the significance, in relation to Johnstone's claim, of the study described above?

(A) Did any of the companies studied switch from private to employee ownership in the middle of the fiscal year?

(B) Did investors assess employee-owned companies more favorably than they assessed privately owned companies?

(C) Were the employee-owned companies performing as well as the privately owned companies before they switched ownership to their employees?

(D) Were the employees of the employee-owned companies that were studied paid at least as much as the employees of the privately owned companies?

(E) Were there significant overlaps in the market interests of the employee-owned and privately owned companies?

Here's how to crack it

All you have to do is turn the questions into statements and use POE. So . . .

(A) Did any of the companies studied switch from private to employee ownership in the middle of the fiscal year?

becomes

"Some of the companies studied switched from private to employee ownership in the middle of the year."

(B) Did investors assess employee-owned companies more favorably than they assessed privately owned companies?

becomes

"Investors assessed employee-owned companies more favorably than privately owned companies in the past year."

(C) Were the employee-owned companies performing as well as the privately owned companies before they switched ownership to their employees?

becomes

"The employee-owned companies were performing as well as the privately owned companies before they switched ownership to their employees."

(D) Were the employees of the employee-owned companies that were studied paid at least as much as the employees of the privately owned companies?

becomes

"The employees of the employee-owned companies were paid at least as much as the employees of the privately owned companies."

(E) Were there significant overlaps in the market interests of the employee-owned and privately owned companies?

becomes

"There were significant overlaps in the market interests of the two groups of companies."

Now, just cross off any answer choices that are out of the scope, then pick the one remaining choice that *either strengthens or weakens* the argument.

The conclusion of the argument is that Johnstone missed the boat: the employee-owned companies that were studied in fact performed better than, not worse than, privately owned companies. Why were the companies successful? Was there any other cause, beyond the workers behaving in a manner other than Johnstone had predicted, for the success of these companies?

Answers (A), (B), and (E) are all out of the scope. We don't care about when they switched, investors' thoughts about the companies, or the market interests of the two groups. That leaves us with (C) and (D). Answer choice (D) mentions salary, but that's also out of the scope. The only one that works is (C). If the companies were performing equally well at the outset, then there must have been some other cause for the strong performances of the employee-owned companies. This effectively strengthens the argument. (C) is the best answer.

15

Games

WHAT YOU WILL SEE

There are 21 to 25 games questions on 5 to 7 games, so each game comes with 3 or 4 questions.

PRACTICE!

Doing games is like arranging tables at a wedding:"Aunt Sylvia can't sit next to Grandma; Tony and Tina must sit together."

Although games can be boiled down to a simple step-by-step procedure, improving your score on games will require practice. Our techniques should help you considerably, but you'll still need to work on games a little each day. The only way you will feel comfortable with games during the actual exam is by practicing them again and again. Our techniques are all aimed at helping you become methodical and efficient in your approach.

Try to practice a game or two every day. Be sure to concentrate on using the step-by-step method, but have fun with games. They're like puzzles, which is exactly how you should treat them.

ETS's Directions

Here are the directions for the analytic section as they will appear on your GRE:

> Directions: Each question or group of questions is based on a passage or set of conditions. In answering some of the questions, it may be useful to draw a rough diagram. For each question, select the best answer choice given.

Our Own Directions

After reading those directions from ETS you may be thinking that in answering "some" questions it may not be useful to draw rough diagrams. Don't be fooled!

> Directions: Use diagrams to answer all games questions!

That's what makes this section Scratch Paper City. You must write down everything!

THE STRUCTURE OF A GAME

Games begin with a "setup" followed by conditions, or what we will call "clues," which will apply to all of the questions of a game. The setup and clues are the rules of the game. They cannot be violated or changed. Often a question will provide an additional clue, which will only apply to that particular question. But an additional clue will never break the original rules.

The best way to get a feel for GRE games is to look at a simple example:

> A pastry shop will feature five desserts—V, W, X, Y, and Z—to be served Monday through Friday, one dessert each day, in an order that conforms to the following restrictions:
>
> Dessert Y must be served before Dessert V.
> Desserts X and Y must be served on consecutive days.
> Dessert Z may not be the second dessert to be served.

That first paragraph is the setup, and the restrictions are the clues.

OUR STEP-BY-STEP STRATEGY

We'll outline the strategy first. Then we'll discuss each step in it at greater length. Then we'll show you how the strategy applies to actual games. Here's the outline:

1. Read the whole setup and all the clues, and draw a diagram on your scratch paper.
2. Symbolize the clues on your scratch paper.
3. Double-check your work and draw deductions.
4. Attack the questions.
5. Keep your pencil moving.

Put what doesn't change at the top of the diagram.

STEP 1: READ THE SETUP AND CLUES, AND DRAW A DIAGRAM

Don't begin to diagram a game before you've read the setup and the clues. The clues are in no particular order. Sometimes the most revealing clue—the one you'll want to use as the starting point for your diagram—is the last one given. Read through all the clues before you begin to make your diagram.

Make a diagram that visually represents the information in the game. You'll use this diagram as a model, or template, so you want it to include information that's always true for the game.

Most of the games on the GRE CAT involve assigning the elements to places. We call these **assignment games**. For all of these games, the best diagram to use is a simple grid. The places go on top of the grid, and you'll assign the elements to those places. So the first question to ask yourself is: What am I assigning to what? Let's look at our example again:

A pastry shop will feature five desserts—V, W, X, Y, and Z—to be served Monday through Friday, one dessert each day, in an order that conforms to the following restrictions:

Dessert Y must be served before Dessert V.
Desserts X and Y must be served on consecutive days.
Dessert Z may not be the second dessert to be served.

Here's how to crack it

Notice that the days of the week are the places, and the desserts are the elements that will be assigned to those places (we'll deal with the clues shortly). Generally, put the things that don't change at the top of the grid. Often things that don't change have a natural order, such as days of the week, times of day, and the like. So, the diagram for this game looks like this:

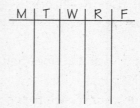

STEP 2: SYMBOLIZE THE CLUES

Make a separate symbol for each element.

The most important skill in getting good at games is the ability to translate the language of the clues into clear visual symbols. You want to be able to work through the questions in a game using your symbols—not the words! Symbolize the clues in a way that's consistent with your diagram. For example, since the days of the week go from left to right, symbolize the clues so that the elements that have to be earlier are to the left of those that have to be later. Let's go back to our example.

Here's that first clue again:

> Dessert Y must be served before Dessert V.

And here's the symbol:

$$Y...V$$

Since Dessert Y must be served before Dessert V, we put it on the left. The ellipsis (...) shows that Y must be sometime before V, but that other desserts could be served between those two. Or they could be adjacent.

Here's the next clue:

> Desserts X and Y must be served on
> consecutive days.

And here's the symbol:

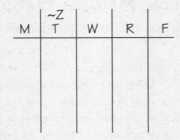

We put a block around Desserts X and Y to show that no other desserts can be served in between those two. We also symbolized the block both ways, since the clue does not indicate that X must be served before Y, or vice versa.

Here's the next clue:

> Dessert Z cannot be the second
> dessert to be served.

And here's the symbol:

Since Dessert Z can never be the second dessert served, we put that information in our model diagram to show that Z can never be served on Tuesday. The wavy negative sign (~) means "not."

> When two elements are always together, that's a **BLOCK**.

SOME SYMBOLIZING GUIDELINES

- Make a separate symbol for each element. For example, if a clue says there are four chocolate bars, the symbol is CCCC, not 4C. You want to be able to see exactly how many items you have to worry about.

- When two elements are always next to each other, put a block around them. Blocks make games much easier. Remember, those two elements have to be together, and there has to be room on the diagram for them.

- When two elements can never be next to each other, use an anti-block symbol. That's just a block with a slash through it.

- For conditional clues (If . . . then . . .), use an arrow. The element that depends on something goes on the left, the independent element goes on the right side of the arrow.

- In some cases, it's just not possible to symbolize a clue. Be sure to write down some shorthand summary of the clue so that you don't forget to check that clue as you do each question.

STEP 3: DOUBLE-CHECK YOUR WORK AND DRAW DEDUCTIONS

After you've symbolized the clues, take the time to double-check everything. Look at your symbols and then tell yourself what they mean. Then read the words of the clues to make sure you've symbolized correctly.

This may seem time-consuming, but it will actually save you time, and will be crucial to your success in solving games. If you go very slowly and carefully at the start of the game, you'll be much more familiar with it and the questions will be much easier to solve. On the other hand, if you go too quickly at the beginning of a game, you'll be much more likely to miss a crucial piece of information or to misrepresent some of the clues. Then the questions will seem impossible to solve!

The major cause of problems with games is misreading the clues!

ELEMENTARY DEDUCTION, MY DEAR WATSON!

Double-checking saves time in the long run.

To draw deductions, ask yourself some questions about the information you have about the game:

- What are your most definite clues? What are your most restricted elements? Does any element always go in one place? If so, put that element in your model diagram. Are there certain places in the diagram where some elements could never go? If so, note that in those places in the model diagram.

- Do you have any blocks? Elements in blocks are very restricted. Are there any places in the diagram where the elements in the block could never go?

- Do certain elements always have to be before other elements? If so, which places in the diagram would be closed to these elements? Make notes in your model diagram.

- Do you have clues about all the elements? If not, which elements have no restrictions? Make notes about any unrestricted elements. Always determine which elements are the least restricted.

- Which places in the diagram are the most restricted? Which are the least restricted?

SOME DEDUCING TIPS

- Always identify the most restricted elements in a game. If one of the elements always has to be in one of the places, you'll start every question by putting that element in place. If the most restricted elements can't go in certain places, then there are only a few places they can go. You should start every question in the game by concentrating on the most restricted elements.

- If you have elements in a block, concentrate on assigning that block rather than on assigning the individual elements.

- If some elements have no restrictions, it's good to write that down so that when you are doing the questions you'll know that you didn't overlook any clues about those elements. You'll also know that unrestricted elements can be assigned to any place that's still open after you've assigned the more restricted elements.

Can you make any deductions on this game?

Draw deductions and add them to your diagram.

A pastry shop will feature five desserts—V, W, X, Y, and Z—to be served Monday through Friday, one dessert each day, in an order that conforms to the following restrictions:

Dessert Y must be served before Dessert V.

Desserts X and Y must be served on consecutive days.

Dessert Z may not be the second dessert to be served.

Well, if we know that Y comes before V on the diagram, are there any restrictions on which dessert can be served Monday? Right, V can't be. If it were on Monday, where would you put Y? And by the same token, do we know anything about Friday? Yes—Y can't be served on Friday. If Y were to be served on Friday, where would you put V? Congratulations, you've just made deductions. Let's put them on the diagram:

```
  ~V   ~Z             ~Y
  M    T    W    R    F
  |    |    |    |    |
  |    |    |    |    |
  |    |    |    |    |
  |    |    |    |    |
  |    |    |    |    |
```

THE ONLY "LOGIC" YOU'LL NEED

Sometimes a clue will say something like "If B is selected, then D is selected." To symbolize that, use an arrow, like this:

$$B \rightarrow D$$

This is called a conditional clue, or an "if-then" clue. It means that whatever is on the left side of the arrow depends, or is conditional, on what's on the right side of the arrow. But whatever is on the right side of the arrow can be assigned independently. Remember, the arrow is not an equal sign. It only goes in one direction. The clue above means "If you have B, it can't be alone. You must have D too." But it doesn't mean if you have D, you must have B; D is independent.

THE CONTRAPOSITIVE

The deduction you make from a conditional clue is called the contrapositive. You can also call it "flip and negate."

Here's an example:

> If A is on the team, B must also be
> on the team.

First symbolize:

$$A \rightarrow B$$

Write everything down on scratch paper! Don't do anything in your head!

Then draw the contrapositive deduction by reversing the order of the letters and negating both letters (flip and negate):

$$\sim B \rightarrow \sim A$$

In other words, if B is not on the team, then A cannot be on the team. This is the only thing that must follow from the clue!

You may be tempted to say that if B is on the team, then A is on the team, but that's not necessarily true. B could be on the team without A. Remember, the restriction is on A, not on B. A cannot be on the team without B.

It works the same way even when the original clue includes a negative component. Just remember to flip and negate!

For example:

If C is selected, D cannot be selected.

You would symbolize:

$$C \rightarrow \sim D$$

So the contrapositive deduction would be:

$$D \rightarrow \sim C$$

Or, If D is selected, then C cannot be selected. Always draw the contrapositive deduction when you see "if-then" clues.

STEP 4: ATTACK THE QUESTIONS

As usual on the GRE, you have to read the questions very carefully. Understanding exactly what the questions are asking is where you have to start in solving them. First, make sure you understand the difference between a COULD question and a MUST question.

A "could" question asks which answer choice could be true (that is, is it possible once?). Only one of the choices could be true, according to the rules of the game. The wrong answers to a could question cannot be true.

A "must" question asks which answer choice is always true, not which choice could be true once. Several of the choices could be true, only one choice cannot be false. The wrong answer choices could be false.

STEP 5: KEEP YOUR PENCIL MOVING

Don't think, draw! Don't look for mental shortcuts, just get busy. Keep trying things on your scratch paper. Try one arrangement, eliminate answer choices, then try another arrangement. You'll get the right answer faster by trying something than by sitting and staring at the question.

Don't even THINK about trying to do games in your head!

PUT THE STRATEGY TO WORK

Here's a relatively simple game, followed by three questions. Read the game and try answering the questions. Don't worry about how much time it takes you. Refer to the strategy we've just outlined as you do the game. Concentrate on doing each step in the process correctly before you go on to the next step. Do it on scratch paper!

Then, when you've finished, carefully read our step-by-step explanations of the strategy, which follow the questions.

ASSIGNMENT GAME 1

Here's a game followed by questions:

A fugue written for six instruments—bass, cello, flute, oboe, piano, and violin—calls for them to enter one by one into the composition. The instruments must enter according to the following conditions:

The piano enters fourth.
The cello enters immediately before the violin enters.
The bass enters sometime before the piano enters and sometime before the oboe enters.
The flute enters sometime before the oboe enters.

Which of the following is an acceptable order, from first to last, in which the instruments could enter?

○ Bass, cello, violin, piano, flute, oboe
○ Bass, flute, oboe, piano, violin, cello
○ Bass, oboe, flute, piano, cello, violin
○ Flute, cello, violin, piano, bass, oboe
○ Flute, cello, violin, bass, piano, oboe

Keep your pencil moving!

If the bass enters third, which of the following must be true?

○ The flute enters first.
○ The flute enters second.
○ The oboe enters fifth.
○ The violin enters second.
○ The violin enters sixth.

If the violin enters sixth, which of the following can be true?

○ The bass enters third.
○ The cello enters second.
○ The flute enters first.
○ The flute enters fifth.
○ The oboe enters second.

Try it yourself first, before you read on!

STEP 1: READ THE SETUP AND CLUES, AND DRAW A DIAGRAM

Okay, we have six instruments and we have to figure out the order. Anything with an order goes on the top of our diagram, so let's draw the diagram like this:

```
 1 | 2 | 3 | 4 | 5 | 6
   |   |   |   |   |
   |   |   |   |   |
   |   |   |   |   |
```

STEP 2: SYMBOLIZE THE CLUES

That first clue is pretty easy, right? Just put the P under the 4:

```
 1 | 2 | 3 | 4 | 5 | 6
   |   |   | P |   |
   |   |   | P |   |
   |   |   | P |   |
   |   |   | P |   |
```

We're filling in Ps all the way down the column so that you never have to worry about P or that column again. It's taken care of for good. The key to games is filling in spaces.

The symbol for the next clue looks like this:

$$\boxed{CV}$$

Notice this block only goes in one direction, because we're told that the cello is immediately before the violin, and we don't have the "after" option.

Next clue:

> B . . . P
> B . . . O

Notice that we separated this clue into two clues, to avoid confusion. Since we don't know the relationship between P and O, it's better to separate the clue.

Next clue:

> F . . . O

Okay, now we're ready for . . .

| Use that paper!

Step 3: Double-Check your Work and Draw Deductions

Use POE in games.

Check everything over by rereading the whole game and checking your diagram and symbols. Then look at the clue symbols to see if you can make any deductions. First check the CV block. This means that V could never be first, because if it were, there would be no place to put C. Also, C could never be sixth, because if it were, there would be no place to put V. Let's put those deductions on the diagram:

~V					~C
1	2	3	4	5	6
			P		
			P		
			P		
			P		

Since we know that B has to come in sometime before P, and we know that P must be fourth, that means that B can never be in 5 or 6. Also, the fact that B has to come sometime before O means that O can never be first. Let's put those deductions in our model diagram:

~O ~V				~B	~B ~C
1	2	3	4	5	6
			P		
			P		
			P		
			P		

Finally, F must come sometime before O, which means that O can never be first (which we have already), and that F can never be sixth. And since both B and F have to come before O, O can never be second either (there has to be room for two instruments to come before it). Let's put those deductions in:

~O ~V	~O			~B	~F ~B ~C
1	2	3	4	5	6
			P		
			P		
			P		
			P		

STEPS 4 AND 5: ATTACK THE QUESTIONS AND KEEP YOUR PENCIL MOVING

Let's go with the first question:

> Which of the following is an acceptable order, from first to last, in which the instruments could enter?
>
> ○ Bass, cello, violin, piano, flute, oboe
> ○ Bass, flute, oboe, piano, violin, cello
> ○ Bass, oboe, flute, piano, cello, violin
> ○ Flute, cello, violin, piano, bass, oboe
> ○ Flute, cello, violin, bass, piano, oboe

Here's how to crack it

All we have to do here is take each clue to the answer choices and check for violations. First of all, according to the first clue, P must be fourth, so we can eliminate any answer choice that doesn't have the piano fourth. Eliminate choice (E). Next, the second clue tells us that C comes immediately before V, so eliminate any choice that doesn't say that. That gets rid of choice (B). The next clue tells us that both P and O have to come after B, so eliminate any choice that doesn't say that. That gets rid of choice (D). Finally, we know that F has to come before O, so that eliminates choice (C). What are we left with? Choice (A), and that's our answer.

Next question:

| Keep your pencil moving!

> If the bass enters third, which of the following must be true?
>
> ○ The flute enters first.
> ○ The flute enters second.
> ○ The oboe enters fifth.
> ○ The violin enters second.
> ○ The violin enters sixth.

Here's how to crack it

First, we have to fill this information in on our diagram (remember, it will only be true for this question):

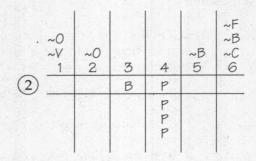

Okay, B is at 3, and we already know that P is at 4, and we also know that O has to come sometime after B. But we also have to save room for that CV block. The only positions where there is going to be room for the CV block, with O in 5 or 6, is 1 and 2. Now the only instruments left are O and F, and the only positions left are 5 and 6, but we already know that F can't be in 6. So, F goes in 5 and O goes in 6:

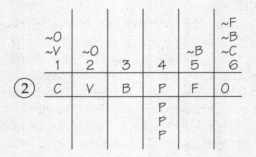

We know where every instrument goes, so let's go to the answers and see what must be true:

(A) Nope, it's fifth.

(B) Nope, it's fifth.

(C) Nope, it's sixth.

(D) Bingo!

(E) Nope, it's second.

Next question:

If the violin enters sixth, which of the following can be true?

- ○ The bass enters third.
- ○ The cello enters second.
- ○ The flute enters first.
- ○ The flute enters fifth.
- ○ The oboe enters second.

Here's how to crack it

First, let's fill in the information we're given:

	~O ~V 1	~O 2	3	4	~B 5	~F ~B ~C 6
②	C	V	B	P	F	O
③				P		V
				P		
				P		

> Write everything down on scratch paper! Don't do anything in your head!

The violin is sixth, which means C has to be fifth. Now let's think about O, since it's very restricted. Check the top of your diagram; the only place you can put O is in 3. That means B and F can fight it out for 1 and 2:

	~O ~V 1	~O 2	3	4	~B 5	~F ~B ~C 6
②	C	V	B	P	F	O
③	B/F	F/B	O	P	C	V
				P		
				P		

Let's go to the answers and see what can be true:

(A) Nope, it's first or second.

(B) Nope, it's fifth.

(C) Bingo!

(D) Nope, it's first or second.

(E) Nope, it's third.

There you go. That's a typical, though relatively easy, GRE CAT game. Congratulations. Notice that it was all about assigning things to places. That's what most GRE CAT games will ask you to do.

ASSIGNMENT GAME 2

Here's another one, a little trickier this time:

Assignment games are by far the most common. Learn them, live them, love them!

A reading group is to choose exactly four books to be read by the group over the summer. The four books must be selected from among seven eligible books: three nonfiction works—P, Q, and R—and four fiction works—T, U, V, and W. The four books must be selected according to the following conditions:

If either Q or R is selected, the other must also be selected.
T and U cannot both be selected.
Q and V cannot both be selected.

Which of the following could be the four books selected by the reading group?

- ◯ P, Q, R, V
- ◯ P, Q, U, W
- ◯ P, U, V, W
- ◯ Q, T, U, W
- ◯ T, U, V, W

If P and T are both selected, which of the following pairs of books could be the other books selected?

- ◯ Q and U
- ◯ Q and W
- ◯ R and V
- ◯ U and V
- ◯ V and W

If R is selected, which of the following CANNOT be selected?

- ◯ P
- ◯ Q
- ◯ T
- ◯ V
- ◯ W

Try it yourself first, then read on. . .

STEP 1: READ THE SETUP AND CLUES, AND DRAW A DIAGRAM

This time, we have elements that fall into different categories—nonfiction and fiction. Let's symbolize them using upper and lower case letters, so we can always tell the difference. Also, we're choosing four books out of a possible seven, so besides putting four spaces across the top of the diagram, we also need a place to put the elements we don't assign. Meet the "out" column:

You CAN improve your scores!

```
P Q R
t u v w    | 1 | 2 | 3 | 4 | OUT
```

Always use the "OUT" column when you're not going to assign every element. Sometimes you can tell which elements are "in" by knowing which ones are "out" first.

STEP 2: SYMBOLIZE THE CLUES

That first clue starts with the word "if". However, it's not really a conditional clue, because they're giving us both directions. So, the first clue is really a block:

$$Q \rightarrow R \qquad R \rightarrow Q \qquad \boxed{QR}$$

The next clue is an anti-block:

And so is the next one:

$$\overline{Qv}$$

STEP 3: DOUBLE-CHECK YOUR WORK AND DRAW DEDUCTIONS

Check over everything. You don't want to forget to put a slash through an anti-block. That would ruin the whole game. Notice that Q is the most restricted element, and that there are no clues about P or W, so those are the least restricted elements. You could also note that, since R is always selected with Q, and since Q and V cannot be selected together, then R and V cannot be selected together. There don't seem to be any further deductions, so move on to . . .

STEPS 4 AND 5: ATTACK THE QUESTIONS AND KEEP YOUR PENCIL MOVING

Practice games every day.

First question:

> Which of the following could be the four books selected by the reading group?
>
> ○ P, Q, R, V
> ○ P, Q, U, W
> ○ P, U, V, W
> ○ Q, T, U, W
> ○ T, U, V, W

Here's how to crack it

All we have to do here is take each clue to the answer choices and eliminate all answer choices that violate each clue. First of all, if we have Q, we have to have R, so eliminate any choice that violates that rule. That gets rid of choices (B) and (D). Next, any choice that contains both T and U must be eliminated. That gets rid of choice (E). Finally, any choice that contains both Q and V must be eliminated. That gets rid of choice (A). That leaves us with the best answer, choice (C).

Next question:

> If P and T are both selected, which of the following pairs of books could be the other books selected?
>
> ○ Q and U
> ○ Q and W
> ○ R and V
> ○ U and V
> ○ V and W

Here's how to crack it

First, fill in what the question tells us:

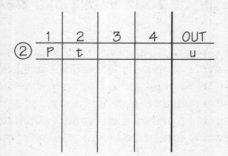

We have a TU anti-block, so that puts U in the out column. It also eliminates choices (A) and (D). We also know that we can only choose two more books. Keep that in mind as we check the answers.

(A) We already eliminated this one.

(B) Nope. We can only choose two more books, and Q brings along R, and choosing Q, R, and W would be too many books.

(C) Nope. We can only choose two more books, and R brings along Q, and choosing R, Q, and V would be too many books. Not only that, but there's a QV anti-block.

(D) We already eliminated this one.

(E) Bingo! This is the only one left; it has to be the answer.

Next question:

If R is selected, which of the following CANNOT be selected?

○ P
○ Q
○ T
○ V
○ W

Here's how to crack it
Fill in the diagram:

	1	2	3	4	OUT
②	P	t			u
	R				

Use POE in games.

We have a QR block, so we can fill Q in. We also have a QV anti-block, so we can put V in the "out" column:

	1	2	3	4	OUT
②	P	t			u
③	R	Q			v

Use that paper!

We have enough to answer the question, don't we? We know which book cannot be selected—book V—so the best answer is choice (D).

ASSIGNMENT GAME 3

Okay, let's try one more assignment game, since most (if not all) of the games you'll see on the GRE CAT will be assignment games:

A window dresser is designing a hat display for the window of a haber-dasher. The display must include one of each of the following five types of hats: fedora, derby, top hat, sombrero, and beret. One hat will displayed each day of a week, Monday through Friday. One of the hats displayed must be red, one must be cobalt, one must be brown, one must be white, and one must be gray. In designing the display, she has made the following decisions:

The derby will be displayed on an earlier day than the top hat.
The beret will be displayed on an earlier day than the fedora.
The white hat will be displayed on an earlier day than the gray hat.
The cobalt hat will be displayed on Wednesday.
The top hat displayed will be brown.

Which of the following could be the colors of the hats displayed on Monday through Friday, respectively?

- ○ White, brown, cobalt, red, gray
- ○ Red, cobalt, white, gray, brown
- ○ Red, brown, cobalt, gray, white
- ○ Cobalt, gray, white, brown, red
- ○ Brown, gray, cobalt, red, white

Always cross off wrong answer choices on your scratch paper.

Any of the hats could be displayed on Wednesday EXCEPT the

- ○ Fedora
- ○ Derby
- ○ Top hat
- ○ Sombrero
- ○ Beret

If the fedora is displayed on an earlier day than the cobalt hat, which of the following must be true?

- ○ The fedora is displayed on Monday.
- ○ The derby is displayed on Tuesday.
- ○ The top hat is displayed on Friday.
- ○ The sombrero is displayed on Wednesday.
- ○ The beret is displayed on Monday.

Try it yourself, then read on . . .

STEP 1: READ THE SETUP AND CLUES, AND DRAW A DIAGRAM

We know the hats are to be displayed throughout a week and, for this game, we have two sets of elements to assign: hats and colors. Let's use uppercase for the hats and lowercase for the colors:

F   D   T   S   B
r   c   b   w   g

Since we have two things to assign to each day, let's modify our diagram a little:

	M	T	W	R	F
hat					
color					
hat					
color					
hat					
color					

This way, we can keep track of horizontal blocks, like if two hats or two colors have to be next to each other, and vertical blocks, like if a hat must be a certain color.

STEP 2: SYMBOLIZE THE CLUES

These clues all look pretty familiar, don't they?

D...T
B...F
w...g

$\boxed{\begin{array}{c} T \\ b \end{array}}$

	M	T	W	R	F
hat					
color			ⓒ		
hat					
color			ⓒ		
hat					
color			ⓒ		

Note that because we have two rows for each setup, the C can't be filled in all the way down the Wednesday column. Make sure you circle it so you know it's always true, and in case you need to add another setup. Also note the vertical Tb block.

STEP 3: DOUBLE-CHECK YOUR WORK AND DRAW DEDUCTIONS

From now on, you can think of the top hat permanently attached to brown. For that reason, the top hat could never be displayed on Wednesday (the cobalt hat is already there). And because of that first clue, we know the Tb block also can't go on Monday. By the same token, D can't be on Friday. You can make the same deductions with the second clue: B can't go on Friday and F can't go on Monday. Also, the gray hat can't go on Monday and the white hat can't go on Friday:

```
        ~g
        ~F                              ~w
     ~ ┌─┐        ~ ┌─┐                 ~B
       │T│          │T│                 ~D
       │b│          │b│
       └─┘          └─┘
        M     T      W      R      F
```

	M	T	W	R	F
hat					
color			ⓒ		
hat					
color			ⓒ		
hat					
color			ⓒ		

STEPS 4 AND 5: ATTACK THE QUESTIONS AND KEEP YOUR PENCIL MOVING

First question:

Use that paper!

Which of the following could be the colors of the hats displayed on Monday through Friday, respectively?

○ White, brown, cobalt, red, gray
○ Red, cobalt, white, red, gray
○ Red, brown, cobalt, gray, white
○ Cobalt, gray, white, brown, red
○ Brown, gray, cobalt, red, white

Here's how to crack it

Check those clues and deductions! The easiest thing to check is that cobalt must be on Wednesday, or third. That was one of our clues. Eliminate any choice that doesn't say that. That gets rid of choices (B) and (D). Now, what else do we know about colors? That white can't go on Friday, or last. Eliminate any choice that doesn't say that. That gets rid of choices (C) and (E). What are we left with? Choice (A), the best answer.

Next question:

Any of the hats could be displayed on Wednesday EXCEPT the

○ Fedora
○ Derby
○ Top hat
○ Sombrero
○ Beret

Here's how to crack it

Hey, check those deductions! We already figured out that the top hat could never be displayed on Wednesday, since it has to be brown, and the hat on Wednesday is cobalt. The answer is (C).

Next question:

> If the fedora is displayed on an earlier day than the cobalt hat, which of the following must be true?
>
> ○ The fedora is displayed on Monday.
> ○ The derby is displayed on Tuesday.
> ○ The top hat is displayed on Friday.
> ○ The sombrero is displayed on Wednesday.
> ○ The beret is displayed on Monday.

Here's how to crack it

Keep your pencil moving!

We know the cobalt hat is displayed on Wednesday, so according to the question, the fedora is either on Monday or Tuesday. But check those deductions; the fedora can't be on Monday. That forces it onto Tuesday. What else do we know about the fedora? It must come after the beret. That forces the beret onto Monday:

```
       ~g
       ~F                              ~w
    ~ ┌─┐        ~ ┌─┐                 ~B
      │T│          │T│                 ~D
      │b│          │b│
      └─┘          └─┘
      M   │  T  │   W   │   R   │   F
```

	M	T	W	R	F
hat					
color			ⓒ		
hat					
color			ⓒ		
hat					
color			ⓒ		

Now check out the answers:

(A) Nope, it's on Tuesday.

(B) We don't know when the derby is displayed.

(C) We don't know when the top hat is displayed.

(D) We don't know when the sombrero is displayed.

(E) Bingo!

Notice we didn't have to fill in the whole diagram to answer this question. Let that be a lesson to you!

MAP GAMES

In an assignment game, you assign elements to places. In a map game, there are no places apart from the elements. Rather, the setup of the game describes something *moving* among the elements, or connections between pairs of elements.

HOW TO APPROACH MAP GAMES

Take plenty of time to symbolize the clues carefully, then combine the clues into one diagram that incorporates all the information. Double-checking before you go to the questions is especially crucial. For map games, you'll refer to this one diagram to answer all of the questions. Here's an example:

In map games, there's no place to ASSIGN the elements. It's all about CONNECTIONS.

> In a corporation, there are seven divisions—A, B, C, D, E, F, and G. These divisions send mail to each other in two ways: by messenger and by fax.
>
> Mail sent by messenger can travel in only one direction, from A to B, from B to D, from D to F, from F to G, and from G to A.
>
> Mail sent by fax can travel in either direction between B and C, between C and G, and between D and E.
>
> The seven divisions cannot send mail by any other means.
>
> Mail that cannot be sent directly to the desired division is passed through one or more intermediate divisions, which pass the mail along according to the conditions stated above.
>
>
> If division D sends mail to division C so that it passes through the fewest possible intermediate divisions, then which of the following must be the order of the intermediate divisions through which the mail passes?
>
> ○ F, G, A, B
> ○ F, B
> ○ F, G
> ○ B, C
> ○ F, G, A

Mail sent from the first to the second division in which of the following pairs can be sent using exactly one intermediate division?

- ◯ A to F
- ◯ C to A
- ◯ D to B
- ◯ E to C
- ◯ G to E

Mail sent from the first to the second division in which of the following pairs requires using both the messenger and the fax?

- ◯ A to F
- ◯ C to G
- ◯ D to C
- ◯ E to D
- ◯ G to B

Try it yourself first, then read on . . .

STEP 1: READ THE SETUP AND CLUES, AND DRAW A DIAGRAM

Don't even THINK about trying to do games in your head!

We know this is a map game because there are no places to put the elements, and we do have to connect them somehow. We can't really draw the diagram until we symbolize the clues, so . . .

STEP 2: SYMBOLIZE THE CLUES

The first clue is about sending mail by messenger. Just draw the connections, noting that they only go in one direction:

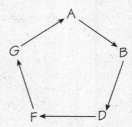

The next clue is about sending mail by fax. Add these connections with a different symbol (in this case, a double line) so you can tell the difference, also noting that these go in both directions:

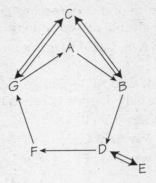

There's your diagram.

STEP 3: DOUBLE-CHECK YOUR WORK AND DRAW DEDUCTIONS

Check everything very carefully!

STEPS 4 AND 5: ATTACK THE QUESTIONS AND KEEP YOUR PENCIL MOVING

First question:

> If division D sends mail to division C so that it passes through the fewest possible intermediate divisions, then which of the following must be the order of the intermediate divisions through which the mail passes?
>
> ○ F, G, A, B
> ○ F, B
> ○ F, G
> ○ B, C
> ○ F, G, A

Here's how to crack it

We have to get from D to C. A messenger can go from D to F, then to G, and then the fax goes from G to C. That's D-F-G-C. The question wants the intermediate divisions between D and C. That's F-G, or choice (C).

Next question:

> Mail sent from the first to the second division in which of the following pairs can be sent using exactly one intermediate division?
>
> ○ A to F
> ○ C to A
> ○ D to B
> ○ E to C
> ○ G to E

Here's how to crack it

The question is asking which of the connections in the answer choices can be achieved by passing through only one other division. Let's try them:

(A)   Nope. To get from A to F, we'd have to go A-B-D-F. That's two divisions in between.

(B)   Bingo! To get from C to A, we can go C-G-A (faxes can go in either direction). G is the only division in between.

(C)   Nope, D is a long way from B.

(D)   Nope, E is a long way from C.

(E)   Nope, G is a long way from E.

Next question:

Need more games practice? Go to your bookstore and pick up a copy of the LSAT/ GRE Analytic Workout.

Mail sent from the first to the second division in which of the following pairs requires using both the messenger and the fax?

- ◯   A to F
- ◯   C to G
- ◯   D to C
- ◯   E to D
- ◯   G to B

Here's how to crack it

Try out the answers:

(A)   Nope. To get from A to F we don't need the fax. The messenger can go A-B-D-F.

(B)   Nope. To go from C to G, we only need the fax.

(C)   Bingo. The messenger goes from D to F to G, and then the fax goes to C.

(D)   Nope. To get from E to D, we only need the fax.

(E)   Nope. We can get from G to B using either the fax (G-C-B) or the messenger (G-A-B), but not both.

PART **V**

How to Crack
The Optional Writing
Assessment

16

The Optional Writing Assessment

WHAT IS THE *OPTIONAL* WRITING ASSESSMENT?

Remember, this test is optional.

The GRE Writing Assessment Test will become available year-round starting in October of 1999. It's a separate, *optional* $50 test that you can take with or apart from your regular GRE CAT. It does NOT count toward your GRE score, but is scored separately, on a scale of 0–6, with 6 being the highest. The test will consist of one 45-minute "Present Your Perspective on an Issue" essay (you get two topics to choose from) and one 30-minute "Analyze an Argument" essay (you don't get a topic choice here).

SHOULD I TAKE IT?

During the next year, graduate departments will be deciding whether to require or recommend that their applicants take the Writing Assessment Test. If you plan to apply to graduate school in the fall of 1999 or beyond, you should check with your prospective graduate schools to see if they want you to take this *optional* test. Or, if you're a great writer, you might choose to take it, to show off a strength that isn't measured by the tyranny of the multiple-choice GRE.

The Writing Assessment Test is a way to "strengthen your application" by testing your ability to express yourself in a cogent, well-organized manner. The essays are graded on your analysis of a topic, your overall organization, and your facility with English grammar and diction. You will be judged not so much by what you write, as by how you write it. What you'll get in this chapter, then, are tips on how to do what ETS expects high scorers to do.

THE BASICS

If you take this test, it's because you want to reveal your writing skills. Even so, this is a pretty rigid assignment—the type of essays we learned to write in junior high school, with an introduction, a two- or three-paragraph body, and a conclusion. You really won't have the time or the freedom to be dazzling (that's what your application essay is for). This test is for showing that you can follow directions, write clearly, and argue persuasively. Here are some general tips:

- **Brush up on your typing.** Yes, you're typing these essays right there at the computer terminal. Don't worry, the word processing is easy. But if you're a slow typist, it's a good idea to practice so you don't waste a lot of time hunting and pecking on test day.

- **Use simple, direct language.** Don't use big words unless you're SURE you're using them properly. You don't have time to be subtle or artful, so it's best to be simple and direct.

- **Make it pretty.** The essay readers look at tons of essays, and spend about three minutes on each one. So cater to the short attention span. Aesthetics, in many ways, are more important than content. Make sure your essays look nice and fill up enough space.

THE ISSUE

The "Present Your Perspective on an Issue" question (we'll call it the **Issue** question) asks for your opinion on some topic. Pick a side and support that position. There is no right or wrong side to pick. The ETS graders don't care what your opinion is. They only want to see if you can argue that position persuasively. So don't be wishy-washy; don't point out the strengths of both sides. Your goal is to present an essay that:

- expresses your viewpoint clearly and resolutely.

- includes examples or other reasoning that supports your views.

- persuades the reader to feel the same way you do.

Here's what you do when you first see the Issue topics:

1. Read the topics and decide which one you can write a better essay about. You don't necessarily have to agree wholeheartedly with what you're writing. You just have to be able to persuade the reader that you do. So, whichever topic you think has better potential is the one to go with.

2. Decide which position you're going to take—for or against.

3. Brainstorm. That means spending a good five minutes coming up with a bunch of supporting ideas and examples. Jot them down on your scratch paper. Make sure you have 3–5 good ones.

4. Start your essay, using a template for structure (more on that in a minute).

5. When you have only a few minutes left, read over your essay and fix any spelling and grammar mistakes you happen to spot.

> The key to a good Issue essay is to be clear about which side of the Issue you're on.

The issue template

Though you can't know what topic you'll get in advance, the essay's structure should be basically the same no matter what you're writing about. The template will be the frame or structure of your Issue essay. If you set up your essay like this (or with your own variations) every time, you'll stay focused.

Here's an example of a simple structural template for an Issue essay. You should write according to your personality, of course, but looking at templates will help keep you focused.

Paragraph 1: "The issue of (whatever the issue is) is a controversial one. On the one hand, (state the side of the issue that you'll be arguing). On the other hand, (state the other side of the issue). However, I believe that (CLEARLY state the position you're taking)."

Paragraph 2: Support your position with one example.

Paragraph 3: Support your position with another example.

Paragraph 4: Support your position with another example.

Paragraph 5: "For all these reasons, I therefore believe that (reiterate your position)."

See? Your first and last paragraph should be quite similar in that they will both state your position (in slightly different words, of course). That way, the reader is sure you've stuck to your position. In fact, because they should say practically the same thing anyway, some people like the **bookends first** approach, in which you write the introduction and the conclusion first, and then the body. This ensures continuity and keeps you focused.

VARIATIONS ON A THEME

Here are some Issue template variations:

Paragraph 1: State your position.

Paragraph 2: Acknowledge the arguments in favor of the other side.

Paragraph 3: Knock down those arguments.

Paragraph 4: Restate your position.

Paragraph 1: State the other side's argument ("Many people believe that...").

Paragraph 2: Contradict that argument ("However, I believe that...").

Paragraph 3: Support your position.

Paragraph 4: Provide more support.

Paragraph 5: Restate your position.

A sample issue

Reacting to statistics of increased crime and violence, some have argued that it is necessary for the entertainment industry to police itself by censoring television programs and popular music lyrics. However, civil liberties advocates argue that it has not been demonstrated that watching violence on television or listening to song lyrics depicting violence leads to real violence.

Which do you find more compelling, the call for censorship of entertainment media, or the civil libertarians' response to it? Explain your position, using relevant reasons and/or examples drawn from your own experience, observations, or reading.

Okay. Say we decide to write an essay about this Issue (remember, you'll get to choose from two topics). First we have to decide which side of the issue we're going to argue for. Let's pick the anti-censorship side. We're going to show that the civil libertarians' argument is more compelling.

Let's do some brainstorming: The fact that it has not been demonstrated that watching violence on television or listening to song lyrics depicting violence leads to real violence is an important point. The passage suggests that the entertainment industry police itself, but how? Who in the industry decides what gets censored? Wouldn't the entertainment industry mainly be concerned with sales? And if it were found that violence sells, would they really not allow violence into the market? Also, if we start censoring violence in TV shows and song lyrics, what's next? Words that might offend someone? Controversial topics? Where do we draw the line? And who decides what gets censored and what doesn't?

Let's see how this essay could be written using one of our templates:

> Paragraph 1: The issue of censorship is a controversial one. On the one hand, freedom of speech is a tenet of our Constitution, and one of our most treasured freedoms. On the other hand, violence is a serious problem in our society that needs to be addressed. However, I believe that the principle of free speech is too important to allow censorship of any kind.
>
> Paragraph 2: (Discuss how watching or listening to violence doesn't make one violent. Give an example.)
>
> Paragraph 3: (Discuss the conflict of interest stemming from the entertainment industry policing itself.)
>
> Paragraph 4: (Discuss the "where do we draw the line" issue.)
>
> Paragraph 5: For all these reasons, I therefore believe that the civil libertarians are right, and that free speech is too precious to allow any kind of censorship.

This is just a rough sketch, of course. You'll be writing your own sparkling prose and brilliant transitions.

THE ARGUMENT

The "Analyze an Argument" question (we'll call it the **Argument** question) asks you to analyze someone else's logic. DO NOT give your opinion of the issue at hand, only of the *structure* of the argument you're given. You'll be using some of the techniques you learned in the Arguments chapter of this book.

Your job is to discuss how convincing you find the argument's line of reasoning and the evidence supporting it. You can also suggest how the argument could be made more convincing. Don't be afraid to really critique the argument they give you. High-scoring essays do the following:

- Clearly identify the components of the argument: conclusion, premises, and assumptions.

- Critique the author's logic and assumptions, not the actual conclusion. Show that the assumptions could be wrong, or that some key term is not adequately identified.

- When possible, suggest ways in which the author could improve the argument. Point out the type of evidence needed to support the assumptions and fill in the gaps.

The key to a good Argument essay is to be clear with your critique of the Argument.

DO NOT give your opinion on the validity of the conclusion—that's what the Issue essay is for. Stick to critiquing the argument at hand.

Here's what you do when you first see the Argument topic:

1. Read the argument *skeptically* and locate the conclusion and the premises (just like you do for an Argument in the Analytic section of the GRE).

2. Brainstorm some assumptions that would weaken the argument, and jot them down on your scratch paper.

3. Assess whether the argument's premises really did a good job supporting the conclusion.

4. Brainstorm some assumptions or premises that might have strengthened the argument.

5. Plug this stuff into a template and start typing.

6. When you have only a few minutes left, read over your essay and fix any spelling and grammar mistakes you happen to spot.

Don't refer to current events in your essay unless you're sure of the facts.

The argument template

Writing this essay should be as automatic as possible, since all Arguments are constructed in the same way. Here's a sample template you can play around with:

Paragraph 1: "The argument that (restate conclusion) is not logically convincing. This argument ignores certain important assumptions."

Paragraph 2: "First, the argument assumes that (insert faulty assumption and explain)."

Paragraph 3: "Second, the argument never addresses (insert missing or faulty assumption and explain)."

Paragraph 4: "Finally, the argument omits (insert missing or faulty assumption and explain)."

Paragraph 5: "Thus, the argument is not logically sound. The evidence in support of the conclusion (restate the problems with the premises/assumptions)."

Paragraph 6: "The argument might have been strengthened by (suggest premises/assumptions that would have better supported the conclusion)."

You don't *have to* stick to this exact structure. But this gives you an idea of what your job is.

Variations on a theme

Here are some Argument template variations:

Paragraph 1: Restate the argument.

Paragraph 2: Discuss the missing information (assumptions) between the conclusion and the premises.

Paragraph 3: Point out three holes in the reasoning of the argument.

Paragraph 4: Explain how those three holes could be filled up by explicitly stating the missing assumptions.

Paragraph 1: Restate the argument, saying that it contains three major flaws.

Paragraph 2: Pick one flaw and state the missing assumption that would fix it.

Paragraph 3: Pick another flaw and state the missing assumption that would fix it.

Paragraph 4: Pick another flaw and state the missing assumption that would fix it.

Paragraph 5: Conclude that because of the three flaws you pointed out, the argument is weak. Perhaps add some suggestions on ways to improve it.

A sample argument

Politicians should be allowed to get free meals in restaurants, even when they are not conducting official business while eating. After all, the salaries they receive are minimal, and without perks such as free food, we cannot expect the most qualified people to desire to run for public office.

Don't refer to literature in your essays unless you know the exact name of the title and author of the book or play.

Discuss how logically convincing you find this argument. In explaining your point of view, be sure to analyze the line of reasoning and the use of evidence in the argument. Also discuss what, if anything, would make the argument more sound and persuasive, or would help you to better evaluate its conclusion.

First of all, what's the conclusion? That politicians should get free meals. What are the premises or reasons supporting that conclusion? One is that they don't make that much money from their salaries, and the other is that we won't get the most qualified people running for office unless there are perks to lure them. Pretty shaky reasoning, huh?

Okay, now let's rip it apart, premise by premise. First, the premise that these politicians don't get big salaries: compared to whom? A local politician might not get paid as much as a high-powered attorney or doctor, but he's not exactly getting minimum wage either. He can probably afford to feed himself. Plus, if he's chosen a life of public service, he already knows that he won't get a big salary, and must learn to budget himself accordingly. And think about it—wouldn't the idea of a politician you voted for, and whose salary you pay with your tax money, getting free meals really annoy you?

The second premise is that we have to lure the most qualified people to run for office with perks. Isn't the opposite really true? Shouldn't the best people be running because they really want to serve the people, and not because they're getting free stuff? Would you vote for someone who was only in it for the free meals?

Also, the argument states that politicians should get free meals in restaurants, even when they are not conducting official business while eating. You mean, even if he's out with his family on the weekend? What does this have to do with politics? If this were part of the deal of holding an office, wouldn't some people abuse it by going out to the finest, most expensive restaurants whenever possible? And who picks up the tab? The taxpayers?

Find out more about the Writing Assessment at www.gre.org or in your registration booklet.

Is there anything that would help this argument? Maybe if it argued for politicians getting *certain* meals during which business is discussed for free. Or maybe there's another, better reason to give them free meals. For example, if a politician knew he was guaranteed a free meal at a restaurant, he wouldn't try to "negotiate" for one in exchange for certain other "services," such as doing the restaurant owner a zoning favor. In that case, maybe the free meal policy *would* attract better people to run—people who wouldn't be looking to make deals for meals!

Whew! Now that we've brainstormed some ideas, let's plug them into one of our templates:

> Paragraph 1: The argument states that politicians should get free meals in restaurants, regardless of whether they are doing business while eating, and is not logically convincing. This argument is based on faulty premises.
>
> Paragraph 2: (Discuss the faulty logic of the "salary" premise.)
>
> Paragraph 3: (Discuss the faulty logic of the "perk" premise.)
>
> Paragraph 4: (Discuss the faulty logic of the any other premise.)
>
> Paragraph 5: Thus, because of the flaws I've enumerated, the argument that politicians should get free meals in restaurants, regardless of whether they are doing business while eating, is illogical and unconvincing.
>
> Paragraph 6: The argument might have been strengthened by (suggest premises/assumptions that would have better supported the conclusion, like the "deals for meals" issue).

This should give you a general idea. You will be writing your own dazzling transitions and scintillating rhetoric.

THE HORSE'S MOUTH

There are sample essays and detailed breakdowns of ETS' essay scoring policy in the GRE CAT registration booklet and on its web site, www.gre.org.

PART VI

Practice Sets

17

Ready for Some GRE CAT Aerobics?

So, you've shaken off some rust, and learned a ton of strategy, and now you're ready for some practice. Well, you can't take a computer adaptive test on paper, but you can, and should, do the following drills that are broken up into "bins" of easy, medium, and hard questions.

TAKE IT EASY

For the latest on the GRE CAT, check www.review.com or www.gre.org.

Everyone should start with the easy bins first. After all, you wouldn't start your exercise program by running five miles. You'd do some jogging and stretching first. Besides, and this can't be stressed enough, your performance on the first few questions on a CAT is CRUCIAL, so no matter what level you're at, you can't afford ANY careless errors on ANY questions, especially the easy ones, where those types of errors most often occur.

So start with the easy bins, check your answers, and see how you do. Then move on to the medium bins, and then, if you dare, the hard ones. Explanations follow in chapter 18. Use the bins to find out if you're still rusty or confused about certain topics or techniques.

Here's some rough scoring information: Just getting the questions in the easy bins correct puts your score roughly at the 400 level; easy and medium bins correct scores roughly 500–600; and easy, medium, and hard pushes your score into the 600–700 and above range. But, this is really about practice. Use real GREs to estimate your score, AFTER you practice.

MAKE IT REAL

Don't time yourself, but move quickly, and use scratch paper as you would if you were taking the real test. DON'T WRITE IN THE BOOK! You might even want to stand up this book when taking the sections, to simulate the experience of looking at a computer screen. Remember, that screen-to-scratch paper conversion is EXTREMELY important; in fact, it's really a technique for doing well on the GRE CAT. Also, try to find a place with no distractions like ringing phones or barking dogs. Simulate the testing environment as much as you can.

DIRECTIONS

The directions aren't included in these practice questions, because, if you've been reading the book, you already know the directions. If you need to brush up on them, find them in each preceding chapter *before* starting the practice questions.

Here we go . . .

18

Bins

1. MOUNT:
    - ⭘ descend
    - ⭘ disassemble
    - ⭘ upset
    - ⭘ hide
    - ⭘ go back

2. PLAYER : TEAM ::
    - ⭘ oil : liquid
    - ⭘ line : drawing
    - ⭘ scales : increase
    - ⭘ hiss : recording
    - ⭘ ingredient : mixture

3. There may be some validity in the facetious recent description of a pundit—a weather-man who talks every day about current events without being able to _____ them.
    - ⭘ outline
    - ⭘ begin
    - ⭘ dissect
    - ⭘ influence
    - ⭘ stop

4. ERADICATE:
    - ⭘ ignore
    - ⭘ undo
    - ⭘ smoke
    - ⭘ introduce
    - ⭘ boil

5. The sparring of the two lawyers appeared _____ ; however, it is well known that, outside the courtroom, the friendship between the two is _____.
    - ⭘ pointless. .cooperative
    - ⭘ hostile. .obvious
    - ⭘ lighthearted. .abrogated
    - ⭘ heightened. .concealed
    - ⭘ brilliant. .precluded

6. EXCRETION : KIDNEY ::
    - ⭘ respiration : lung
    - ⭘ lymphoma : cancer
    - ⭘ propulsion : engine
    - ⭘ information : media
    - ⭘ disinfection : soap

7. In radio, a morning broadcasting time often _____ a larger and more _____ audience and, thus, one that is more appealing to advertisers of expensive products.
    - ⭘ demands. .attractive
    - ⭘ denotes. .agreeable
    - ⭘ indicates. .prosperous
    - ⭘ overlooks. .practical
    - ⭘ encourages. .widespread

8. SNAKE : REPTILE ::
    - ⭘ fish : school
    - ⭘ beetle : insect
    - ⭘ elephant : land
    - ⭘ egg : chicken
    - ⭘ lamb : sheep

Our visual perception depends on the reception of energy reflecting or radiating from that which we wish to perceive. If our eye could receive and measure

5 infinitely delicate sense-data, we could perceive the world with infinite precision. The natural limits of our eyes have, of course, been extended by mechanical instruments; telescopes and microscopes,

10 for example, expand our capabilities greatly. There is, however, an ultimate limit beyond which no instrument can take us; this limit is imposed by our inability to receive sense-data smaller than those

15 conveyed by an individual quantum of energy. Since these quanta are believed to be indivisible packages of energy and so cannot be further refined, we reach a point beyond which further resolution of the

20 world is not possible. It is like a drawing a child might make by sticking indivisible discs of color onto a canvas.

We might think that we could avoid this limitation by using quanta with extremely

25 long wavelengths; such quanta would be sufficiently sensitive to convey extremely delicate sense-data. And these quanta would be useful as long as we only wanted to measure energy, but a

30 completely accurate perception of the world will depend also on the exact measurement of the lengths and positions of what we wish to perceive. For this, quanta of extremely long wavelengths are

35 useless. To measure a length accurately to within a millionth of an inch, we must have a measure graduated in millionths of an inch; a yardstick graduated in inches is useless. Quanta with a wavelength of one

40 inch would be, in a sense, measures that are graduated in inches. Quanta of extremely long wavelengths are useless in measuring anything except extremely large dimensions.

45 Despite these difficulties, quanta have important theoretical implications for physics. It used to be supposed that, in the observation of nature, the universe could be divided into two distinct parts, a

50 perceiving subject and a perceived object. In physics, subject and object were supposed to be entirely distinct, so that a description of any part of the universe would be independent of the observer.

55 Quantum theory, however, suggests otherwise, for every observation involves the passage of a complete quantum from the object to the subject, and it now appears that this passage constitutes an

60 important coupling between observer and observed. We can no longer make a sharp division between the two in an effort to observe nature objectively. Such an attempt at objectivity would distort the

65 crucial interrelationship of observer and observed as parts of a single whole. But, even for scientists, it is only in the world of atoms that this new development makes any appreciable difference in the explanation of observations.

9. The passage as a whole could be best described as

○ a consideration of factors that impede exact observation of the world
○ an acknowledgment of the limitations of conventional units of measurement
○ a criticism of efforts to divide perceiving subjects from perceived objects
○ a report on a conflict between two different scientific theories of visual perception
○ a description of a diminished capacity for sensory perception

10. According to the passage, quanta of extremely long wavelengths can only be used to measure objects with extremely large dimensions because the quanta

○ would be independent of the observer
○ are graduated to within a millionth of an inch
○ lack sufficient magnitude of energy
○ exist in theory, but cannot be observed unless we expand our current mechanical capabilities
○ cannot offer a means of exact measurement of the lengths and positions upon which a completely accurate perception of the world would depend

11. LUCIDITY:
    - ⬭ glistening
    - ⬭ obscurity
    - ⬭ gravity
    - ⬭ attractiveness
    - ⬭ quiescence

12. FERTILIZER : GROWTH ::
    - ⬭ glaze : pottery
    - ⬭ yeast : leavening
    - ⬭ cotton : texture
    - ⬭ illumination : interest
    - ⬭ octane : speed

13. FRUSTRATE:
    - ⬭ facilitate
    - ⬭ moderate
    - ⬭ climb
    - ⬭ judge
    - ⬭ assemble

14. BOLSTER:
    - ⬭ infect
    - ⬭ compound
    - ⬭ untie
    - ⬭ generate
    - ⬭ undermine

15. DISARM : WEAPONS ::
    - ⬭ limit : abilities
    - ⬭ soothe : difficulties
    - ⬭ restrain : movement
    - ⬭ disguise : identity
    - ⬭ usurp : power

Column A   Column B

1. $(3 + 0) \times 4$ $0 \times (3 + 4)$

   ◯   the quantity in Column A is always greater
   ◯   the quantity in Column B is always greater
   ◯   the quantities are always equal
   ◯   it cannot be determined from the information given

Column A   Column B

$$a = 15$$
$$a + b = 29$$

2. a^2 b^2

   ◯   the quantity in Column A is always greater
   ◯   the quantity in Column B is always greater
   ◯   the quantities are always equal
   ◯   it cannot be determined from the information given

3.   Of team A's victories this year, sixty percent were at home. If team A has won a total of twenty games this year, how many of those games were won away from home?

   ◯   5
   ◯   7
   ◯   8
   ◯   12
   ◯   15

Column A   Column B

$$a = b$$

4. $4a + b$ $a + 4b$

   ◯   the quantity in Column A is always greater
   ◯   the quantity in Column B is always greater
   ◯   the quantities are always equal
   ◯   it cannot be determined from the information given

5. $652(523) + 427(652)$ is equal to which of the following?

   ◯ $523 (652 + 427)$
   ◯ $652 (523 + 427)$
   ◯ $(652 + 427)(523 + 652)$
   ◯ $(652 + 523)(427 + 652)$
   ◯ $(652 + 652)(523 + 427)$

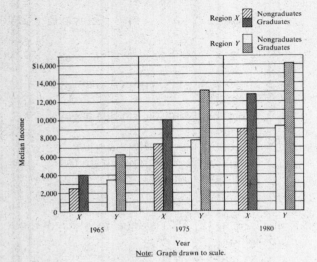

MEDIAN INCOME OF
COLLEGE GRADUATES VS. NONGRADUATES
IN REGIONS X AND Y

Region X Nongraduates / Graduates

Region Y Nongraduates / Graduates

Year

Note: Graph drawn to scale.

6. The median income of graduates in Region Y increased by approximately how much between 1965 and 1980?

○ $6,000
○ $7,000
○ $8,000
○ $10,000
○ $16,000

Column A   Column B

The diameter of circle M is greater than the radius of circle N.

7. The circumference   The circumference
   of circle M of circle N

○ the quantity in Column A is always greater
○ the quantity in Column B is always greater
○ the quantities are always equal
○ it cannot be determined from the information given

8. If $a = 4$ and $4a - 3b = 1$, what is the combined value of a and b?

○ 5

○ $5\frac{2}{3}$

○ 9

○ $14\frac{2}{3}$

○ $21\frac{2}{3}$

Column A   Column B

9. $\frac{3}{4} + \frac{3}{4}$ $\left(\frac{3}{4}\right)^2$

○ the quantity in Column A is always greater
○ the quantity in Column B is always greater
○ the quantities are always equal
○ it cannot be determined from the information given

10. If $k = 6 \times 17$, then which of the following is a multiple of k?

- ○ 68
- ○ 78
- ○ 85
- ○ 136
- ○ 204

Column A	Column B

$$ab = a \text{ and } a = 0.$$

11. a b

- ○ the quantity in Column A is always greater
- ○ the quantity in Column B is always greater
- ○ the quantities are always equal
- ○ it cannot be determined from the information given

12. What is the value of $(4 + a)(4 - b)$ when $a = 4$ and $b = -4$?

- ○ −64
- ○ −16
- ○ 0
- ○ 16
- ○ 64

Column A	Column B

n cases of soda N contain a total of 36 bottles of soda.

13. The total number of bottles in x cases of soda X $\dfrac{36x}{n}$

- ○ the quantity in Column A is always greater
- ○ the quantity in Column B is always greater
- ○ the quantities are always equal
- ○ it cannot be determined from the information given

Column A	Column B

14 more than a is −9

14. $a + 9$ -14

- ○ the quantity in Column A is always greater
- ○ the quantity in Column B is always greater
- ○ the quantities are always equal
- ○ it cannot be determined from the information given

15. The illumination E, in footcandles, provided by a light source of intensity I, in candles, at a distance D, in feet, is given by

$$E = \frac{I}{D^2}.$$

For an illumination of 50 footcandles at a distance of 4 feet from a source, the intensity of the source must be

- ○ 50 candles
- ○ 200 candles
- ○ 800 candles
- ○ 1,600 candles
- ○ 2,500 candles

1. Nonprescription sunglasses shield the wearer's eyes from damaging ultraviolet sunlight. Squinting, however, provides protection from ultraviolet rays that is at least as good as the protection from nonprescription sunglasses. There is, therefore, no health advantage to be gained by wearing nonprescription sunglasses rather than squinting.

   Which of the following, if true, most seriously weakens support for the conclusion above?

   - Many opticians offer prescription sunglasses that not only screen out ultraviolet sunlight but also provide corrective vision.
   - Some nonprescription sunglasses provide less protection from ultraviolet sunlight than does squinting.
   - Squinting strains facial muscles and causes headaches and fatigue.
   - Many people buy sunglasses because they feel that sunglasses are fashionable.
   - Some people squint even when they are wearing sunglasses.

   Questions 2–5

   Two walls of a room in a nursery school are being repainted. There are six colors to choose from—purple, blue, green, yellow, orange, and red. The walls must be painted with three different colors each:

   Purple and yellow must be used on the same wall.

   Blue and orange cannot be used on the same wall.

   The two walls cannot have the same combination of colors as each other.

2. All of the following are possible colors chosen for one wall EXCEPT

   - Purple, blue, red
   - Purple, green, yellow
   - Purple, yellow, red
   - Blue, green, red
   - Green, orange, red

3. Which of the following colors could be chosen for a wall for which purple is chosen?

   - Blue and green
   - Blue and orange
   - Blue and red
   - Green and yellow
   - Orange and red

4. Which of the following is an acceptable way to paint the walls?

Wall 1	Wall 2
Purple, blue, yellow	Purple, yellow, orange
Purple, green, red	Green, yellow, orange
Purple, yellow, orange	Purple, blue, orange
Blue, green, red	Blue, orange, red
Green, yellow, red	Green, yellow, red

5. If one wall is painted with blue, green and red, then the other wall can be painted with each of the following EXCEPT

   - Purple, blue, yellow
   - Purple, green, yellow
   - Purple, yellow, red
   - Blue, green, red
   - Green, orange, red

6. In May 1990, the American airlines serving European destinations substantially reduced the price of flights to those destinations. During the months subsequent to the reductions, the number of tickets sold to European destinations increased to well above the monthly average for the previous year. Despite this fact, the number of tickets sold by American airlines to European destinations was not noticeably different from the previous year's total.

Which of the following, if true, best explains the apparent paradox in the passage above?

○ Many Americans travel to European destinations only when airfares are low.

○ The amount of revenue generated in 1990 by sales of tickets to European destinations remained the same as it was the previous year.

○ For part of 1990, the number of tickets sold to European destinations was lower than the year's monthly average.

○ The larger the number of tickets sold by American airlines in a given one-year period, the lower the per-ticket price during that period.

○ There is a predictable up and down pattern to the volume of tickets sold by American airlines to European destinations.

7. A motion picture by Orson Welles, the director who died in 1985, was edited down from 200 hours of footage abandoned by Welles into a 100-minute final form. The film, composed solely of shots directed by Welles, and edited according to Welles' shooting script and preliminary director's notes, is therefore a legitimate Orson Welles motion picture.

Which of the following, if true, is most damaging to the contention that the new film is a legitimate Orson Welles motion picture?

○ Part of the found footage not included by the editors in the new film had previously been seen in a documentary completed by Welles before his death.

○ Film scholars have maintained that the footage was shot during a period during which Welles created some of his least successful works.

○ A motion picture can only legitimately be attributed to a director if the director decides what final footage should be selected for inclusion in it and what weight should be given in post-production to material selected for inclusion.

○ A legitimate motion picture contains visual motifs, subject matter, and editorial patterns similar to those present in a director's outstanding motion pictures.

○ Few of the films directed by Orson Welles were fewer than 120 minutes in duration.

Questions 8–11

A haberdasher is displaying colored hats in two windows, one on the left and one on the right. Each window will display three hats. There are seven hats from that to choose: a red one, an orange one, a yellow one, a green one, a blue one, a purple one, and a white one. The following conditions must be met:

The red hat must be displayed, and it must go in the left window.

The orange hat must be displayed, and it must go in the right window.

The purple hat cannot be displayed in the same window as the orange hat, nor can it be displayed with the green hat.

Both the yellow hat and the white hat must be displayed, and they must go in the same window.

8. Which of the following is an accurate list of hats that can be displayed in the left window?
    ○ Red, blue, purple
    ○ Red, yellow, blue
    ○ Red, green, white
    ○ Red, orange, purple
    ○ Orange, yellow, white

9. If the white hat is displayed in the left window, which of the following is a pair of hats that must be displayed in the right window?
    ○ Yellow and green
    ○ Green and blue
    ○ Red and orange
    ○ Blue and purple
    ○ Yellow and purple

10. Which of the following is an accurate list of hats that can be displayed in the right window?
    ○ Orange, green, blue
    ○ Orange, green, purple
    ○ Orange, purple, white
    ○ Red, orange, blue
    ○ Orange, yellow, green

11. If the white hat is displayed in the right window, which of the following is a pair of hats that could be displayed in the left window?
    ○ Yellow and green
    ○ Yellow and blue
    ○ Yellow and purple
    ○ Green and purple
    ○ Blue and purple

12. During the War of 1812, the United States Congress licensed privateers (armed pirates) who were empowered to plunder enemy ships. Those privateers financed their ventures through the sale of the seized cargo. A Florida man has petitioned Congress to license modern privateers to mount a private "war-for-profit" against seagoing smugglers of illegal drugs.

    Which of the following, if true, is a drawback to the Florida man's proposal?
    ○ Modern ships are much faster than those of the nineteenth century.
    ○ Although the United States Constitution still authorizes the licensing of privateers, no licenses have been issued for over 150 years.
    ○ Modern privateers would be unable to finance their operations by selling the seized cargo without being in violation of the law.
    ○ The 1812 privateers plundered ships that belonged to citizens of another country.
    ○ Most of the ships used by drug smugglers are modified fishing boats.

Four children—Amy, Ben, Cindy, and Dennis—are choosing among six different flavored lollipops which are lined up on the counter of the candy store in the following order from left to right: cherry, orange, lemon, grape, raspberry, and strawberry. Each lollipop must be chosen by a child. The following information is known about the choices:

Each child chooses at least one lollipop.

No child can choose two lollipops that are adjacent to each other.

13. If Amy chooses the cherry and the strawberry lollipops, which one of the following must be true?
   - ○ Another child besides Amy chooses two lollipops.
   - ○ The child who chooses lemon cannot also choose raspberry.
   - ○ Cindy chooses a lollipop that is located to the left of the lollipop that Ben chooses.
   - ○ The orange lollipop is chosen by either Ben or Cindy.
   - ○ The raspberry lollipop is chosen by either Cindy or Dennis.

14. If Cindy chooses two lollipops, and Ben and Dennis both choose lollipops that are located somewhere to the left of the first lollipop that Cindy chooses, which of the following could be the two lollipops that Cindy chooses?
   - ○ Cherry and lemon
   - ○ Orange and grape
   - ○ Orange and strawberry
   - ○ Lemon and strawberry
   - ○ Raspberry and strawberry

15. If Amy chooses the orange lollipop and two other lollipops, which one of the following CANNOT be true?
   - ○ Amy chooses the strawberry lollipop.
   - ○ Amy and Cindy choose lollipops that are adjacent to each other.
   - ○ Ben and Cindy choose lollipops that are adjacent to each other.
   - ○ Ben and Cindy choose lollipops that are located somewhere to the left of the grape lollipop.
   - ○ Amy chooses lollipops that are immediately to the left of the one Ben chooses and immediately to the left of the one Dennis chooses.

1. DODGE:

    ○ release
    ○ create
    ○ assert aggressively
    ○ admire greatly
    ○ face directly

2. TEETH : SAW ::

    ○ cog : wheel
    ○ pick : ice
    ○ bit : drill
    ○ pulley : rope
    ○ wood : screw

3. INDUSTRY:

    ○ politics
    ○ density
    ○ lethargy
    ○ tolerance
    ○ vastness

4. Although the candidate obviously wanted to
    _____ the euphoria that has infused her
    campaign of late, she refrained from imply-
    ing that the momentum had turned against
    her and might result in her defeat.

    ○ authenticate
    ○ moderate
    ○ maintain
    ○ clarify
    ○ revive

Questions 5–6

Tillie Olsen's fiction and essays have
been widely and rightly acknowledged as
major contributions to American literature.
Her work has been particularly valued by
contemporary feminists. Yet few of
Olsen's readers realize the extent to which
her vision and choice of subject are rooted
in an earlier literary heritage—the tradition
of radical political thought, mostly socialist
and anarchist, of the 1910s and 1920s, and
the Old Left tradition of the 1930s. I do
not mean that one can adequately explain
the eloquence of her work in terms of its
political origins, or that left-wing politics
were the single most important influence
on it. My point is that its central
consciousness—its profound
understanding of class and gender as
shaping influences on people's lives—
owes much to that earlier literary heritage,
a heritage that, in general, has not been
sufficiently valued by most contemporary
literary critics.

5. The best description of the passage is

    ○ an argument that Olsen's success as a
      writer is due to her class and gender
      consciousness
    ○ a statement that Olsen's radical political
      background is the most important
      influence on her work
    ○ an attempt to place Olsen's work in a
      broader literary context
    ○ a call to literary critics to investigate the
      beginnings of a literary tradition
    ○ a suggestion that Olsen's work has
      been mistakenly understood in terms of
      a particular literary heritage

6. According to the passage, which of the following is an accurate statement about the literary heritage referred to by the author?

○ It considers gender to be the determining factor in people's lives.

○ It has been the single most important source of Olsen's work.

○ It belongs to a political tradition that includes different strains of radical thought.

○ It provides the intellectual stimulus, but not the emotional force behind Olsen's work.

○ It owes more to socialist thought of the early twentieth century than to anarchist thought of that period.

7. CONTRITION : PENITENT ::

○ caution : driver
○ speculation : philosopher
○ obstinacy : athlete
○ sanguinity : partner
○ wisdom : sage

8. LUMINOUS:

○ distant
○ broken
○ dull
○ impractical
○ inconsiderate

9. Until about 1980, almost all economists assumed that economic growth is fueled by demand pressure at the level of the consumer; after the combination of high inflation and unemployment experienced in the 1990s, however, economists detected no _____ this previously _____ view of economic growth.

○ deviations from. .revolutionary
○ ground for. . ubiquitous
○ preference for. .unquestioned
○ forerunners of. .modern
○ disagreements with. .popular

10. TEMERITY : TREPIDATION ::

○ oration : publicity
○ strength : permanence
○ superfluity : necessity
○ axiom : confidence
○ indemnity : security

11. The treatment of waste water has been _____ through _____ the contaminants, but perhaps it may be more practical to neutralize the pollution in the water by adding certain chemical compounds that cause the harmful waste particles to become inert.

○ authorized. .screening
○ attempted. .tracing
○ initiated. .avoiding
○ simplified. .identifying
○ undertaken. .removing

12. COUNTERMAND : ORDER ::

○ corroborate : document
○ restate : claim
○ reopen : investigation
○ prejudice : testimony
○ revoke : license

13. PREDISPOSED:

○ directed
○ stubborn
○ disinclined
○ nostalgic
○ tranquil

14. Recent investigation into business and morality reveals the way in which apparently _____ business decisions, typically lost sight of in the ordinary operations of commerce, in reality _____ moral choices of major importance.

○ unimportant. .cloak
○ unreliable. .provoke
○ unparalleled. .symbolize
○ unprecedented. .allow
○ untrammeled. .impel

15. SHEARING : WOOL ::

○ shredding : paper
○ breathing : wine
○ trimming : hedge
○ reaping : grain
○ weaving : silk

Column A   Column B

$$3 + k = 5 - k$$

1. k 2

     ◯ the quantity in Column A is always greater
     ◯ the quantity in Column B is always greater
     ◯ the quantities are always equal
     ◯ it cannot be determined from the information given

Column A   Column B

2. $\dfrac{7}{8} - \dfrac{1}{6}$ $\dfrac{3}{4} - \dfrac{1}{8}$

     ◯ the quantity in Column A is always greater
     ◯ the quantity in Column B is always greater
     ◯ the quantities are always equal
     ◯ it cannot be determined from the information given

3. $\dfrac{0.2\left(0.0002\right)}{0.002}$

     ◯ 0.02
     ◯ 0.002
     ◯ 0.0002
     ◯ 0.00002
     ◯ 0.000002

Column A   Column B

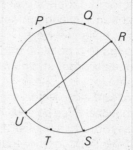

P, Q, R, S, T, and *U* are points on the circle as shown.

4.   The length of   The length of
       arc *PQR*   arc *STU*

     ◯ the quantity in Column A is always greater
     ◯ the quantity in Column B is always greater
     ◯ the quantities are always equal
     ◯ it cannot be determined from the information given

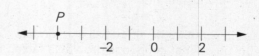

Note: Drawn to scale.

5.   If *Q* is a point to the right of 0 on the number line above and the distance between *P* and *Q* is 11, then the coordinate of *Q* is

     ◯ −15
     ◯ 7
     ◯ 8
     ◯ 11
     ◯ 15

Column A	Column B

6. The number of minutes in y weeks

   The number of hours in $60y$ weeks

   ○ the quantity in Column A is always greater
   ○ the quantity in Column B is always greater
   ○ the quantities are always equal
   ○ it cannot be determined from the information given

Column A	Column B

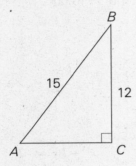

7. The area of $\triangle ABC$

   90

   ○ the quantity in Column A is always greater
   ○ the quantity in Column B is always greater
   ○ the quantities are always equal
   ○ it cannot be determined from the information given

MEDIAN INCOME OF
COLLEGE GRADUATES *VS.* NONGRADUATES
IN REGIONS X AND Y

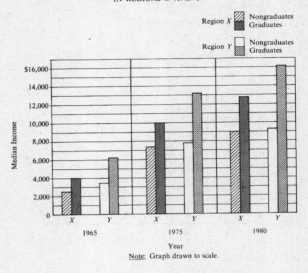

Note: Graph drawn to scale.

8. In 1975, the median income of nongraduates in Region X was approximately what fraction of the median income for graduates in Region X?

   ○ $\dfrac{3}{5}$

   ○ $\dfrac{5}{8}$

   ○ $\dfrac{3}{4}$

   ○ $\dfrac{10}{13}$

   ○ $\dfrac{4}{5}$

9. $12m^2 - 8m - 64 =$

- ⃝ $4(3m + 8)(m - 2)$
- ⃝ $4(3m - 8)(m + 2)$
- ⃝ $4(3m - 2)(m + 8)$
- ⃝ $4m^2 - 64$
- ⃝ $4m - 64$

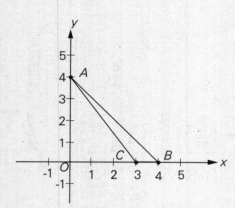

10. What is the area of triangle ABC in the figure above?

- ⃝ 2
- ⃝ 4
- ⃝ $4\sqrt{2}$
- ⃝ 7
- ⃝ 8

Column A   Column B

It takes Michael 3 hours at an average rate of 60 miles per hour to drive from his home to the state park. In contrast, it takes 2.5 hours at an average speed to 65 miles per hour for Michael to drive from his home to his lake house.

11. Michael's driving distance from his home to the state park

Michael's driving distance from his home to his lake house

- ⃝ the quantity in Column A is always greater
- ⃝ the quantity in Column B is always greater
- ⃝ the quantities are always equal
- ⃝ it cannot be determined from the information given

Column A   Column B

$$100 = \frac{10}{x}$$

12. x 10

- ⃝ the quantity in Column A is always greater
- ⃝ the quantity in Column B is always greater
- ⃝ the quantities are always equal
- ⃝ it cannot be determined from the information given

13. What is the greatest possible value of integer n if $6^n < 10,0000$

- ⃝ 5
- ⃝ 6
- ⃝ 7
- ⃝ 8
- ⃝ 9

Column A   Column B

$$x^2 + 8x = -7$$

14. x 0

- ⃝ the quantity in Column A is always greater
- ⃝ the quantity in Column B is always greater
- ⃝ the quantities are always equal
- ⃝ it cannot be determined from the information given

15. In the equation $ax + b = 26$, x is a constant. If $a = 3$ when $b = 5$, what is the value of b when $a = 5$?

- ⃝ −11
- ⃝ −9
- ⃝ 3
- ⃝ 7
- ⃝ 21

1. Environmental noise, produced by cars, planes, heavy machinery, and small appliances, has been shown to cause frustration, stress, and permanent hearing loss. A government health agency has recommended that people limit their exposure to noise to 8 hours of 90-decibel noise or 4 hours of 95-decibel noise. Many health care professionals, however, feel that even these limits do not adequately protect the public from the ill effects of noise pollution.

   Which of the following, if true, would most support the health care professionals' view as described above?

   ○ The numbers of 8 and 4 hours include cumulative short-term exposure to noise such as that experienced during a commute, while listening to music, or as a result of sudden or unexpected sounds.

   ○ Many manufacturers are capable of producing products that run more quietly, but public demand for these products is low.

   ○ White-noise machines produce sound that covers or filters disruptive noises.

   ○ The government has neglected efforts to mandate more stringent standards for environmental noise.

   ○ Noise of less than 90 decibels can disrupt sleep patterns and increase hypertension, while brief exposure to noise above 100 decibels can cause permanent hearing trauma.

2. Ironically, those companies that require prospective employees to undergo stringent drug testing before being hired have a higher incidence of dismissals attributed to drug use by employees than do companies that administer no drug testing at all.

   Which of the following, if true, helps to explain the apparent paradox in the statement above?

   ○ In most areas of business, more companies choose not to administer drug tests than choose to do so.

   ○ The decision of companies not to test prospective employees for drug use is a reflection of their belief that employees are unlikely to engage in drug use.

   ○ Companies that administer drug tests often contract work to companies that do not require drug testing.

   ○ The number of dismissals attributed to drug use has no relationship to the number of employees at the company.

   ○ Companies that are highly concerned with drug use by employees are more likely to monitor employees' behavior and attribute that behavior to drug use.

Questions 3–5

At an amusement resort, the different pavilions—the Zoo, the Rides, and the Food Area—are arranged in a circle, and can be reached by tram. The tram goes to the Zoo and stops at the Apes, the Reptiles, the Big Cats, and the Zebras, in that order. Then it goes to the Rides and stops at the Roller Coaster, the Water Ride, and the Ferris Wheel, in that order. Then it goes to the Snack Bar, and on to the Apes, to repeat the circle. There is also a double-decker bus that travels back and forth between the Big Cats and the Snack Bar, and another double-decker bus that travels back and forth between the Water Ride and the Snack Bar. The tram and the double-decker buses are the only means of transportation available at the resort.

3. In order to get from the Snack Bar to the Zebras while making as few stops as possible, one must take the

    ○ tram only
    ○ double-decker bus to the Zoo only
    ○ tram, and then the double-decker bus to the Zoo
    ○ double-decker bus to the Zoo, and then the tram
    ○ double-decker bus to the Rides, and then the tram

4. Which one of the following could be the second intermediate stop for someone travelling from the Reptiles to the Ferris Wheel?

    ○ Big Cats
    ○ Ferris Wheel
    ○ Roller Coaster
    ○ Snack Bar
    ○ Water Ride

5. Using both a double-decker bus and the tram, which one of the following trips can be made with the fewest stops?

    ○ The Reptiles to the Big Cats
    ○ The Snack Bar to the Reptiles
    ○ The Snack Bar to the Water Ride
    ○ The Snack Bar to the Zebras
    ○ The Zebras to the Roller Coaster

Questions 6–8

A book-of-the-month club is offering a special deal for new members. Over a one-year period, January to December, the club will send a free book each month for nine months of the year. There will be three months in which no free books are sent. The books—R, S, T, U, V, W, X, Y, and Z—fall into three categories: three are biographies, two are art books, and four are novels.

Books of two different categories may not be sent in consecutive months.

A month in which no book is sent cannot separate months in which books of the same category are sent.

S and U are in different categories.

U, V, and W are all in the same category.

A book is never sent in May.

R and X are biographies.

Y is an art book.

6. If no book is sent in April, which one of the following must be true?

    ○ No book is sent in October.
    ○ The books are sent in this order: biographies, art books, novels.
    ○ The book sent in March is a biography.
    ○ The book sent in January is an art book.
    ○ The book sent in December is a novel.

7. If the books are sent in this order—novels, art books, biographies—which of the following could be the months in which no books are sent?

    ○ January, May, and October
    ○ January, June, and October
    ○ April, July, and August
    ○ May, August, and December
    ○ May, September, and October

8. All of the following are months in which an art book can be sent EXCEPT

    ○ January
    ○ June
    ○ August
    ○ November
    ○ December

Dale is taking six classes at school—geography, history, journalism, kinetics, linguistics, and math. She gets a different grade in each class. The possible grades are, from highest to lowest, A, B, C, D, E, and F. The following information is known about the grades she receives:

Her grade in geography is higher than her grade in linguistics.

She receives a B in journalism.

Her grade in kinetics is either exactly one grade higher or exactly one grade lower than her grade in history.

9. If Dale receives a D in history, which of the following is the highest grade she can receive in linguistics?

○ A
○ B
○ C
○ E
○ F

10. If Dale receives an E in math, which of the following is the grade she must receive in geography?

○ A
○ B
○ C
○ D
○ F

11. If Dale receives a D in kinetics, which of the following is the lowest grade she can receive in geography?

○ A
○ B
○ C
○ E
○ F

12. In which of the following classes can Dale receive an A?

○ History
○ Journalism
○ Kinetics
○ Linguistics
○ Math

13. The coach of one of the league's best teams is amused by all of the publicity his coaching methods have received. He believes that coaches receive too much credit for winning games and claims that "fans assume too easily that coaches are geniuses when a team wins and morons when a team loses."

According to the coach's statement, it can be inferred that he believes which one of the following to be true?

○ A winning coach should attempt to manipulate the press.
○ No coach can justifiably be called a genius.
○ His own coaching methods would most likely not succeed with other teams.
○ Coaches are less important during a losing streak than they are when a team is winning.
○ The success of a team cannot be completely determined by its coach.

14. A recent medical study found that women who exercised more than three hours per week were more likely than other women to have high levels of a certain chemical compound in their blood. High levels of this compound can be one of the first warning signs of skin cancer, which is almost always caused by excessive exposure of the skin to sunlight.

Which one of the following, if true, would cast doubt on the study's implication that exercising more than three hours per week increases the odds of contracting skin cancer?

○ Lack of exercise increases the rate of absorption of many dangerous chemical compounds into the blood stream.

○ Exercise increases the rate of blood flow through the circulatory system, thereby increasing the rate at which contaminants spread through the body.

○ The most common form of exercise among the women in this study was swimming in an indoor pool.

○ Women contract skin cancer at a significantly higher rate than men do.

○ Women who exercised more than three hours per week also spent more time outdoors than did women who exercised fewer than three hours per week.

15. To many environmentalists, the extinction of plants—accompanied by the increasing genetic uniformity of species of food crops—is the single most serious environmental problem. Something must be done to prevent the loss of wild-food plants or no-longer-cultivated food plants. Otherwise, the lack of genetic food diversity could allow a significant portion of a major crop to be destroyed overnight. In 1970, for example, southern leaf blight destroyed approximately 20 percent of the United States corn crop, leaving very few varieties of corn unaffected in the areas over which the disease spread.

Which of the following can be inferred from the passage above?

○ Susceptibility to certain plant diseases is genetically determined.

○ Eighty percent of the corn grown in the United States is resistant to southern leaf blight.

○ The extinction of wild food plants can in almost every case be traced to destructive plant diseases.

○ Plant breeders focus on developing plants that are resistant to plant disease.

○ Corn is the only food crop threatened by southern leaf blight.

1. FLAG:

   ○ break down
   ○ regain energy
   ○ resume course
   ○ push forward
   ○ show pride

2. SYNOPSIS : CONDENSED ::

   ○ digression : repeated
   ○ mystery : enticing
   ○ excursion : pleasant
   ○ antiquity : forgotten
   ○ plagiarism : pirated

3. To examine the _____ of importing concepts from one discipline to enhance another, merely look at the degree to which words from the first may, without distortion, be _____ the second.

   ○ danger. .meaningless for
   ○ popularity. .created within
   ○ etiquette. .revitalized by
   ○ pace. .supplanted by
   ○ validity. .employed by

4. CONSUMMATE:

   ○ refuse
   ○ undermine
   ○ satiate
   ○ abrogate
   ○ suspect

5. ADMONISH : COUNSEL ::

   ○ mollify : intensity
   ○ necessitate : generosity
   ○ enervate : vitality
   ○ manufacture : opinion
   ○ remunerate : payment

Our visual perception depends on the reception of energy reflecting or radiating from that which we wish to perceive. If our eye could receive and measure

5 infinitely delicate sense-data, we could perceive the world with infinite precision. The natural limits of our eyes have, of course, been extended by mechanical instruments; telescopes and microscopes,

10 for example, expand our capabilities greatly. There is, however, an ultimate limit beyond which no instrument can take us; this limit is imposed by our inability to receive sense-data smaller than those

15 conveyed by an individual quantum of energy. Since these quanta are believed to be indivisible packages of energy and so cannot be further refined, we reach a point beyond which further resolution of the

20 world is not possible. It is like a drawing a child might make by sticking indivisible discs of color onto a canvas.

We might think that we could avoid this limitation by using quanta with extremely

25 long wavelengths; such quanta would be sufficiently sensitive to convey extremely delicate sense-data. And these quanta would be useful as long as we only wanted to measure energy, but a

30 completely accurate perception of the world will depend also on the exact measurement of the lengths and positions of what we wish to perceive. For this, quanta of extremely long wavelengths are

35 useless. To measure a length accurately to within a millionth of an inch, we must have a measure graduated in millionths of an inch; a yardstick graduated in inches is useless. Quanta with a wavelength of one

40 inch would be, in a sense, measures that are graduated in inches. Quanta of extremely long wavelengths are useless in measuring anything except extremely large dimensions.

45 Despite these difficulties, quanta have important theoretical implications for physics. It used to be supposed that, in the observation of nature, the universe could be divided into two distinct parts, a

50 perceiving subject and a perceived object. In physics, subject and object were supposed to be entirely distinct, so that a description of any part of the universe would be independent of the observer.

55 Quantum theory, however, suggests otherwise, for every observation involves the passage of a complete quantum from the object to the subject, and it now appears that this passage constitutes an

60 important coupling between observer and observed. We can no longer make a sharp division between the two in an effort to observe nature objectively. Such an attempt at objectivity would distort the

65 crucial interrelationship of observer and observed as parts of a single whole. But, even for scientists, it is only in the world of atoms that this new development makes any appreciable difference in the

70 explanation of observations.

6. The author employs the metaphor of a child's drawing (lines 20–22) mainly to

   ○ highlight the eventual limitation of the resolution of sense-data using quanta
   ○ reveal the sense of frustration scientists feel when confronted by the limits of accurate measurement
   ○ reply to the criticisms of certain skeptics who hold the view that any mechanical extensions of perception necessarily introduce distortions of the sense-data
   ○ explain the relationships between discs of color and units of energy
   ○ discredit those scientists who argue that precise perception of the world is possible through the use of quanta

7. According to the passage, previous theories in theoretical physics differed from quantum theory in that these theories assumed that

○ the natural limits of human perception cannot be overcome by using quanta of extremely long wavelengths

○ the observer and the object perceived can be separately identified

○ the use of mechanical instruments is more useful to physics than theoretical speculation

○ the interrelationship between the perceiver and perceived makes no difference in observations of the world of atoms

○ scientific method is independent of the actual practices of physicists

8. HYPERBOLE:

○ dietary supplement
○ strange sensation
○ direct route
○ employee
○ understatement

9. Just as midwifery was for hundreds of years _____ practice, something that women retained control over for themselves, so too the increasingly independent role of the midwife in the process of childbirth is a _____ domination by institutional medicine.

○ a personal. .reaction of
○ a controversial. .tolerance of
○ an autonomous. .liberation from
○ a communal. .celebration of
○ a dangerous. .protection from

10. EPIDEMIOLOGY : DISEASE ::

○ radiology : fracture
○ paleontology : behavior
○ epistemology : knowledge
○ ichthyology : religion
○ numerology : formulas

11. Modernity appears to be particularly _____ mistaken notions, perhaps because in breaking free from the fetters of convention, the result is that we are very likely to be _____ unexamined hypotheses and unprepared actions.

○ immune to. .accepting of
○ contrary to. .reliant on
○ fraught with. .susceptible to
○ disposed of. .suspicious of
○ insensitive to. .liberated from

12. PUISSANCE:

○ impotence
○ poverty
○ flexibility
○ grace
○ vigor

13. OFFICIOUS : OBLIGING ::

○ dubious : peculiar
○ malevolent : corrupt
○ effusive : demonstrative
○ placid : merciful
○ radical : cautious

14. The _____ issues that arise inherently from the very nature of social scientific investigation must be judged separately from the solely _____ issues, which are hotly debated one moment and forgotten the next.

○ reiterated. .pragmatic
○ innate. .realistic
○ habitual. .discerning
○ theoretical. .arbitrary
○ perpetual. .temporal

15. EFFERVESCENT:

○ vapid
○ intercepted
○ dispersed
○ disaffected
○ disconcerted

HARD MATH BIN

Column A   **Column B**

Triangle A Triangle B

1. The area of   The area of
   Triangle A Triangle B

   ○ the quantity in Column A is always
      greater
   ○ the quantity in Column B is always
      greater
   ○ the quantities are always equal
   ○ it cannot be determined from the
      information given

Column A   **Column B**

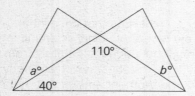

2. a b

   ○ the quantity in Column A is always
      greater
   ○ the quantity in Column B is always
      greater
   ○ the quantities are always equal
   ○ it cannot be determined from the
      information given

3. How many square tiles, each with a perimeter of 64 inches, must be used to completely cover a bathroom floor with a width
   of 64 inches and a length of 128 inches?

   ○ 2
   ○ 4
   ○ 8
   ○ 32
   ○ 128

Column A   **Column B**

a is a positive number and $ab < 0$.

4. $a(b + 1)$ $a(b - 1)$

   ○ the quantity in Column A is always
      greater
   ○ the quantity in Column B is always
      greater
   ○ the quantities are always equal
   ○ it cannot be determined from the
      information given

5. Which of the following CANNOT be an
   integer if the integer k is a multiple of 12 but
   not a multiple of 9?

   ○ $\dfrac{k}{3}$

   ○ $\dfrac{k}{4}$

   ○ $\dfrac{k}{10}$

   ○ $\dfrac{k}{12}$

   ○ $\dfrac{k}{36}$

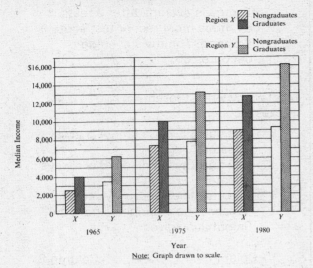

MEDIAN INCOME OF
COLLEGE GRADUATES *VS.* NONGRADUATES
IN REGIONS *X* AND *Y*

Region *X* — Nongraduates / Graduates
Region *Y* — Nongraduates / Graduates

Median Income: $16,000 / 14,000 / 12,000 / 10,000 / 8,000 / 6,000 / 4,000 / 2,000 / 0

X *Y* (1965) *X* *Y* (1975) *X* *Y* (1980)

Year

Note: Graph drawn to scale.

6. For how many of the four categories given did the median income increase by at least 30 percent from 1975 to 1980?

   ○ None
   ○ One
   ○ Two
   ○ Three
   ○ Four

7. Which of the following is equivalent to $(3a - 5)(a + 6)$?

   I. $(3a + 5)(a - 6)$

   II. $-5(a + 6) + 3a(a + 6)$

   III. $3a^2 - 30$

   ○ II only
   ○ III only
   ○ I and II only
   ○ II and III only
   ○ I, II, and III

Column A   Column B

A rectangular bathroom measures $9\frac{1}{2}$ feet by 12 feet. The floor is covered by rectangular tiles measuring $1\frac{1}{2}$ inches by 2 inches.

8. The number of $6 \times 48 \times 19$
   tiles on the
   bathroom floor

   ○ the quantity in Column A is always greater
   ○ the quantity in Column B is always greater
   ○ the quantities are always equal
   ○ it cannot be determined from the information given

9. An office supply store charged $13.10 for the purchase of 85 paper clips. If some of the clips were 16¢ each and the remainder were 14¢ each, how many of the paper clips were 14¢ clips?

   ○ 16
   ○ 25
   ○ 30
   ○ 35
   ○ 65

Column A   Column B

k is an integer such that
$9(3)^3 + 4 = k.$

10. The average   16
    of the prime
    factors of *k*

   ○ the quantity in Column A is always greater
   ○ the quantity in Column B is always greater
   ○ the quantities are always equal
   ○ it cannot be determined from the information given

Column A   Column B

$$y > 0 \text{ and } (-1)^y = 1$$

11. y 2

- ○ the quantity in Column A is always greater
- ○ the quantity in Column B is always greater
- ○ the quantities are always equal
- ○ it cannot be determined from the information given

Column A   Column B

$$a = b + 2$$

12. $a^2 - 2ab + b^2$ $2a - 2b$

- ○ the quantity in Column A is always greater
- ○ the quantity in Column B is always greater
- ○ the quantities are always equal
- ○ it cannot be determined from the information given

13. If the dimensions of a rectangular crate, in feet, are 5 by 6 by 7, which of the following CANNOT be the total surface area, in square feet, of two sides of the crate?

- ○ 60
- ○ 70
- ○ 77
- ○ 84
- ○ 90

Column A   ColumnB

Tommy's average after 8 tests is 84. If his most recent test score is dropped, Tommy's average becomes 85.

14. Tommy's most recent   83
test score

- ○ the quantity in Column A is always greater
- ○ the quantity in Column B is always greater
- ○ the quantities are always equal
- ○ it cannot be determined from the information given

Column A   Column B

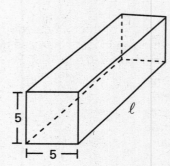

A rectangular box has a surface area of 190 square feet.

15. The length ℓ 7 feet
of the box

- ○ the quantity in Column A is always greater
- ○ the quantity in Column B is always greater
- ○ the quantities are always equal
- ○ it cannot be determined from the information given

1. On the basis of a study it conducted, a research group concluded that managers in division A of a certain company authorize more discretionary spending than do managers in division B. These conclusions are based on an analysis of the number of non-budgeted expense reports that each manager approved.

   The statistics used by the group will not be useful as a measure of which division spends more on non-budgeted expenses if which of the following is true?

   ○ The group counts each expense report equally, regardless of the dollar value of the report.
   ○ The group records all expenses, including those made by the managers themselves.
   ○ Most expense reports submitted to managers for approval are in fact approved.
   ○ Most non-budgeted expenses are incurred by the managers themselves.
   ○ All non-budgeted expense reports are subject to approval by someone who works for neither division.

2. Geographers and historians have traditionally held the view that Antarctica was first sighted around 1820, but some sixteenth-century European maps show a body that resembles the polar landmass, even though explorers of the period never saw it. Some scholars, therefore, argue that the continent must have been discovered and mapped by the ancients, whose maps are known to have served as models for the European cartographers.

   Which of the following, if true, is most damaging to the inference drawn by the scholars?

   ○ The question of who first sighted Antarctica in modern times is still much debated, and no one has been able to present conclusive evidence.
   ○ Between 3,000 and 9,000 years ago, the world was warmer than it is now, and the polar landmass was presumably smaller.
   ○ There are only a few sixteenth-century global maps that show a continental landmass at the South Pole.
   ○ Most attributions of surprising accomplishments to ancient civilizations or even extraterrestrials are eventually discredited or rejected as preposterous.
   ○ Ancient philosophers believed that there had to be a large landmass at the South Pole to balance the northern continents and make the world symmetrical.

Questions 3–5

Seven foods—A, B, C, D, E, F, and G—are to be chosen for the creation of a menu which is to include either three or four foods. A, B, C, and D are hot foods, and E, F, and G are cold foods. There must be at least one hot food and at least one cold food on the menu, but there cannot be an equal number of hot and cold foods. The entree on the menu must be a food whose temperature is not the temperature of the majority of the other foods on the menu. The following conditions must also be met:

If A is on the menu, then D cannot be on the menu.

If B is on the menu, then E cannot be on the menu.

D and F cannot be on the menu unless they are both on the menu.

If G is on the menu, then E must be on the menu.

3. Which one of the following represents an acceptable menu?
    - ◯ A, B, C
    - ◯ C, E, G
    - ◯ D, F, G
    - ◯ A, C, D, F
    - ◯ B, D, E, F

4. If B is on the menu, which one of the following must be true?
    - ◯ There are three foods on the menu.
    - ◯ There are four foods on the menu.
    - ◯ B is the entree on the menu.
    - ◯ D is the entree on the menu.
    - ◯ F is the entree on the menu.

5. Which one of the following could NOT be the entree on the menu?
    - ◯ C
    - ◯ D
    - ◯ E
    - ◯ F
    - ◯ G

6. The Natural Bounty Market, an organic food cooperative, solicits two-thirds of its new members by running ads on the local public radio station between the hours of 6 a.m. and noon. The Natural Bounty's membership committee, in an effort to increase its member base, resolves to run radio ads around the clock. The committee expects that, because of the increased number of radio ads, the number of new members will increase by at least 100 percent.

The membership committee's expected goal would be most strongly supported if which of the following were true?

- ◯ The ads run between 6 a.m. and noon were heard by fewer than 40 percent of the listeners of the public radio station who would be interested in joining The Natural Bounty Market.
- ◯ Grocery shoppers typically listen to the radio in the morning hours.
- ◯ Most of the public radio station listeners with an interest in The Natural Bounty Market are already members of that cooperative organization.
- ◯ The majority of those who become members of The Natural Bounty Market do so as a result of the solicitations on the public radio station.
- ◯ The total number of listeners to the public radio station is fairly constant throughout the day and evening.

Questions 7–11

In the English department at a certain university, a final paper's grade is determined after one full week, Sunday to Saturday, of consideration by the staff. Each day one member of the staff—Professor X, Professor Y, Professor Z, Teaching Assistant K and Teaching Assistant L—reads the paper and passes it on to the next person to read the next day.

Teaching assistants use two consecutive days to read final papers, and professors each use one day.

The final paper is handed in on Sunday.

If, on any day, a final paper is determined to be a failure, it is no longer passed on to the next person.

Only a professor can determine that a final paper is a failure. However, a final paper cannot be determined to be a failure on Sunday.

7. Which one of the following is an acceptable sequence of staff members to read the final paper?

Sun	Mon	Tue	Wed	Thu	Fri	Sat
L	L	Y	X	Z	K	K
K	L	Z	K	L	X	Y
Z	K	K	X	L	Y	L
Y	Z	L	K	L	K	X
X	Y	K	K	L	Z	Y

8. If Professor Z reads the paper on Friday, which one of the following must be true?

- Professor X reads the paper on either Sunday or Saturday.
- Professor Y reads the paper on either Tuesday or Thursday.
- Either Professor X or Professor Y must read the paper on either Monday or Wednesday.
- Professor X and Professor Y must read the paper on consecutive days.
- Professor Y does not read the paper on either Monday or Wednesday.

9. If Teaching Assistant L notices a problem with a paper on Wednesday, and the paper is determined to be a failure on Friday, Professor Y could have read the paper on any of the following days EXCEPT

- Sunday
- Monday
- Tuesday
- Thursday
- Friday

10. If Teaching Assistant K reads a paper on Tuesday, and Professor X is the only member of the staff who can fail a paper after it is passed on by Teaching Assistant K, which one of the following must be true?

- Professor X reads the paper on Wednesday.
- Professor X reads the paper on Thursday.
- Professor Y reads the paper on Sunday.
- Teaching Assistant K reads the paper on Wednesday.
- Teaching Assistant L reads the paper on Thursday.

11. Suppose it is known that Teaching Assistant K reads a paper on either Tuesday or Wednesday, but not both days, and that Teaching Assistant L reads the paper on either Thursday or Friday, but not both days. All of the following are possible schedules for the teaching assistants EXCEPT:

- Teaching Assistant K reads the paper on Monday, and Teaching Assistant L reads the paper on Wednesday.
- Teaching Assistant K reads the paper on Tuesday, and Teaching Assistant L reads the paper on Thursday.
- Teaching Assistant K reads the paper on Tuesday, and Teaching Assistant L reads the paper on Friday.
- Teaching Assistant K reads the paper on Wednesday, and Teaching Assistant L reads the paper on Thursday.
- Teaching Assistant K reads the paper on Thursday, and Teaching Assistant L reads the paper on Friday.

Questions 12–13

How does an architect most easily maintain a client base interested in commissioning her for new projects? She relies on the design features and building materials utilized in the projects with which she initially won her following. Unfortunately, the result is that she will never experience measurable artistic development as an architect.

12. The argument depends upon which of the following assumptions about an architect's maintenance of a client base?
    - ○ An architect is never more interested in artistic development than with reliance on the design features and materials with which she developed her following.
    - ○ An architect is always careful to replicate a part of her original design when commissioned by a former client for a new project.
    - ○ An architect pays scant attention to the artistic development of her contemporaries in the field.
    - ○ An architect talks with her clients specifically about the design features and building materials that drew them to the architect's work in the first place.
    - ○ An architect is capable of predicting any trends or shifting preferences in the field before turning in final designs for a new project.

13. Which of the following, if true, is most damaging to the conclusion above?
    - ○ Frequently among those in an architect's client base are former architects and students of architecture.
    - ○ Those commissioning architects for new projects are pressured to commission works of broad-based appeal.
    - ○ Former clients commissioning architects for new projects most frequently cite "innovative design" as their most desired attribute for the new project.
    - ○ Alienation of a client base through refusal to draw upon signature design features and building materials can cost an architect a great deal of income.
    - ○ The favored design features and building materials of one nation's architectural industry can be widely divergent from those of another nation.

14. Several large steel companies in the United States have requested that tariffs be imposed on imported foreign steel. These companies usually incorporate high-tech refining processes in their steel production, which, while creating a higher grade of steel, also cause significant price increases. These companies fear they will lose a substantial portion of the domestic market to foreign competitors in the next few years. They contend that foreign steel, while generally of a lower grade, will be highly competitive in the United States due to its low price. Those companies requesting the tariffs should instead consider a return to more primitive, and profitable, refinement techniques.

Which of the following, if true, would most seriously weaken the conclusion drawn above?

○ An increase in the quality of steel used in an industry tends to result in higher customer satisfaction and assurance levels.
○ Tariffs have been shown to be an ineffective method of stymieing foreign competition in the electronics industry.
○ Domestic purchasers of steel will not buy low-grade foreign steel if strict tariffs are applied to its importation.
○ The United States automotive industry, which accounts for almost all domestic steel purchases, only uses steel of the highest grades.
○ The technologically advanced refining processes used in the production of American steel tend to be less environmentally sound than the processes used to produce low-grade steel.

15. At a certain university, of the last fifty women considered for full-time positions, only eighteen percent of them held these positions at the university after three years. Comparably, of the last fifty men considered, sixty percent of them are still working full-time after three years. Over forty percent of all full-time positions in the academic profession are currently held by women. An examination of these statistics makes it clear that this university's hiring practices are gender biased and should be altered to promote the full-time employment of women.

Which of the following, if true, most seriously weakens the force of the evidence cited above?

○ Almost all of the women who were considered for full-time positions at the university were hired, then left of their own accord after a few months.
○ When compared with the overall academic profession, the board of directors of the university seems to have an unbiased attitude toward women.
○ The definition of full-time employment has been altered several times over the last decade.
○ Most women who hold full-time academic positions have received multiple degrees.
○ Forty percent of the women who were not retained for full-time employment have expressed outrage at what they consider unfair hiring practices.

19
Answers and Explanations

EASY VERBAL BIN EXPLANATIONS

1. MOUNT:
   - descend
   - disassemble
   - upset
   - hide
   - go back

1. **A** It's A. Remember to make your own opposites for the stem words instead of looking at the choices ETS gives you right away. Also, if it helps, "translate" the stem word they give you into another word you are more comfortable with before making an opposite. So an opposite for MOUNT might be "get off," or "dismount." Choice A will be closest, but make sure you look at all the choices.

2. PLAYER : TEAM ::
   - oil : liquid
   - line : drawing
   - scales : increase
   - hiss : recording
   - ingredient : mixture

2. **E** It's E. Make a sentence expressing the relationship between the stem words. PLAYER is part of a TEAM is okay. Now try on the answer choices. A) OIL is part of a LIQUID? Yuck. B) LINE is part of a DRAWING? Not awful. Keep it for now. C) SCALES are part of an INCREASE? Huh? D) HISS is part of a RECORDING? Remember clear and necessary, and lose D! E) INGREDIENT is part of a MIXTURE? Not bad. We could make another sentence with the stem words to help decide between B and E. Something like a TEAM is a group of PLAYERs. Just remember to reverse the words in the answers now. B— DRAWING is a group of LINEs does not sound as good as MIXTURE is a group of INGREDIENTs. LINE and DRAWING is also not a particularly strong relationship. That's E!

3. There may be some validity in the facetious recent description of a pundit—a weatherman who talks every day about current events without being able to _____ them.

- ○ outline
- ○ begin
- ○ dissect
- ○ influence
- ○ stop

3. **D** The best answer is D. Remember to cover the answer choices. We can get a good idea of what the answer should be without even looking at them. Look for trigger words that indicate the direction of the sentence, and clues that tell us what's going on. The dash is a trigger here; it tells us that the first part of the sentence says the same thing as the later part. So a pundit, even if you don't know what it means, is like a weatherman, who can tell us about the weather (or current events in the case of a pundit) without being able to _____ it. How about something like "control"? Check answers. Choice A is awful, as is C. B and E aren't quite like control, and either one suggests that the other is just as good (or bad). D, "influence," is much like our "control."

4. ERADICATE:

- ○ ignore
- ○ undo
- ○ smoke
- ○ introduce
- ○ boil

4. **D** Remember to make synonyms for the stem, translating into language you're a bit more comfortable with. THEN make the opposite, and look at the answers for the choice that best matches. ERADICATE means get rid of. The opposite of get rid of is something like "cause" or "start." Check answers—A) IGNORE stinks. So does B) UNDO. Not much like opposites, these two. C) SMOKE? Maybe if we're smoking something. Otherwise . . . lose it. D) INTRODUCE is a lot like "cause" or "start." We like it. Good thing, too, because E is nuts. Boil indeed. Pick D.

5. The sparring of the two lawyers appeared _____ ; however, it is well known that, outside the courtroom, the friendship between the two is _____ .

○ pointless. .cooperative
○ hostile. .obvious
○ lighthearted. .abrogated
○ heightened. .concealed
○ brilliant. .precluded

5. **B** The best answer is B. This sentence has a nice changing direction trigger, "however," in the middle of it. So we know the two parts of the sentence are saying two opposing things. The first part of the sentence discusses the sparring, or fighting, of the two lawyers and how it appeared. It probably looked like fighting. A word like "nasty" or "fighting" or "real" might be good for that first blank. Look at the first words in the answers. Choice A stinks. Choice B's first word, "hostile," is a good word to keep. C—if they were fighting, is "light-hearted" good? No. D—"heightened" isn't awful; it could be that the fighting seemed intense. Choice E, "brilliant," is not. On to the other blank. Oh, now we know that despite their seeming to fight, these guys are really friends? That changes things. That's what "however" is doing here. So what do we do with the second blank? Outside the court, their friendship is good, well known, strong. We have a choice now between B's "obvious," and D's "concealed." If it's well known, it's not concealed! B is the only answer for which for both words work. Read it through to make sure.

6. EXCRETION : KIDNEY ::

○ respiration : lung
○ lymphoma : cancer
○ propulsion : engine
○ information : media
○ disinfection : soap

6. **A** It's A. EXCRETION is regulated by the KIDNEY. Try A) RESPIRATION is regulated by the LUNG? Okay. B) LYMPHOMA is regulated by the CANCER? No. C) PROPULSION is regulated by the ENGINE? Not. D) INFORMATION is regulated by the MEDIA? Only if you're fond of conspiracy theories. E) DISINFECTION is regulated by SOAP? Nope. That leaves A. Another sentence you might have used is KIDNEY performs EXCRETION, or KIDNEY is the organ of EXCRETION.

7. In radio, a morning broadcasting time often
_____ a larger and more _____ audience
and, thus, one that is more appealing to
advertisers of expensive products.

- ◯ demands. .attractive
- ◯ denotes. .agreeable
- ◯ indicates. .prosperous
- ◯ overlooks. .practical
- ◯ encourages. .widespread

7. **C** The answer is C. Do this one blank at a time, whichever one you think is easier to come up with a word for first. How about the first blank? Something like "gets" or "draws"? Now look at only the first words; we want to get rid of the ones that are nothing like our word. "Overlooks" in D is pretty bad. Cross off answer choice D completely, making sure you don't consider it when we look at the rest of the answers' second words. But the other choices aren't that bad; leave them alone, and we'll go to the other blank. The second blank describes the audience, and the second part of the sentence tells us that this audience is "appealing to advertisers of expensive products." This is here to tell us that the audience can afford the advertised products. "Wealthy" is a good word. Look for something like it and remember—we're looking only at the second words in the answers! A—"attractive" is nice, as is B—"agreeable," but these don't address the "expensive products" mentioned. C—"prosperous" is like wealthy. We like it. E is likewise far from "wealthy." Both words in C are good. Make sure to read the sentence through with your answer choice; make sure it sounds reasonable.

8. SNAKE : REPTILE ::

- ⟩ fish : school
- ⟩ beetle : insect
- ⟩ elephant : land
- ⟩ egg : chicken
- ⟩ lamb : sheep

8. **B** It's B. SNAKE is a type of REPTILE, right? Let's go. A) FISH is a type of SCHOOL? How about B? BEETLE is a type of INSECT? Sure. Keep it. C) ELEPHANT is a type of LAND? No way. D) EGG is a type of CHICKEN? Not really. Of course, they are related, but remember we are looking to see if they have the same relationship as the stem words. They don't. And choice E) LAMB is a type of SHEEP is okay. We have two choices that work; we can either make a more specific sentence with the stem, or work backwards with the answers, making different sentences for them. B's sentence pretty much needs to be something like BEETLE is a type or kind of INSECT, which certainly works with the stem words. But D's sentence is something like a LAMB is a baby SHEEP, which doesn't work with the stem. Therefore, B is the best answer.

Our visual perception depends on the reception of energy reflecting or radiating from that which we wish to perceive. If our eye could receive and measure

5 infinitely delicate sense-data, we could perceive the world with infinite precision. The natural limits of our eyes have, of course, been extended by mechanical instruments; telescopes and microscopes,

10 for example, expand our capabilities greatly. There is, however, an ultimate limit beyond which no instrument can take us; this limit is imposed by our inability to receive sense-data smaller than those

15 conveyed by an individual quantum of energy. Since these quanta are believed to be indivisible packages of energy and so cannot be further refined, we reach a point beyond which further resolution of the

20 world is not possible. It is like a drawing a child might make by sticking indivisible discs of color onto a canvas.

We might think that we could avoid this limitation by using quanta with extremely

25 long wavelengths; such quanta would be sufficiently sensitive to convey extremely delicate sense-data. And these quanta would be useful as long as we only wanted to measure energy, but a

30 completely accurate perception of the world will depend also on the exact measurement of the lengths and positions of what we wish to perceive. For this, quanta of extremely long wavelengths are

35 useless. To measure a length accurately to within a millionth of an inch, we must have a measure graduated in millionths of an inch; a yardstick graduated in inches is useless. Quanta with a wavelength of one

40 inch would be, in a sense, measures that are graduated in inches. Quanta of extremely long wavelengths are useless in measuring anything except extremely large dimensions.

45 Despite these difficulties, quanta have important theoretical implications for physics. It used to be supposed that, in the observation of nature, the universe could be divided into two distinct parts, a

50 perceiving subject and a perceived object. In physics, subject and object were supposed to be entirely distinct, so that a description of any part of the universe would be independent of the observer.

55 Quantum theory, however, suggests otherwise, for every observation involves the passage of a complete quantum from the object to the subject, and it now appears that this passage constitutes an

60 important coupling between observer and observed. We can no longer make a sharp division between the two in an effort to observe nature objectively. Such an attempt at objectivity would distort the

65 crucial interrelationship of observer and observed as parts of a single whole. But, even for scientists, it is only in the world of atoms that this new development makes any appreciable difference in the

70 explanation of observations.

9. The passage as a whole could be best described as

○ a consideration of factors that impede exact observation of the world

○ an acknowledgment of the limitations of conventional units of measurement

○ a criticism of efforts to divide perceiving subjects from perceived objects

○ a report on a conflict between two different scientific theories of visual perception

○ a description of a diminished capacity for sensory perception

9. **A** It's A. Don't forget to find the main idea before doing the questions. This passage is about quanta and the limits of visual perception. Question 9 is a main idea question. Let's match the main idea we formulated above with the answer choices. Choice A is a good paraphrase of our main idea. We like it. B mentions only limits on units of measurement. The passage is mainly about visual perception, even though units of measurement are discussed. So B really can't be the main idea. C talks about a criticism of efforts to divide perceiver from perceived. There are no such efforts in the passage. Lose C. D talks about two conflicting theories of perception. While another is briefly mentioned around line 47, the passage concentrates on describing one theory. So D isn't good as the main idea. Choice E? The passage is not a description of diminished capacity for sensory perception. First of all, it concentrates on visual perception only. Also, the passage does not describe reduced capacities of perception, but rather addresses limitations of perception. So A is the best version of the main idea here.

10. According to the passage, quanta of extremely long wavelengths can only be used to measure objects with extremely large dimensions because the quanta

- ⭘ would be independent of the observer
- ⭘ are graduated to within a millionth of an inch
- ⭘ lack sufficient magnitude of energy
- ⭘ exist in theory, but cannot be observed unless we expand our current mechanical capabilities
- ⭘ cannot offer a means of exact measurement of the lengths and positions upon which a completely accurate perception of the world would depend

10. **E** E is best. In order to answer this question about quanta of "extremely long wavelength" it would be good idea to see where that phrase, or one much like it, is used in the passage. Skim the passage quickly looking for the phrase. These lead words first appear around line 25. And the question asks why quanta of extremely long wavelengths can only be used to measure large things. Read around the place you found the lead words, from about line 20 to line 30, looking for the answer to the question. It doesn't really get answered there, so you look for the next occurrence of the phrase, and find it in line 34. Read around that. It starts to get good around line 36, but we really don't have the answer yet. "Extremely large" shows up again in line 43. The real answer is in lines 34–44. Measuring with long wavelengths is like using a really big ruler, divided into kinda big units. It's on the wrong scale, and can't be precise for anything small. Choice E covers this best. Incidentally, choice B is contradicted in the passage, so it really stinks. C isn't addressed.

11. LUCIDITY:

- ⭘ glistening
- ⭘ obscurity
- ⭘ gravity
- ⭘ attractiveness
- ⭘ quiescence

11. **B** It's B. LUCIDITY means clarity. The opposite of this could be "unclearness." Not an elegant word, but it will do the trick. Don't even worry if the word you make is real, as long as it will help you get an answer. OBSCURITY, choice B, partially or completely hidden from sight, is best.

12. FERTILIZER : GROWTH ::
   ○ glaze : pottery
   ○ yeast : leavening
   ○ cotton : texture
   ○ illumination : interest
   ○ octane : speed

12. **B** B is the answer. A good sentence for the stem would be FERTILIZER encourages or causes GROWTH. Now try the answer choices: A) GLAZE encourages or causes POTTERY. No good for this sentence. Dump A. B) YEAST causes or encourages LEAVENING. It sure does. Keep it. C) COTTON causes or encourages TEXTURE? Nonsense. D) ILLUMINATION causes or encourages INTEREST—totally unrelated. E) OCTANE causes or encourages SPEED? Octane in gasoline has no relationship to speed. Go away, E. So, the only answer that made any sense with the sentence we made with the stem was B. We're happy.

13. FRUSTRATE:
   ○ facilitate
   ○ moderate
   ○ climb
   ○ judge
   ○ assemble

13. **A** It's A. FRUSTRATE means to annoy, make difficult. "Make easier" would be a good opposite. A—FACILITATE means just that—to make easier. But we need to look at all the answers. Don't take the chance of screwing this up. We might also like B—MODERATE. But that means make less severe. If you couldn't decide between these two choices, you'd make opposites for the answer choices, and see which is closer to the stem. The opposite for choice A would be to make harder. The opposite for choice B would be to make more severe. A is better.

14. BOLSTER:
   ○ infect
   ○ compound
   ○ untie
   ○ generate
   ○ undermine

14. **E** E is correct. BOLSTER means support. The opposite of that would be "take away support." That gives us "undermine."

15. DISARM : WEAPONS ::

- ○ limit : abilities
- ○ soothe : difficulties
- ○ restrain : movement
- ○ disguise : identity
- ○ usurp : power

15. **E** E is the best answer. A good sentence defining this relationship might be DISARM is to take away WEAPONS. How's A) LIMIT is to take away ABILITIES? Well, it's not taking them away. B) SOOTHE is to take away DIFFICULTIES? No, it just makes us feel better. C) RESTRAIN is to take away MOVEMENT? It's not awful, so keep it. D) DISGUISE is to take away IDENTITY? No, just to hide it. E) USURP is to take away POWER? Looks good. Now we need to choose between C and E. We could make another sentence for the stem, or we can work backwards with C and E. A good relationship sentence for C is RESTRAIN is to prevent MOVEMENT. Is DISARM to prevent WEAPONS? Not really. E) USURP is to forcibly take away POWER. Is DISARM to forcibly take away WEAPONS? Yes it is, and it's a better choice than C.

EASY MATH BIN EXPLANATIONS

Column A	Column B
1. $(3 + 0) \times 4$	$0 \times (3 + 4)$

○ the quantity in Column A is always greater
○ the quantity in Column B is always greater
○ the quantities are always equal
○ it cannot be determined from the information given

Column A	Column B
$a = 15$
$a + b = 29$
2. a^2	b^2

○ the quantity in Column A is always greater
○ the quantity in Column B is always greater
○ the quantities are always equal
○ it cannot be determined from the information given

3. Of team A's victories this year, sixty percent were at home. If team A has won a total of twenty games this year, how many of those games were won away from home?

○ 5
○ 7
○ 8
○ 12
○ 15

1. **A** It's A. The first thing to do is to write down A, B, C, D. In this case, we can ditch D because all there are here are numbers, no variables. Now we need to evaluate each side. Remember PEMDAS, the order of operations. In Column A, we do the parentheses first, which will be 3. Then 3 times 4 is 12. So Column A is 12. In Column B, we also do the parentheses first—that will be 7. But then we multiply that times 0. And anything times 0 = 0. That's what Column B is. So A will always be larger.

2. **A** The answer is A. Write down ABCD to use process of elimination. They tell us that $a = 15$ and $a + b = 29$. Plug the given value of a into the equation with a and b, and solve for b. It's 14. Now Column A is 15 squared. Don't multiply this yet! Column B is 14 squared. Without actually multiplying out for each column, you should see that A will be larger. We were given a value for a—it was fixed, so we didn't really need to plug in to know that A is always larger.

3. **C** It's C. We are told that the team won 20 games, and that 60 percent of these were won at home. But we are being asked how many games the team won AWAY from home. That's the other 40 percent. To find exactly how many games were won AWAY from home, we need to take 40 percent of 20. Use translation for this:

40 percent of 20 is . . . can be translated as

$\dfrac{40}{100} \times 20$, which will equal 8—choice C.

<u>Column A</u>   <u>Column B</u>

$$a = b$$

4. $4a + b$ $a + 4b$

- ○ the quantity in Column A is always greater
- ○ the quantity in Column B is always greater
- ○ the quantities are always equal
- ○ it cannot be determined from the information given

5. 652(523) + 427(652) is equal to which of the following?

- ○ 523 (652 + 427)
- ○ 652 (523 + 427)
- ○ (652 + 427)(523 + 652)
- ○ (652 + 523)(427 + 652)
- ○ (652 + 652)(523 + 427)

4. **C** The answer is C. Here we will need to plug in, so write down A, B, C, D. ETS tells us that a and b are equal. So let's pick something, like $a = b = 4$. So Column A in this case is $4(4) + 4 = 20$. Column B is $4 + 4(4)$ which will also equal 20. So far they're equal. So cross out A and B. Are they always equal? Let's plug in again, trying to make a mess. Maybe $a = b = -1$? So Column A will give $4(-1) + (-1)$ which will equal -5. And Column B is $-1 + 4(-1)$, which will also be -5. Looks equal indeed. So it's C that's best.

5. **B** The answer is B. Hope you didn't feel inclined to multiply this out! The ugliness of the numbers should deter you. Annoying multiplication is not what this test is about; avoiding it is. Can we rearrange this? After all, that's what the answers are: rearranged numbers, not actual products. We can factor a 652 out of each term like this: 652 (523 + 427), which is the same thing as (652) (523) + (652) (427). And that's B.

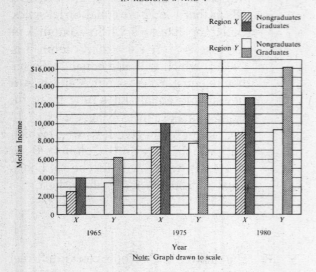

MEDIAN INCOME OF
COLLEGE GRADUATES *VS.* NONGRADUATES
IN REGIONS *X* AND *Y*

Note: Graph drawn to scale.

6. The median income of graduates in Region *Y* increased by approximately how much between 1965 and 1980?

- ○ $6,000
- ○ $7,000
- ○ $8,000
- ○ $10,000
- ○ $16,000

6. **D** The answer is D. To find the *amount* that the median income of graduates in region Y increased from 1965 to 1980, find each individual amount. In 1965, median income was about $6,200. In 1980, it was about $16,200. So it increased by about $10,000. We don't really know the exact numbers, but the question says approximately. So don't make yourself crazy.

Column A | Column B

The diameter of circle M is greater than the radius of circle N.

7. The circumference of circle M | The circumference of circle N

○ the quantity in Column A is always greater
○ the quantity in Column B is always greater
○ the quantities are always equal
○ it cannot be determined from the information given

8. If $a = 4$ and $4a - 3b = 1$, what is the combined value of a and b?

○ 5

○ $5\frac{2}{3}$

○ 9

○ $14\frac{2}{3}$

○ $21\frac{2}{3}$

7. **D** The answer is D. Write down A, B, C, D to use the Process of Elimination. We're told the diameter of circle M is greater than the radius of circle N. Plug in some values for the diameter and radius of these circles, making sure that they fit the info we're given. Let's say the diameter of M is 10, and the radius of N is 3. Column A asks for the circumference of circle M. Circumference = 2 times π times radius, or π times diameter. Using the 10 we picked for the diameter of M, the circumference of circle M is 10π. Using 3 for the radius of circle N will get us 6π as its circumference. For the time being it looks like A is larger, so eliminate B and C, since neither of these can always be true. We're left with A and D as choices. So plug in again, trying to make a different answer happen. If we keep the diameter of M as 10, but make the *radius* of $N = 9$, Column A is still 10π, but Column B becomes 18π. Now B is larger, so A cannot be the correct answer, since we found a case where Column A is not larger than Column B. So dump A. The only choice left is D.

8. **C** The answer is C. Put the value of a that they give us into the equation. It will become $4(4) - 3b = 1$. That's $16 - 3b = 1$. Subtract 16 from each side, and we now have $-3b = -15$. Divide each side by -3, and we find that $b = 5$. Make sure to read the question before picking an answer! ETS wants "the combined value of a and b." That's $4 + 5 = 9$—choice C. Notice how the value of b is sitting there also, waiting for us to be in a hurry and pick it. Don't.

Column A | Column B

9. $\dfrac{3}{4} + \dfrac{3}{4}$ $\qquad$ $\left(\dfrac{3}{4}\right)^2$

○ the quantity in Column A is always greater
○ the quantity in Column B is always greater
○ the quantities are always equal
○ it cannot be determined from the information given

10. If $k = 6 \times 17$, then which of the following is a multiple of k?

○ 68
○ 78
○ 85
○ 136
○ 204

9. **A** A is correct. Write down A, B, C, D. Here again we know to eliminate D, because all we have is numbers. Column A is $\dfrac{3}{4}$ + $\dfrac{3}{4}$, which we don't even need to use the bowtie for, because the bottom numbers are the same. $\dfrac{3}{4} + \dfrac{3}{4} = \dfrac{6}{4}$, which we can also say is $1\dfrac{1}{2}$. Column B, even though it also has $\dfrac{3}{4}$ in it, is asking us to *square* it.

For multiplying $\dfrac{3}{4}$ by $\dfrac{3}{4}$, remember we multiply the top numbers across to get a top number. It'll be 9 in this case. And we multiply across the bottom for the bottom number, in this case 16. So the product is $\dfrac{9}{16}$. We don't need to use the bowtie to compare these either. Column A is clearly larger than 1, and Column B is less. So, A is the answer.

10. **E** It's E. Here we really can't easily escape doing the multiplication, but multiplying 17 by 6 shouldn't kill us. It's 102. And we are looking for a multiple of 102, in other words, what we get when we multiply 102 by any integer. It could be –102, or 102, not that either of those are here. Of the ones that are here, only 204 is a multiple of 102. It's 102 times 2. So, choice E is the winner.

Column A   Column B

$$ab = a \text{ and } a = 0$$

11. a b

- ⬭ the quantity in Column A is always greater
- ⬭ the quantity in Column B is always greater
- ⬭ the quantities are always equal
- ⬭ it cannot be determined from the information given

12. What is the value of $(4 + a)(4 - b)$ when $a = 4$ and $b = -4$?

- ⬭   –64
- ⬭   –16
- ⬭   0
- ⬭   16
- ⬭   64

11. **D** The answer is D. Don't forget to write A, B, C, D on your scratch paper, and plug in! They tell us that $ab = a$, and that $a = 0$. Put in that value of a in the first equation. We now know that 0 times $b = 0$. Plug in a value of b that makes this true. Yes, it can be just about anything! Say we make $b = 5$. Then Column A is 0 and Column B is 5. Column B is larger, so we can eliminate choices A and C. But you know we're not done; we must plug in again. So, try another value for b, maybe something a bit wacky, like 0. Column A is still 0, but now so is Column B. So the columns can be equal. We've already crossed out A and C, and now we can cross out B, because we just found a case when the answer could be C. We're left with D, because we really had two different answers depending on what we plugged in for b.

12. **E** E is the correct answer. Watch the signs carefully. In order to evaluate this expression, we need to put in the values of a and b we are given. The $(4 + a)$ becomes $(4 + 4) = 8$. And the $(4 - b)$ becomes $(4 - (-4))$ which is also 8. Subtracting a negative number is the same thing as adding, remember? To finish this problem, don't forget that we need to multiply the 8s together, getting 64. That's E.

Column A   Column B

n cases of soda *N* contain a total
of 36 bottles of soda.

13. The total number of
bottles in *x* cases $\dfrac{36x}{n}$
of soda *x*

○ the quantity in Column A is always
  greater
○ the quantity in Column B is greater
○ the quantities are always equal
○ it cannot be determined from the
  information given

Column A   Column B

14 more than *a* is –9

14.   *a* + 9   –14

○ the quantity in Column A is always
  greater
○ the quantity in Column B is greater
○ the quantities are always equal
○ it cannot be determined from the
  information given

15. The illumination *E*, in footcandles, provided
by a light source of intensity *I*, in candles, at

a distance *D*, in feet, is given by $E = \dfrac{I}{D^2}$.

For an illumination of 50 footcandles at a
distance of 4 feet from a source, the intensity of the source must be

○ 50 candles
○ 200 candles
○ 800 candles
○ 1,600 candles
○ 2,500 candles

13. **D** This is D. Write down A, B, C, D! The question says that *n* cases of soda *N* have a total of 36 bottles of soda. We can decide that *n* = 6, for example, so each case has 6 bottles. Now we go to the two columns. Column A asks us the total number of bottles in *x* cases of soda *X*. That's right, a different number of cases of a different soda. Cute, huh? It could be *anything*—the conditions above only apply to soda *N*. So even though we made *n* = 6, we can pick anything for *x*. And we can change our *n*, too, for that matter. So the answer is D.

14. **C** The correct answer is C. We are told that 14 more than *a* is –9. Let's translate this into an equation. Moving left to right, we see that this equation is 14 + *a* = –9. Now solve it by subtracting 14 from each side; *a* equals –23. So put it into the columns. Column A is –23 + 9, which is –14. Ooh! Look at Column B! It's –14, too. We can't use any other values for *a*—it was a set value and we've plugged it in. Both columns are always –14, so the answer is C.

15. **C** C is correct. Be careful here about which variable is which. Set up the equation as it's given, and substitute the numbers in the problem:

$E = \dfrac{I}{D^2}$ becomes $50 = \dfrac{I}{4^2}$, or $50 = \dfrac{I}{16}$.

To solve, we multiply both sides by 16. *I* will equal 50 times 16, or 800. Bingo. That's C. Don't be thrown by the sciencey sounding wording. We just need to put in the given values.

EASY ANALYTIC BIN EXPLANATIONS

1. Nonprescription sunglasses shield the wearer's eyes from damaging ultraviolet sunlight. Squinting, however, provides protection from ultraviolet rays that is at least as good as the protection from nonprescription sunglasses. There is, therefore, no health advantage to be gained by wearing nonprescription sunglasses rather than squinting.

Which of the following, if true, most seriously weakens support for the conclusion above?

○ Many opticians offer prescription sunglasses that not only screen out ultraviolet sunlight but also provide corrective vision.

○ Some nonprescription sunglasses provide less protection from ultraviolet sunlight than does squinting.

○ Squinting strains facial muscles and causes headaches and fatigue.

○ Many people buy sunglasses because they feel that sunglasses are fashionable.

○ Some people squint even when they are wearing sunglasses.

1. **C** The answer is C. The argument concludes that there is no health advantage to wearing nonprescription sunglasses rather than squinting, and we are asked to weaken support for the conclusion. We're told that both methods protect from ultraviolet radiation, but if there were a reason that one of the methods were harmful, or that wearing sunglasses would truly afford a health advantage which squinting could not, we would be in business. Choice A discusses prescription sunglasses, and is out of scope. B would strengthen the contention that there's no advantage to wearing glasses—there would be a *disadvantage*. Choice C tells us something bad about squinting, making glasses seem better. This does the job. D addresses fashion, which is out of scope. E does nothing to distinguish squinting from wearing sunglasses.

Questions 2–5

Two walls of a room in a nursery school are being repainted. There are six colors to choose from—purple, blue, green, yellow, orange, and red. The walls must be painted with three different colors each:

Purple and yellow must be used on the same wall.

Blue and orange cannot be used on the same wall.

The two walls cannot have the same combination of colors as each other.

2. All of the following are possible colors chosen for one wall EXCEPT

   ○ Purple, blue, red
   ○ Purple, green, yellow
   ○ Purple, yellow, red
   ○ Blue, green, red
   ○ Green, orange, red

2–5 A typical assignment game with nice blocks. We have six colors, and we choose combos of three for each of two walls:

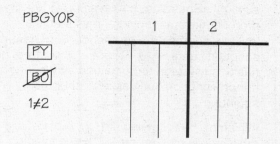

PBGYOR

PY

BO

1≠2

There's only one tricky bit we need to notice. The last clue should alert us that something's up. If the two walls cannot have the same combination of colors as each other, this sounds like we can use colors more than once. Indeed, nowhere in the setup or clues do we read that we have to use all 6 colors. So using one color more than once must be okay. Now get out those paintbrushes . . .

2. **A** The correct answer is A. An EXCEPT question, about possible "lineups," and here we want to know which one is no good. Take it one clue at a time. In the set up, we are told three different colors. So far, so good. First clue says purple and yellow must be used together. Uh oh. Choice A is a problem. And since we want the one that's bad, we're done. We found it. All of the other choices have okay combos.

3. Which of the following colors could be chosen for a wall for which purple is chosen?

   ◯ Blue and green
   ◯ Blue and orange
   ◯ Blue and red
   ◯ Green and yellow
   ◯ Orange and red

3. **D** D is the answer. What can be the other colors if we pick purple? Gotta have yellow; start there. Wow. Only D has yellow; the others don't. We are done. Gee, that was frighteningly easy.

4. Which of the following is an acceptable way to paint the walls?

   Wall 1   Wall 2
   ◯ Purple, blue, yellow   Purple, yellow, orange
   ◯ Purple, green, red   Green, yellow, orange
   ◯ Purple, yellow, orange   Purple, blue, orange
   ◯ Blue, green, red   Blue, orange, red
   ◯ Green, yellow, red   Green, yellow, red

4. **A** It's A. Here we are asked for an acceptable lineup. Take it one clue at a time. After we get rid of the junk, we should only have one answer left. We know there are three different colors per wall. No violations. Next—purple and yellow must be used together. B has a problem with this, so eliminate it. In C, Wall 2 uses purple without yellow—no good. And E uses yellow alone (not to mention that it's the same combo twice). So we have A and D left. Next clue—no blue and orange together. There goes D in the garbage. Choice A is the only one left. Bingo!

5. If one wall is painted with blue, green and red, then the other wall can be painted with each of the following EXCEPT

   ◯ Purple, blue, yellow
   ◯ Purple, green, yellow
   ◯ Purple, yellow, red
   ◯ Blue, green, red
   ◯ Green, orange, red

5. **D** It's D. Remember, this is an EXCEPT question, and we are asked to find the bad seed among the answer choices. We're told that one wall has blue, green and red. Check the clues against the answer choices for violations. We know from the setup that there must be three different colors on each wall; that's okay in all of the choices. Next: purple and yellow must be together. That's not violated anywhere. Next: blue and orange can't be together. That's not violated. Last clue: the two walls can't have the same color combos as each other. That's bad news for D; it's the exact same as the other wall, and violates the condition, which makes it our answer.

6. In May 1990, the American airlines serving European destinations substantially reduced the price of flights to those destinations. During the months subsequent to the reductions, the number of tickets sold to European destinations increased to well above the monthly average for the previous year. Despite this fact, the number of tickets sold by American airlines to European destinations was not noticeably different from the previous year's total.

Which of the following, if true, best explains the apparent paradox in the passage above?

○ Many Americans travel to European destinations only when airfares are low.

○ The amount of revenue generated in 1990 by sales of tickets to European destinations remained the same as it was the previous year.

○ For part of 1990, the number of tickets sold to European destinations was lower than the year's monthly average.

○ The larger the number of tickets sold by American airlines in a given one-year period, the lower the per-ticket price during that period.

○ There is a predictable up and down pattern in the volume of tickets sold by American airlines to European destinations.

6. **C** The correct answer is C. Here's the deal—the price of tickets goes down in May 1990, and more are sold than were the previous year. But the overall number of tickets sold does not change much from 1989 to 1990. Why? It seems weird. Resolving the paradox will mean coming up with an explanation that allows both of these seemingly contradictory situations to coexist. Think about how it could happen—ticket sales went up after May, but we don't really know what happened before then. If ticket sales at the beginning of 1990 were really slow, then that might explain how the overall number of tickets sold in each of the years didn't change much. Let's look for that. Choice A doesn't help us—we don't know what the fares were like in 1989, and this doesn't resolve our paradox. Choice B doesn't take care of our paradox—it is kind of the same thing. Choice C is our pal. If the beginning of 1990 was slow for ticket sales, and the second half was high, the average can still be the same as that of the previous year. In D, we don't know which given one year period this is, and it doesn't explain the paradox. Choice E pretty much reinforces the problem we are presented with, but does nothing to explain it. It's C, folks.

7. A motion picture by Orson Welles, the director who died in 1985, was edited down from 200 hours of footage abandoned by Welles into a 100-minute final form. The film, composed solely of shots directed by Welles, and edited according to Welles's shooting script, and preliminary director's notes, is therefore a legitimate Orson Welles motion picture.

Which of the following, if true, is most damaging to the contention that the new film is a legitimate Orson Welles motion picture?

- ○ Part of the found footage not included by the editors in the new film had previously been seen in a documentary completed by Welles before his death.
- ○ Film scholars have maintained that the footage was shot during a period during which Welles created some of his least successful works.
- ○ A motion picture can only legitimately be attributed to a director if the director decides what should be selected for inclusion in it and what weight should be given to in post-production material selected for inclusion.
- ○ A legitimate motion picture contains visual motifs, subject matter, and editorial patterns similar to those present in a director's outstanding motion pictures.
- ○ Few of the films directed by Orson Welles were fewer than 120 minutes in duration.

7. **C** It's C. We are being asked to damage the conclusion that this is a legitimate Orson Welles movie. We're told that Welles directed the footage, and his notes and shooting script were used. But does that make it a legitimate Welles film? Let's look for an answer choice that says it doesn't. Choice A just tells us that Welles had actually used some of the footage before. This barely strengthens the argument, and certainly does not weaken it, which is what we are trying to do. In B, scholars say that this footage is among Welles's lamest. Still his. This doesn't address the issue of what is sufficient for "legitimacy," though. C—this does address the issue of "legitimacy," and the film described above does not meet the criteria. Welles, because he was dead, did not actually select the shots or decide what would be included. For all we know, the footage may have been intended for six different films, and the big guy is spinning in his grave. This is the answer we want, but keep looking. Choice D *strengthens* the contention that this film could be considered legit. Lose it. Choice E does a poor job of weakening the argument, especially when compared to choice C. It merely mentions one way that the new film is not characteristic of most of Welles's other works. Choice C, by far, does the best job of weakening the argument.

A haberdasher is displaying colored hats in two windows, one on the left and one on the right. Each window will display three hats. There are seven hats from which to choose: a red one, an orange one, a yellow one, a green one, a blue one, a purple one, and a white one. The following conditions must be met:

The red hat must be displayed, and it must go in the left window.

The orange hat must be displayed, and it must go in the right window.

The purple hat cannot be displayed in the same window as the orange hat, nor can it be displayed with the green hat.

Both the yellow hat and the white hat must be displayed, and they must go in the same window.

8–11   Ah, lovely hats. Your diagram should be divided into two sections: left and right, with space for three hats in each. One hat will not be used in each case.

ROYGBPW

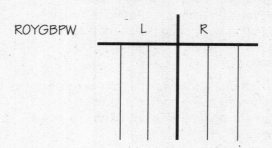

Make sure you double-check your clues after symbolizing them. Incorporate clues into your diagram if you can. Here we know that the red hat is on the left and the orange hat is on the right. We also can deduce that since the purple hat and the orange hat can't be in the same window, the purple hat will never be on the right. Everything else is a block or an anti-block. All of this can be shown like this:

ROYGBP

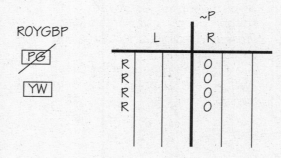

Now we can do the questions.

8. Which of the following is an accurate list of hats that can be displayed in the left window?
- ○ Red, blue, purple
- ○ Red, yellow, blue
- ○ Red, green, white
- ○ Red, orange, purple
- ○ Orange, yellow, white

9. If the white hat is displayed in the left window, which of the following is a pair of hats that must be displayed in the right window?
- ○ Yellow and green
- ○ Green and blue
- ○ Red and orange
- ○ Blue and purple
- ○ Yellow and purple

8. **A** It's A. This is a possible line-up question. Handle it by taking the clues one at a time, and checking the answer choices for violations. We're being asked which hats can go in the left window. First clue says the red hat must be on the left. Answer choice E violates this, so out it goes. The second clue says the orange hat must go in the right window, so it can't go in the left one. Answer choice D violates this, so eliminate it. The third clue, which should be broken into two separate parts, tells us that purple and orange can't go together and that purple and green can't be together, but no answer violates this clue. Next, yellow and white must be together. Both B and C violate this, so A is all that's left.

9. **B** It's B. Take a look:

If the white hat is on the left, so is yellow. The left side is then red, white, and yellow. On the right we already have orange and can't have purple. Therefore the other two on the right must be green and blue. That's B for Bingo.

10. Which of the following is an accurate list of hats that can be displayed in the right window?

- ○ Orange, green, blue
- ○ Orange, green, purple
- ○ Orange, purple, white
- ○ Red, orange, blue
- ○ Orange, yellow, green

11. If the white hat is displayed in the right window, which of the following is a pair of hats that could be displayed in the left window?

- ○ Yellow and green
- ○ Yellow and blue
- ○ Yellow and purple
- ○ Green and purple
- ○ Blue and purple

10. **A** A is the answer. This is a nice possible lineup question for the right window. Go through clue by clue: Red must be on the left, not right, so eliminate choice D. The "orange must be on the right" clue is okay in all lineups in the answers. We can't have purple and orange together, so get rid of B and C. We can't have purple and green together, but that doesn't help us right now. Yellow and white must be together, and they are not in choice E, so eliminate it. A is all that's left, and it doesn't violate any clues.

11. **E** E is the correct answer. Take a look:

If the white hat is on the right, so must be the yellow. And we know the orange is already there. We're being asked about the left hand side, so we can eliminate any answers that have yellow, white, or orange; that gets rid of A, B, and C. We have green, purple, and blue to pick from for the other two hats on the left. The question asks us which _could_ be on the left. And green and purple together is a no-no. That eliminates D, so E is left. Blue and purple is fine; so is blue and green, but that's not a choice, and E was the only one left anyway after we used process of elimination.

12. During the War of 1812, the United States Congress licensed privateers (armed pirates) who were empowered to plunder enemy ships. Those privateers financed their ventures through the sale of the seized cargo. A Florida man has petitioned Congress to license modern privateers to mount a private "war-for-profit" against seagoing smugglers of illegal drugs.

Which of the following, if true, is a drawback to the Florida man's proposal?

- ◯ Modern ships are much faster than those of the nineteenth century.
- ◯ Although the United States Constitution still authorizes the licensing of privateers, no licenses have been issued for over 150 years.
- ◯ Modern privateers would be unable to finance their operations by selling the seized cargo without being in violation of the law.
- ◯ The 1812 privateers plundered ships that belonged to citizens of another country.
- ◯ Most of the ships used by drug smugglers are modified fishing boats.

12. **C** The answer is C. Asking us for a drawback to the proposal is similar to asking us to weaken the argument. This is an argument by analogy, which assumes that the situation during the War of 1812 is comparable to the situation in the war on drugs. To weaken the argument, look for an answer choice that suggests that this similarity is not valid, and that allowing privateering will not help the war against drugs. Choice A says that ships now are faster than they were then. This really makes no difference, as all ships are probably faster. That won't make it any easier or harder to privateer. Choice B won't weaken the argument; in fact, it says privateering is technically still legal. C says that privateers would be breaking the law selling cargo seized from drug smugglers. This small legal hitch blows the writer's notion that privateering is a good idea out of the water; looks good for weakening. Choice D mentions that in 1812 the ships were those of a different country, which is out of scope. And choice E is also irrelevant. Knowing what kind of boats the smugglers use makes no difference to the argument, or us. We like C.

Questions 13–15

Four children—Amy, Ben, Cindy, and Dennis—are choosing among six different flavored lollipops which are lined up on the counter of the candy store in the following order from left to right: cherry, orange, lemon, grape, raspberry, and strawberry. Each lollipop must be chosen by a child. The following information is known about the choices:

Each child chooses at least one lollipop.

No child can choose two lollipops that are adjacent to each other.

13. If Amy chooses the cherry and the strawberry lollipops, which one of the following must be true?

○ Another child besides Amy chooses two lollipops.

○ The child who chooses lemon cannot also choose raspberry.

○ Cindy chooses a lollipop that is located to the left of the lollipop that Ben chooses.

○ The orange lollipop is chosen by either Ben or Cindy.

○ The raspberry lollipop is chosen by either Cindy or Dennis.

13–15 This is an assignment game, so we need a grid. Remember to put whatever doesn't change and/or has an order on top of your diagram. We're given the order of the lollipops, so that's the top of the grid:

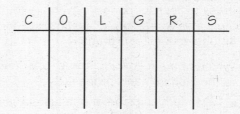

And the elements are the kids—A, B, C, and D.

13. A Okay, time for question 13. Fill in what you know:

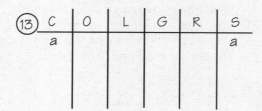

Now, notice we have four spaces left to fill, and three kids to fill them with. The clues tell us that each kid chooses at least one lollipop. So, in order for three kids to fill four spaces, one of the kids is going to have to choose two lollipops. Bingo! That's choice A.

14. If Cindy chooses two lollipops, and Ben and Dennis both choose lollipops that are located somewhere to the left of the first lollipop that Cindy chooses, which of the following could be the two lollipops that Cindy chooses?

- ○ Cherry and lemon
- ○ Orange and grape
- ○ Orange and strawberry
- ○ Lemon and strawberry
- ○ Raspberry and strawberry

15. If Amy chooses the orange lollipop and two other lollipops, which one of the following CANNOT be true?

- ○ Amy chooses the strawberry lollipop.
- ○ Amy and Cindy choose lollipops that are adjacent to each other.
- ○ Ben and Cindy choose lollipops that are adjacent to each other.
- ○ Ben and Cindy choose lollipops that are located somewhere to the left of the grape lollipop.
- ○ Amy chooses lollipops that are immediately to the left of the one Ben chooses and immediately to the left of the one Dennis chooses.

14. **D** If Ben and Dennis both have to choose lollipops to the left of Cindy's two lollipops, Cindy must be choosing lollipops toward the right end of the lollipop line. She's definitely NOT choosing the two left most lollipops, cherry and orange. So, eliminate A, B, and C. The second clue tells us that she can't choose lollipops that are adjacent; that gets rid of E. We're left with D.

15. **C** Amy's choosing orange, and two others that can't be next to each other, so the diagram will look like this:

	C	O	L	G	R	S
⑬	a					a
⑮		a		a		a

Now, every kid has to choose a lollipop, and there are three kids left, and three spaces to fill. It doesn't matter who goes where, but since Amy has every other lollipop, the other kids can't choose lollipops that are adjacent to each other; one gets cherry, one gets lemon, and one gets raspberry. So, the answer that CANNOT be true is C—Ben and Cindy can't choose adjacent lollipops. The other choices can or must be true. What else is true? These kids should go to the dentist!

MEDIUM VERBAL BIN EXPLANATIONS

1. DODGE:

   ○ release
   ○ create
   ○ assert aggressively
   ○ admire greatly
   ○ face directly

1. **E**   E is the answer. Maybe we can't define DODGE right away. Word association will help us here. Where have you seen this word used?

   Ever play dodgeball? What's the idea? Not getting hit. The opposite of that would be getting hit. Look for something like that. Or, if we can dodge a ball, we ought also to be able to do its opposite with a ball. A) RELEASE ball? Okay. B) CREATE ball? Out of what? Not so good. C) ASSERT AGGRESSIVELY ball, or ASSERT ball AGGRESSIVELY? This is plain weird. D) ADMIRE GREATLY a ball? Sure it's lovely and round, but does it make much sense? No. E) FACE DIRECTLY a ball, or FACE a ball DIRECTLY? Sounds good. And that's it. You could also use DODGE the draft. But you can't dodge the question even if you can't come up with a perfect definition of the word.

2. TEETH : SAW ::

   ○ cog : wheel
   ○ pick : ice
   ○ bit : drill
   ○ pulley : rope
   ○ wood : screw

2. **C**   C is best. Careful with the sentence here. We don't want to get too specific too quickly. Let's try TEETH are part of a SAW. A) COG is part of a WHEEL? Could be. Don't chuck it yet. B) PICK is a part of ICE? No. C) BIT is part of a DRILL. Yes. D) PULLEY is part of a ROPE? Well, it works with one sometimes, but it's not part of one. E) WOOD is a part of a SCREW? No way. So there's A and C to look at more closely. Can we make a more specific sentence with the stem? What do teeth have to do with a saw besides being a part of one? They cut. TEETH are the cutting part of a SAW. Back to A) COG is the cutting part of a WHEEL? There is no cutting part of a wheel. C? BIT is the cutting part of a DRILL? Yes, that's the part that does the damage. C is our answer.

3. INDUSTRY:

○ politics
○ density
○ lethargy
○ tolerance
○ vastness

4. Although the candidate obviously wanted to _____ the euphoria that has infused her campaign of late, she refrained from implying that the momentum had turned against her and might result in her defeat.

○ authenticate
○ moderate
○ maintain
○ clarify
○ revive

3. **C** C is correct. INDUSTRY has at least two meanings, one of which does not have a clear opposite. It won't be used here in the sense of "I'm in the plastics industry." Here it will mean hard work, diligence. The opposite of that will be something like lazy, without hard work. The closest to that is choice C—LETHARGY.

4. **B** The answer is B. Here we have "although" acting as a trigger, telling us that the start of the sentence is not the same as the end. The blank is in the first part, and we know the first part should be different from the second part of the sentence. The second part of the sentence says the candidate didn't want to let on that she might lose. What would she want to do to the "euphoria that has infused her campaign?" Calm it down, but not completely destroy it. She wanted to be realistic without being defeatist. Look for something like "calm." A is no good. B, "moderate" is a lot like calm. Keep it. C—"maintain" is keeping the same, which she didn't want to do. Lose it. D and E are not like "calm." That's B.

Tillie Olsen's fiction and essays have been widely and rightly acknowledged as major contributions to American literature. Her work has been particularly valued by contemporary feminists. Yet few of Olsen's readers realize the extent to which her vision and choice of subject are rooted in an earlier literary heritage—the tradition of radical political thought, mostly socialist and anarchist, of the 1910s and 1920s, and the Old Left tradition of the 1930s. I do not mean that one can adequately explain the eloquence of her work in terms of its political origins, or that left-wing politics were the single most important influence on it. My point is that its central consciousness—its profound understanding of class and gender as shaping influences on people's lives— owes much to that earlier literary heritage, a heritage that, in general, has not been sufficiently valued by most contemporary literary critics.

Remember, the first thing we need to do when dealing with a reading passage is get the main idea. This does not require particularly careful reading. Remember, the passage isn't going anywhere. It will always be there on the screen for you to look for the answers. The main idea of this passage is something like "Olsen's thinking draws on early twentieth-century radical political thought." That's not everything the passage says, but it's enough to start dealing with the questions.

5. The best description of the passage is

- ⭕ an argument that Olsen's success as a writer is due to her class and gender consciousness
- ⭕ a statement that Olsen's radical political background is the most important influence on her work
- ⭕ an attempt to place Olsen's work in a broader literary context
- ⭕ a call to literary critics to investigate the beginnings of a literary tradition
- ⭕ a suggestion that Olsen's work has been mistakenly understood in terms of a particular literary heritage

5. **C** The answer is C. This question pretty much asks for the main idea. The main idea is above. What answer choice matches this best? Choice A is supported nowhere in the passage. It never says her success is related to her influences. Choice B is specifically contradicted in lines 11–16, where the writer says it wasn't the most important influence. So that's not it. Choice C—an attempt to put her work in a broader context? Hmm. Author says feminists like her work, but in lines 5–8 mentions that not many people know about one of Olsen's significant influences. That sounds like putting her work in a broader context. Choice D doesn't happen here. There's not really an overall literary tradition being discussed. And while the author of the passage says that the literary heritage that influenced Olsen is undervalued, he really doesn't urge all to go research it. We're reading about Tillie Olsen. Choice E? Has Olsen's work "been mistakenly understood in terms of a particular literary heritage?" What heritage would that be? The passage says that many don't realize that she was influenced by that earlier tradition. The best answer is C.

6. According to the passage, which of the following is an accurate statement about the literary heritage referred to by the author?

   ⬯ It considers gender to be the determining factor in people's lives.
   ⬯ It has been the single most important source of Olsen's work.
   ⬯ It belongs to a political tradition that includes different strains of radical thought.
   ⬯ It provides the intellectual stimulus, but not the emotional force behind Olsen's work.
   ⬯ It owes more to socialist thought of the early twentieth century than to anarchist thought of that period.

6. **C**   It's C. We are asked here which is an accurate statement about the literary heritage mentioned by the author. It's a good idea to try and formulate an answer to the question BEFORE you look at the answers. This helps avoid the tricky nature of some of the answers. What does the author say about the tradition? It's radical political thought, from the early 1900s, and isn't valued by literary critics. Let's try to match some of that. A—Gender as the determining factor in people's lives? This is an answer that should offend our common sense. The passage itself cites class right next to where it cites gender, so gender isn't *the* determining factor. Choice B—single most important source? No, this is explicitly contradicted in lines 11–16. C—belongs to a tradition that includes radical political thought. We saw that and said that. Keep it. The emotional force mentioned in choice D isn't really discussed here at all. Choice E says that Olsen's writing owes more to one type of radical thought than another. The passage just says she was influenced by thought that included both socialist and anarchist thought. So C best matched what we had come up with in advance.

7. CONTRITION : PENITENT ::
- ○ caution : driver
- ○ speculation : philosopher
- ○ obstinacy : athlete
- ○ sanguinity : partner
- ○ wisdom : sage

7. **E** It's E. A good sentence is a PENITENT is characterized by CONTRITION. Since we reversed the order of the stem words, remember to do the same when we look at the answer choices. So, choice A gives us a DRIVER is characterized by CAUTION. You'd hope so, but you can't define the words in terms of each other. Strike A. A PHILOSOPHER is characterized by SPECULATION? Contemplation, perhaps, but not speculation. Out goes B. ATHLETE is characterized by OBSTINACY? All athletes are stubborn? No. Eliminate C. D—A PARTNER is characterized by SANGUINITY? If you don't know what sanguinity means, leave this choice in. If you do know the word, you should want to eliminate the choice. And E—a SAGE is characterized by WISDOM. Yup. E is the best choice whether or not you knew what sanguinity meant. At least we know E has a good relationship. If you also didn't know what sage meant, then just pick between D and E. But learn that vocab!

8. LUMINOUS:
- ○ distant
- ○ broken
- ○ dull
- ○ impractical
- ○ inconsiderate

8. **C** It's C. LUMINOUS has something to do with light, specifically "filled with light" or "giving off light." So we are looking for something that means "not giving off light" or "not being filled with light." Don't fall for A—DISTANT—which at a glance might be interesting. Make sure you look at all of the answers. That way we won't miss DULL, choice C, which is used here in the sense that something dull has no shine, or light coming off it.

9. Until about 1980, almost all economists assumed that economic growth is fueled by demand pressure at the level of the consumer; after the combination of high inflation and unemployment experienced in the 1990s, however, economists detected no _____ this previously _____ view of economic growth.

- ⬭ deviations from. .revolutionary
- ⬭ ground for. . ubiquitous
- ⬭ preference for. .unquestioned
- ⬭ forerunners of. .modern
- ⬭ disagreements with. .popular

9. **B** B is best. There is a colon separating the two parts of the sentence, suggesting the second part continues in the same direction as the first, but there's also a "however" in the second part, which tells us something changes direction there. So the first part is telling us about "until about 1980" and the second part about the 1990s. If the economists believed that "growth is fueled. . . consumer" before 1980, the "however" suggests their view was different in the 1990s. The second part of the sentence should say this. It has two blanks—let's try the second first, since it talks about the economists' view. We know "almost all economists presumed" it. Let's look for something for the second blank that means assumed by nearly all. A—"revolutionary" may sound good in the blank, but it doesn't mean something assumed by most. Dump A and don't look back. For B—how's "ubiquitous"—everywhere at once? Okay. Leave it. C—"unquestioned" is also much like assumed by all. D—"modern" isn't supported by the rest of the sentence. E—"popular" isn't terrible. So we still have B, C, and E. Time for the first blank. Before 1980 the economists held the view that economic growth blah, blah, blah. After the 1990s, *however*, that changed—and economists detected no ____ this view. Support for? Belief in? Look at the first words in our remaining choices. B—"ground for" is lovely. C—"preference for" is not as good. And E—"disagreements with"—is way off. So B is the choice that works best in each blank. Be sure to read the sentence through after you've picked an answer, making certain it makes sense.

10. TEMERITY : TREPIDATION ::
    ◯ oration : publicity
    ◯ strength : permanence
    ◯ superfluity : necessity
    ◯ axiom : confidence
    ◯ indemnity : security

10. **C** It's C. Here we've got a couple of harder words as the stem. A good sentence to make would be TEMERITY is lacking TREPIDATION. Then go through the answer choices. Choice A doesn't work and has no relationship to boot. Same with B. C—SUPERFLUITY is lacking NECESSITY? Okay. D—AXIOM is lacking CONFIDENCE? No, but if you didn't know what "axiom" meant, you should leave it. E—INDEMNITY is lacking SECURITY is no good; if anything, "indemnity" would be more like "security." So C is best. If you didn't know one of the stem words, you could work backwards from the answer choices, making sentences with each and trying out the sentences on the stem. Or if you didn't know either of the stem words, eliminate non-relationships like A, B, and D (if you knew "axiom"), and guess. It's not bad to get a question down to two or three answer choices when you don't even know what the stem words mean!

11. The treatment of waste water has been _____ through _____ the contaminants, but perhaps it may be more practical to neutralize the pollution in the water by adding certain chemical compounds that cause the harmful waste particles to become inert.

- ○ authorized. .screening
- ○ attempted. .tracing
- ○ initiated. .avoiding
- ○ simplified. .identifying
- ○ undertaken. .removing

11. **E**   E is correct. It's a two–blanker; do one at a time, whichever you like better first. In this case, it's probably the second that most people find easier to deal with. We have a "but" partway through the sentence, telling us that what comes before the "but" is different from what comes after it. What comes after it tells us that another way to neutralize pollution is to add something to the water that will combine with the pollutants and make them harmless. The treatment alluded to in the first part of the sentence must be different. Second blank? Treating waste water is probably done by taking out, removing, or getting rid of the pollutants. Look for something like that for the second blank. Choice A's "screening" isn't bad. Keep it and go on. B's "tracing" is nothing like getting rid of. Lose it. C— "avoiding"? Oh look, here comes the pollution! Let's avoid it! Don't think so. And choice D? "Identifying" contaminants is not a way of treating waste water. But E's "removing" is fine. Now to the other blank. This is a bit weird. Seems like the blank doesn't even need to be here, but it is and we need to fill it. The treatment has been accomplished, or done by taking out the icky stuff? Look for something like either of those words. We only have two choices remaining. Choice A is "authorized" and we are authorized to dump it because it isn't much like the words we want. E's "undertaken" means done or accomplished. We are happy with E.

12. COUNTERMAND : ORDER ::
- ◯ corroborate : document
- ◯ restate : claim
- ◯ reopen : investigation
- ◯ prejudice : testimony
- ◯ revoke : license

13. PREDISPOSED:
- ◯ directed
- ◯ stubborn
- ◯ disinclined
- ◯ nostalgic
- ◯ tranquil

12. **E** It's E. The sentence would be COUNTERMAND is to take back an ORDER. Try it out. A) CORROBORATE is to take back a DOCUMENT? No. Maybe to agree with it, or verify it? B) RESTATE is to take back a CLAIM? No. Let me restate that: No. C) REOPEN is to take back an INVESTIGATION? A bunch of hooey. D) PREJUDICE is to take back TESTIMONY? No, it stinks, and isn't related to boot. We boot it. E) REVOKE is to take back a LICENSE? You bet. Go with E.

13. **C** It's C. PREDISPOSED means likely to do something, as in "When I guess on a multiple choice test, I'm predisposed to picking C." So the opposite of this will be a word that will convey the idea of "unlikely to do something." Careful here. B and C may interest us. Make precise opposites for them if you're not sure which to pick. For B—STUBBORN—the opposite might be easy to lead, which is not that close to PREDISPOSED. For C—DISINCLINED—however, an opposite might be liking or likely to do something. Hello, sailor. See you at C.

14. Recent investigation into business and morality reveals the way in which apparently _____ business decisions, typically lost sight of in the ordinary operations of commerce, in reality _____ moral choices of major importance.

- ○ unimportant. .cloak
- ○ unreliable. .provoke
- ○ unparalleled. .symbolize
- ○ unprecedented. .allow
- ○ untrammeled. .impel

14. **A** It's A. When you see a two-blank sentence completion, do whichever blank first you feel you know more about. The first blank, which describes the business decisions, looks good. What else do we know about the business decisions? The sentence says they are "apparently" something, and that they are "typically lost sight of." These clues help us put something like "lost sight of" in the first blank. Now go to the first words in the answer choices, looking for something comparable to "lost sight of." In A, "unimportant" is okay. In B, "unreliable" is not like "lost sight of," so lose it. Choices C and D, "unparalleled" and "unprecedented," don't describe something easy to lose sight of—more the opposite, so eliminate them. And in E, "untrammeled" may be a word we don't know, so keep it. (If you do know it, you'll want to eliminate it.) On to the second blank. This blank describes the moral choices; what else do we know about them? The sentence changes direction, which we can see in the "apparently" this, but "in reality" that construction. So the decisions that are apparently no big deal, in reality are moral choices. Let's try something like "hide" for the second blank. In A, "cloak" is good; that means they're hidden. But in E, "impel" is not like "hide." So dump it. A is left, and if you knew "untrammeled," you'd pretty much be done after doing one blank. But make sure you check the other anyway. Why get a question wrong by being lazy?

15. SHEARING : WOOL ::
    ○ shredding : paper
    ○ breathing : wine
    ○ trimming : hedge
    ○ reaping : grain
    ○ weaving : silk

15. **D** It's D. Make a sentence for the stem, such as SHEARING is how you get WOOL. SHREDDING is how you get PAPER? No, so kill A. In B, is BREATHING how you get WINE? Um, no. TRIMMING is how you get HEDGE? No—bye, C. REAPING is how you get GRAIN? It works if you know the words, and if you don't know what reaping is, you leave it anyway. WEAVING is how you get SILK? Nope. So D is either the only one that worked, or the only one left. Because another good sentence would be SHEARING is the harvesting of WOOL, and yes, REAPING is the harvesting of GRAIN.

Column A | Column B

$$3 + k = 5 - k$$

1. k 2

- ○ the quantity in Column A is always greater
- ○ the quantity in Column B is always greater
- ○ the quantities are always equal
- ○ it cannot be determined from the information given

Column A | Column B

2. $\dfrac{7}{8} - \dfrac{1}{6}$ $\dfrac{3}{4} - \dfrac{1}{8}$

- ○ the quantity in Column A is always greater
- ○ the quantity in Column B is always greater
- ○ the quantities are always equal
- ○ it cannot be determined from the information given

1. **B** B is correct. We are given an equation with one variable, k. Solve it by adding k to each side, so the k on the right of the equal sign goes away. Now we have $3 + 2k = 5$. Subtract 3 from each side, and we end up with $2k = 2$. So $k = 1$. Now put that into the columns. Column A is 1, and Column B is 2. There's only that one value, so there's nothing else to do. Column B will always be larger, so B's the answer.

2. **A** It's A. Remember to write down A, B, C, D, and realize that there are only numbers here, no variables, so D is not a viable option. Lose it. Use the bowtie to subtract the fractions. In Column A, multiply 6 and 8 for a bottom number of 48. The top will be $42 - 8 = 34$. So, $\dfrac{34}{48}$. We can reduce this to $\dfrac{17}{24}$. In Column B, the bottom number is 32, and the top will be $24 - 4 = 20$. We reduce this to $\dfrac{5}{8}$. Now bowtie to compare the values for Columns A and B.

   Eight times 17 is 136 for Column A, and 24 times 5 is 120 for Column B. The Column A number is larger, and so is Column A.

3. $\dfrac{0.2(0.0002)}{0.002} =$

○ 0.02
○ 0.002
○ 0.0002
○ 0.00002
○ 0.000002

3. **A** It's A. Lots of numbers with decimals, all in a fraction. Yikes. We can't have decimals in a fraction, and the answer choices are all decimals, so we need to convert this to a decimal. In order to do this, we need first to multiply out the top: 0.2 (0.0002). The most important thing is to keep track of the number of decimal places. The product will be 4, with a total of five decimal places. So that's 0.00004 on top. Now we have:

$$\frac{0.00004}{0.002}$$

We still need to get rid of decimals. In order to turn this into a decimal with no fractions, we need to get rid of the bottom number. Do this by moving the decimal three places to the right on the bottom, and three places to the right on the top. It's all right to move the decimals as long as we do it the same number of places on the top and bottom. So now we have:

$$\frac{0.04}{2}$$

and can just do "long" division to get the decimal:

$$2\overline{)0.04} \quad = 0.02$$

So it's 0.02, choice A.

Column A   Column B

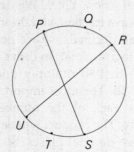

P, Q, R, S, T, and U are points on
the circle as shown.

4.   The length of   The length of
     arc *PQR*   arc *STU*

- ◯ the quantity in Column A is always greater
- ◯ the quantity in Column B is always greater
- ◯ the quantities are always equal
- ◯ it cannot be determined from the information given

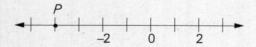

Note: Drawn to scale.

5.   If Q is a point to the right of 0 on the number line above and the distance
between P and Q is 11, then the coordinate of Q is

- ◯ −15
- ◯ 7
- ◯ 8
- ◯ 11
- ◯ 15

4. **D** The answer is D. The two arcs certainly look equal, don't they? But we are really not given information that tells us this is the case. While ETS's instructions tell us that points can be "assumed to be in the order shown," they don't tell us some things that would be useful in this problem. If we were told that PS and RU intersect at the center, then we'd know that the arcs were the same length. That point might be the center, or it might not, so the best answer here is D. In this case, we really don't have enough info.

5. **B** B is correct. The picture says it's drawn to scale, which might be useful. Each mark on the number line is 1, which means P is −4. If we are told that Q is to the right of the 0, and the distance between P and Q is 11, all you need to do is count it off, extending the line. Mark Q, and then just see what it's coordinate is by counting again from 0. It will be 7. That's B. Just read carefully, but you always do that anyway, right? Or you could have said that Q is the result of adding 11 to P, or −4 + 11, which is also 7.

Column A	Column B
6. The number of minutes in y weeks	The number of of hours in $60y$ weeks

○ the quantity in Column A is always greater

○ the quantity in Column B is always greater

○ the quantities are always equal

○ it cannot be determined from the information given

6. C It's C. This looks really frightening; we might have to do some serious multiplying here. Avoid it. Don't try and set up any proportions, either. It'll just make you nuts. Go with common sense and write it all down. In Column A, we want to know the number of minutes in y weeks. "Lots," is the answer, but let's get specific and plug in, say, $y = 2$. So, how many minutes in 2 weeks? That's 14 days. Each day is 24 hours, so that's really how many minutes in 14 times 24 hours. And if there are 60 minutes in each hour, then there are 14 times 24 times 60 minutes in those 2 weeks. Don't multiply this out. Leave it for now.

Do the same thing in Column B. Use the same value for y. So how many hours in 120 weeks? Well, each of those weeks is 7 days, so they really want to know how many hours there are in 7 times 120 days. And there's 24 hours in a day, so it's 7 times 120 times 24 hours in those 120 weeks. Don't multiply that out either. We can compare these without multiplying. How? Remember that we can do anything we want to each side in a quant comp question, as long as we do it to both sides. So now the columns are really this:

Column A	Column B
(14) (24) (60)	(120) (7) (24)

There's a 24 on each side; cancel them out. What we're really doing here is dividing each side by 24, but who cares—as long as we do it on both sides it's cool. Now:

Column A	Column B
(14) (60)	(120) (7)

And if we divide both sides by 60 now, Column A is just 14, and Column B is 7 times 2, which is also 14. They're equal. Dump A and B. We can do it again with a different y, and should, but guess what happens. Equal every time, so, it's C. Anytime you're getting what look like potentially big ugly numbers that will need to be multiplied out, see if you can deal with them by factoring or dividing both sides of a quant comp by the same number.

Column A | Column B

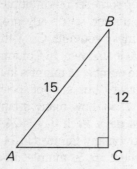

7. The area of △ABC   90

○ the quantity in Column A is always greater
○ the quantity in Column B is always greater
○ the quantities are always equal
○ it cannot be determined from the information given

7. **B** It's B. We need to find the area of the triangle, but we only know the height. Never fear—it's a right triangle. Guess what will get us that third side. The Pythagorean theorem—that $a^2 + b^2 = c^2$ thing. The a side and the b side are the legs, and c is the hypotenuse. We have two of the three, and can solve for the third. So, $12^2 + b^2 = 15^2$, or $144 + b^2 = 225$. Subtract 144 from each side. Now it's $b^2 = 81$. So $b = 9$, and we now have both the base and height of the triangle. For area, we do $\frac{1}{2}$ × the base times the height. So $\frac{1}{2}$ × 9 × 12 = 54. That's the area. And Column B is 90, which is larger. The answer is B.

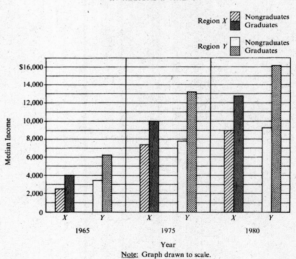

MEDIAN INCOME OF COLLEGE GRADUATES *VS.* NONGRADUATES IN REGIONS *X* AND *Y*

8. In 1975, the median income of nongraduates in Region X was approximately what fraction of the median income for graduates in Region X?

○ $\dfrac{3}{5}$

○ $\dfrac{5}{8}$

○ $\dfrac{3}{4}$

○ $\dfrac{10}{13}$

○ $\dfrac{4}{5}$

8. **C** It's C. To find the fraction, just put the first amount over the second. The median income of nongraduates in Region X in 1975 was approximately $7,500. The median income for graduates in Region X in the same year was $10,000. So it's $\dfrac{7500}{10000}$, which will reduce to $\dfrac{3}{4}$. Choice C.

9. $12m^2 - 8m - 64 =$
   ○ $4(3m + 8)(m - 2)$
   ○ $4(3m - 8)(m + 2)$
   ○ $4(3m - 2)(m + 8)$
   ○ $4m^2 - 64$
   ○ $4m - 64$

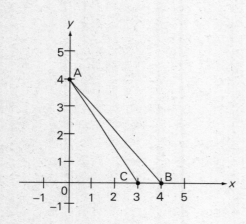

10. What is the area of triangle ABC in the figure above?

   ○ 2
   ○ 4
   ○ $4\sqrt{2}$
   ○ 7
   ○ 8

9. **B** This is B. It's meant to be a case of factoring, but we don't even really need to do it that way. We could plug in for m, picking a value like $m = 2$. In that case $12m^2 - 8m - 64$ would equal $12(4) - 8(2) - 64 = 48 - 16 - 64 = -32$. Then put $m = 2$ into each of the answer choices and see which gives you a value of -32:

A) $4(6 + 8)(2 - 2) = 0$. No.

B) $4(6 - 8)(2 + 2) = -8(4) = -32$. Okay!

C) $4(6 - 2)(10) = 160$. Nope.

D) $4(4) - 64 = -48$. Uh uh.

E) $8 - 64 = -56$. No.

Isn't plugging in splendid? When you see algebra-ish questions with variables in the answer choices, plug in!

10. **A** The answer is A. There are two ways to find the area of triangle ABC. We can find it directly using the area of a triangle formula: Area $= \frac{1}{2} bh$. In this case, the base of the triangle, segment CB, is 1. The height of the triangle, segment AO, is 4. Yes, that's right, the height can be outside the triangle, as long as it is drawn from the base to the vertex (corner) of the angle opposite the base. So now it's just $\frac{1}{2}$ times 1 times 4, which equals 2. Voila! An equally valid but slightly more laborious way to get the area would be to find the area of large triangle AOB: $\frac{1}{2}$ times 4 times 4 = 8, and then subtract the area of smaller triangle AOC. Triangle AOC's area would be $\frac{1}{2}$ times 3 times 4 = 6. Subtracting the area of the larger triangle from the smaller would leave us with 2. That's still A.

It takes Michael 3 hours at an average rate of 60 miles per hour to drive from his home to the state park. In contrast, it takes 2.5 hours at an average speed of 65 miles per hour for Michael to drive from his home to his lake house.

11. Michael's driving distance from his home to the state park | Michael's driving distance from his home to his lake house

- ○ the quantity in Column A is always greater
- ○ the quantity in Column B is always greater
- ○ the quantities are always equal
- ○ it cannot be determined from the information given

Column A   Column B

$$100 = \frac{10}{x}$$

12. x 10

- ○ the quantity in Column A is always greater
- ○ the quantity in Column B is always greater
- ○ the quantities are always equal
- ○ it cannot be determined from the information given

11. **A** The answer is A. To find the value of Column A, multiply Michael's rate of 60 mph by his time of three hours. That's 180 miles. From his home to his lake house (Column B), he travels for 2.5 hours at a speed of 65 miles. That will be a distance of 2.5 times 65 = 162.5 miles. So, Column A is larger. Notice that we didn't plug in; we were given the numbers, so we can't fool around with them, and so, we're done.

12. **B** It's B. Write A, B, C, D on that scratch paper! In order to compare x and 10, we need to solve for the value of x. Here we can cross-multiply to get $100x = 10$. Divide both sides by 100, and $x = 1/10$. So Column A is 1/10 and Column B is 10, so Column B is bigger. We're done here; there's only one value for x, and we have to use it.

13. What is the greatest possible value of integer n if $6^n < 10{,}000$?

○ 5
○ 6
○ 7
○ 8
○ 9

13. **A** It's A. Don't forget to look at the answers; they're part of the question. We've got a question that smells like algebra with numbers in the answer choices. What to do? Plug in the answer choices. Though we usually start with the middle value, we want 6 to the n power to be less than 10,000. So we're going to start with A, which will yield the smallest number. The last number that gives us a number under 10,000 is the answer. Yes, we have to do a bit of multiplication, but we can also do some approximating. Six times 6 is 36, and 6 times that is 216. That's 6 to the third power. But let's just call it 200 now. Six to the fourth power is 200 times 6 = 1,200. Six to the fifth power is 1,200 times 6, or 7,200. That's still under 10,000. But is 5 the greatest possible value of integer n? Try $n = 6$. That would be 7,200 times 6. More than 40,000. So A is the greatest integer value for n that makes this less than 10,000. Nice of ETS to suggest answers, isn't it?

Column A   Column B

$$x^2 + 8x = -7$$

14. x 0

○ the quantity in Column A is always greater
○ the quantity in Column B is always greater
○ the quantities are always equal
○ it cannot be determined from the information given

14. **B** The answer is B. Did you recognize this? It's a quadratic equation, meaning that one of the terms is a variable that's been squared. This also means that there are <u>two</u> values of x. First, we need to arrange the equation so it equals 0, so we need to add 7 to each side. Now we have $x^2 + 8x + 7 = 0$. To find the values of x here, we now need to factor this, or unF.O.I.L. it. So set up two sets of parentheses:

( ) ( )

Since the last sign in the expression is positive, both signs will be the same in each set of parentheses. And, since the other sign in the expression is positive, that means that each of the signs in the parentheses will be a plus sign. So now it's

(+) (+)

Each of the first terms needs to be x, because that's where the x squared comes from when we F.O.I.L.

$(x +)(x +)$

So now we play with the factors of the last term, the 7, and using trial and error, see what will give us the original expression when we F.O.I.L. Not a big problem here, because there's only one pair of factors for 7. So it will be

$(x + 7)(x + 1) = 0$

In order for this to equal 0, either the first set of parentheses or the second set of parentheses needs to equal 0. $x = -7$ is the value that will make the first equal 0, and $x = -1$ is the value that works for the second. So the solution is $x = -1$ or -7. Plug each of these values in and compare the columns. Column A can be -1, and if Column B is 0, then Column B is larger in this case. And if Column A is -7, Column B is still 0, and is still larger. So no matter what, Column B is still larger, giving us B as the answer.

15. In the equation $ax + b = 26$, x is a constant. If $a = 3$ when $b = 5$, what is the value of b when $a = 5$?

○ −11
○ −9
○ 3
○ 7
○ 21

15. **B** B is correct. X is a constant, and all that means is that it stands for a number—the *same number* no matter what the values of the other variables are. We can figure out the value of x with the first set of a and b that we're given. Put in $a = 3$ and $b = 5$, and we have $3x + 5 = 26$. Now we do a little solving. Subtract 5 from each side, and it's $3x = 21$, so $x = 7$. Always. No matter what a and b are later. And later $a = 5$, and we want to know the value of b. We can put $a = 5$, and $x = 7$ into the original equation, and solve for b. That would be $5(7) + b = 26$. $35 + b = 26$, so $b = -9$. And that's choice B.

MEDIUM ANALYTIC BIN EXPLANATIONS

1. Environmental noise, produced by cars, planes, heavy machinery, and small appliances, has been shown to cause frustration, stress, and permanent hearing loss. A government health agency has recommended that people limit their exposure to noise to 8 hours of 90-decibel noise or 4 hours of 95-decibel noise. Many health care professionals, however, feel that even these limits do not adequately protect the public from the ill effects of noise pollution.

   Which of the following, if true, would most support the health care professionals' view as described above?

   ○ The numbers of 8 and 4 hours include cumulative short-term exposure to noise such as that experienced during a commute, while listening to music, or as a result of sudden or unexpected sounds.
   ○ Many manufacturers are capable of producing products that run more quietly, but public demand for these products is low.
   ○ White noise machines produce sound that covers or filters disruptive noises.
   ○ The government has neglected efforts to mandate more stringent standards for environmental noise.
   ○ Noise of less than 90 decibels can disrupt sleep patterns and increase hypertension, while brief exposure to noise above 100 decibels can cause permanent hearing trauma.

1. **E** It's E. We want to support the health care professionals' claim that these noise limits do not give the public adequate protection from noise pollution. We support by strengthening; we need to find an answer that says these limits are not sufficient. Choice A just tells us more about what the recommended limits include. B is out of scope—we don't care about products. C doesn't address the limits. D doesn't strengthen the health professionals' claims. It just picks on the government and is thereby out of scope. E tells us that even the recommended limits may not be adequate. An 85-decibel noise, for example, can disturb sleep patterns, says answer E. If this is true, then 4 hours of exposure to such noise might be considered harmful by the health professionals in question.

2. Ironically, those companies that require prospective employees to undergo stringent drug testing before being hired have a higher incidence of dismissals attributed to drug use by employees than do companies that administer no drug testing at all.

Which of the following, if true, helps to explain the apparent paradox in the statement above?

- ○ In most areas of business, more companies choose not to administer drug tests than choose to do so.
- ○ The decision of companies not to test prospective employees for drug use is a reflection of their belief that employees are unlikely to engage in drug use.
- ○ Companies that administer drug tests often contract work to companies that do not require drug testing.
- ○ The number of dismissals attributed to drug use has no relationship to the number of employees at the company.
- ○ Companies that are highly concerned with drug use by employees are more likely to monitor employees' behavior and attribute that behavior to drug use.

2. **E** This is E. It's a "resolve the paradox" question. So, something seemingly weird happens; the companies that do the drug testing when hiring employees also end up firing the most employees for drug use. How could that happen if they've screened them!?! We need to look for a choice that allows the two situations to coexist. Choice A says that more companies don't test for drugs than do. Who cares? This resolves nothing. Choice B talks about the companies that don't test. Our paradox involves those that do—out of scope. Choice C—the issue here is contracting. We care about actual employees—out of scope. Choice D—that's all well and good, and we don't care. Ahh, but E! Choice E does the job—tells us the same companies that are testing at hiring KEEP testing, or otherwise monitor employees' behavior, and attribute problems to drugs. Paranoid weasels. It's E.

Questions 3–5

At an amusement resort, the different pavilions—the Zoo, the Rides, and the Food Area—are arranged in a circle, and can be reached by tram. The tram goes to the Zoo and stops at the Apes, the Reptiles, the Big Cats, and the Zebras, in that order. Then it goes to the Rides and stops at the Roller Coaster, the Water Ride, and the Ferris Wheel, in that order. Then it goes to the Snack Bar, and on to the Apes, to repeat the circle. There is also a double-decker bus which travels back and forth between the Big Cats and the Snack Bar, and another double-decker bus which travels back and forth between the Water Ride and the Snack Bar. The tram and the double-decker buses are the only means of transportation available at the resort.

3–5 Okay, this is a map game. Spend time making the map before looking at any of the questions. We symbolize and make our diagram at the same time here. Just be ready with the eraser to make adjustments. Don't use double-headed arrows for routes that go both ways, but rather two arrows. It's easier to see at a glance that the route is two-way.

The map should look something like this:

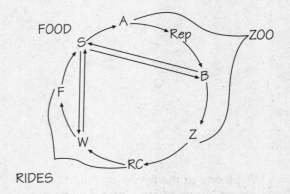

Question time!

3. In order to get from the Snack Bar to the Zebras while making as few stops as possible, one must take the
   - ⬭ tram only
   - ⬭ double-decker bus to the Zoo only
   - ⬭ tram, and then the double-decker bus to the Zoo
   - ⬭ double-decker bus to the Zoo, and then the tram
   - ⬭ double-decker bus to the Rides, and then the tram

4. Which one of the following could be the second intermediate stop for someone travelling from the Reptiles to the Ferris Wheel?
   - ⬭ Big Cats
   - ⬭ Ferris Wheel
   - ⬭ Roller Coaster
   - ⬭ Snack Bar
   - ⬭ Water Ride

3. **D** The answer is D. We want to make as few stops as possible. We could look at the map to see what looks like it might do that, or try the answers and count the number of stops. We need to make sure that when counting the stops that we are consistent—count the in-between stops only, or the origin, intermediate stops, and destination, but do it the same way every time. From the Snack Bar to the Zebras, we can take the bus to Big Cats, then the tram to the Zebras—one intermediate stop. Since there is no way to travel directly from the Snack Bar to Zebras, we will be hard pressed to beat one stop. So, that was the bus and then the tram. Match it in the answer choices. We can dump all but D and E. Where do we take the bus to? The Big Cats in the Zoo, so that's D. Bingo.

4. **D** It's D again. We're going from the Reptiles to the Ferris Wheel. There are a couple of ways to do it, and we are being asked for the SECOND INTERMEDIATE STOP. We could do it all on the tram—Reptiles, Big Cats, Zebras, Roller Coaster, Water Ride, Ferris Wheel. In that case the second intermediate stop would be Zebras. Which isn't there. Well, that would be nice of them, wouldn't it? What else can we try? We could also do the dizzying Reptiles, Big Cats (via tram), Snack Bar (via bus), Water Ride (via the other bus), Ferris Wheel (via tram again). In this case, the second intermediate stop would be the Snack Bar, which is choice D. Good thing, too; with all that schlepping around, we could use a bite to eat.

5. Using both a double-decker bus and the tram, which one of the following trips can be made with the fewest stops?

○ The Reptiles to the Big Cats
○ The Snack Bar to the Reptiles
○ The Snack Bar to the Water Ride
○ The Snack Bar to the Zebras
○ The Zebras to the Roller Coaster

5. **D** D again. Here we just need to count the stops, remembering that the question says to use both a double-decker bus and the tram. The fewest stops is what we need. Choice A—Reptiles to Big Cats: to do this with the fewest stops, we'd use only the tram, not both. And to do it by using both would require two intermediate stops (once at the Big Cats after a train ride, and once at the Snack Bar via the bus). Choice B, Snack Bar to Reptiles, also would either use the tram only, or become incredibly convoluted. Ditch it. C—Snack Bar to Water Ride? Uses a bus only, or is fairly complicated: Snack Bar to Big Cats (bus), Zebras (tram), Roller Coaster (tram), Water Ride (tram). That would be three intermediate stops, which is still more than A. Two intermediate stops is our number to beat. Choice D, Snack Bar to Zebras, could go Snack Bar to Big Cats (bus), Zebras (tram). Ooh—that's one intermediate stop. Looks good. Since we have to use both kinds of transportation, we must have at least one stop, so it's unlikely that any other choice can beat that! Look at E— Zebras to Roller Coaster. The most direct route is by tram only, with no intermediate stops, but that's not what we want. D is best.

A book-of-the-month club is offering a special deal for new members. Over a one-year period, January to December, the club will send a free book each month for nine months of the year. There will be three months in which no free books are sent. The books—R, S, T, U, V, W, X, Y, and Z—fall into three categories: three are biographies, two are art books, and four are novels.

Books of two different categories may not be sent in consecutive months.

A month in which no book is sent cannot separate months in which books of the same category are sent.

S and U are in different categories.

U, V, and W are all in the same category.

A book is never sent in May.

R and X are biographies.

Y is an art book.

6–8 Another assignment game. We are assigning nine books and three empty spaces to twelve months. The months, which have a natural order, should be on the top of the diagram, and the books or spaces are assigned to them. The books are R, S, T, U, V, W, X, Y, and Z, and let's call the spaces –, –, and –:

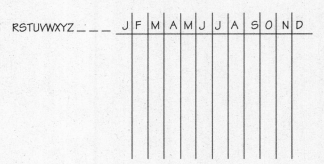

The books are known by letters, but each is also biography, art, or novel. Subscripts might be a good way to deal with this. And there are some books we don't have identified by type. All of this must be kept track of. We are told there are three biographies, two art books, and four novels. And we are told some things about which books are which.

R and X are both bios, Y is an art book, and U, V, and W are all in the same category, so we can deduce that they must be novels, or else there would be too many of one of the other types of books. And since S and U are different types of books, we know S must be either art or bio. The books we don't know about are T and Z. We might also notice that since books of different categories can't be in consecutive months, and books of the same type can't be separated by empty months, the books must be sent in groups—the art books in two consecutive months, the novels in four consecutive months, and the bios in three consecutive months—and that these groups must be separated by empty months. Whew. Thinking about this now will save us trouble later.

So, here's what we have:

RSTUVWXYZ _ _ _

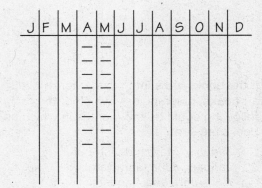

```
bbb

aa

nnnn

S ≠ U

Rb Xb Ya Un Vn Wn

Sa/b
```

```
  J F M A M J J A S O N D
            —
            —
            —
            —
            —
            —
            —
```

6. If no book is sent in April, which one of the following must be true?

- ○ No book is sent in October.
- ○ The books are sent in this order: biographies, art books, novels.
- ○ The book sent in March is a biography.
- ○ The book sent in January is an art book.
- ○ The book sent in December is a novel.

6. **C** The answer to question 6 is C. No book is sent in April, and we can put that in the diagram:

```
J F M A M J J A S O N D
    — —
    — —
    — —
    — —
    — —
    — —
    — —
```

So what must happen? In order to keep the groups separate, we must have the bios in the first three months. Then we can have the art books, an empty month, and then the novels. Or we could have novels, empty month, art books. Since we are not being asked about individual books, only types of books, let's just skip assigning individual books for now. Here's what we can do:

⑥

J	F	M	A	M	J	J	A	S	O	N	D
b	b	b	—	—	n	n	n	—	a	a	
b	b	b	—	—	a	a	—	n	n	n	

Now we can see what the answers offer. A doesn't have to be true, nor does B. It is true that the March book is a biography in either case. We like C. D isn't going to be true because the first three months will be bios. And E doesn't have to be true, although it can. Best answer to this *must* question is C.

7. If the books are sent in this order—novels, art books, biographies—which of the following could be the months in which no books are sent?

- ◯ January, May, and October
- ◯ January, June, and October
- ◯ April, July, and August
- ◯ May, August, and December
- ◯ May, September, and October

7. **D** It's D. If we send the books in that order, novels must be January, February, March, and April. So, eliminate choices A and B. The rest of the year has some flexibility, but we also know that May is an empty month. This allows us to eliminate C, since it doesn't include May. How can we finish the year? They don't ask us about specific books, so let's not worry about them. It's a "could" question, so let's look at the remaining two answers and try to prove one possible. For D, the diagram would look like this:

J	F	M	A	M	J	J	A	S	O	N	D
n	n	n	n	—	a	a	—	b	b	b	—

Is it okay? Sure, and we're done. We don't have to check E if we know D is possible.

8. All of the following are months in which an art book can be sent EXCEPT
- ○ January
- ○ June
- ○ August
- ○ November
- ○ December

8. **A** The answer is A. We want to know which month we can't send an art book in. Eliminate D and E, because we sent art books in November and December in question 6, and eliminate B, since we sent one in June in question 7. That leaves us with January or August. Try them. If we send one in January (choice A), then we send the second art book in February. That leaves March and April empty, along with May. We couldn't fit the block of three bios or the block of four novels in March and April, especially since we need to separate the blocks with empty months. If we made March, April, and May all empty, no empty months would be left to separate bios and novels later in the year. January is our month.

Dale is taking six classes at school—geography, history, journalism, kinetics, linguistics, and math. She gets a different grade in each class. The possible grades are, from highest to lowest, A, B, C, D, E, and F. The following information is known about the grades she receives:

Her grade in geography is higher than her grade in linguistics.

She receives a B in journalism.

Her grade in kinetics is either exactly one grade higher or exactly one grade lower than her grade in history.

9–12　Yes, that's right, another assignment game. Six classes and six different grades. This belongs on a grid, with grades (which have a natural order) on top, to which we will assign classes. Here's the diagram and the clues so far:

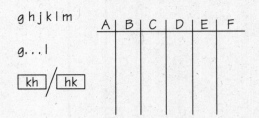

There are a few deductions to make. If Dale's grade in geography is higher than her grade in linguistics, she can't get an A in linguistics and can't get an F in geography. And if her grades in history and kinetics are consecutive, *and* she has a B in journalism, there's no room for kinetics or history to be an A, since B is already taken up. So we have this:

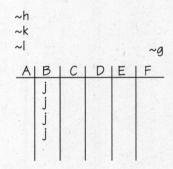

Now it's time to kill and eat.

9. If Dale receives a D in history, which of the following is the highest grade she can receive in linguistics?

○ A
○ B
○ C
○ E
○ F

9. **C** It's C. If she gets a D in history, her grade for kinetics has to be either a C or an E. Let's entertain both possibilities, and see how high a grade we can get her in linguistics. We deduced she can't get an A, and journalism is hogging up B, so we can eliminate those answers. Can she get a C in linguistics? Give it to her. That forces kinetics under E, geography under A, and math under F.

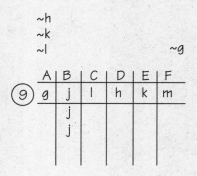

So she can get a C in linguistics, and that's the highest grade she can get in that subject. Choice C.

10. If Dale receives an E in math, which of the following is the grade she must receive in geography?

○ A
○ B
○ C
○ D
○ F

10. **A** A is correct. Work with blocks first when placing things in the chart—they are harder to fit, and the possibilities are limited. If she gets an E in math, that only leaves us one place to put the hk/kh block—in C and D. It doesn't matter which order we do history and kinetics in, but it only leaves two other open spaces—the A and the F. Geography can't be her lowest grade, so she must again get an A in geography. Linguistics ends up under F, but we actually don't need that, since the question is about geography:

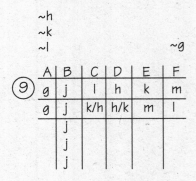

So that's A.

11. If Dale receives a D in kinetics, which of the following is the lowest grade she can receive in geography?

- ○ A
- ○ B
- ○ C
- ○ E
- ○ F

11. **D** It's choice D. Before we do anything else, let's eliminate choice E; we've already deduced that she can't get an F in geography. Okay, we are looking for Dale's lowest possible grade in geography, so let's try giving her the next lowest available grade for geography—the E. If she gets a D in kinetics, her history grade must be either a C or E. Let's try it in C, since we're trying to put geography in E. So, if she gets an E for geography, then the F is for linguistics. That means the A must be in math:

	A	B	C	D	E	F
⑨	g	j	l	h	k	m
⑩	g	j	k/h	h/k	m	l
⑪	m	j	h	k	g	l

~h
~k
~l
~g

This is fine. So, an E is the lowest grade she can get in geography, which is choice D. We don't have to try anything else.

12. In which of the following classes can Dale receive an A?

- ○ History
- ○ Journalism
- ○ Kinetics
- ○ Linguistics
- ○ Math

12.   **E**   E is correct. If you've got past setups, use them. We have some complete setups for the last few questions. What subjects do they have as As? Geography and math. Geography isn't here, but math is. That's E. Yes, we're done. Don't forget that your previous work in games can be helpful in future questions. Make sure that the set-ups you have on paper are legit, and cross out any that don't work, so you don't reuse them by accident. If we didn't use our past setups here, we'd just have more work to do, trying out all of the answers.

13. The coach of one of the league's best teams is amused by all of the publicity his coaching methods have received. He believes that coaches receive too much credit for winning games and claims that "fans assume too easily that coaches are geniuses when a team wins and morons when a team loses."

According to the coach's statement, it can be inferred that he believes which one of the following to be true?

- ○ A winning coach should attempt to manipulate the press.
- ○ No coach can justifiably be called a genius.
- ○ His own coaching methods would most likely not succeed with other teams.
- ○ Coaches are less important during a losing streak than they are when a team is winning.
- ○ The success of a team cannot be completely determined by its coach.

13.   **E**   The answer is E. This modest coach is saying that coaches get too much credit. On this inference question, we need to find the answer that we KNOW is true from the coach's statements. Choice A is completely out of scope; there is absolutely nothing in this argument about manipulation. In B, he's not saying that no coach is a genius, he's saying that coaches are assumed to be geniuses too easily by the fans. In C, other teams are outside the scope, and he's not talking about his methods. In D, no comparison is made between the necessity for coaches during a winning streak or a losing streak. That leaves us with E, which is a nice paraphrase of "coaches get too much credit."

14. A recent medical study found that women who exercised more than three hours per week were more likely than other women to have high levels of a certain chemical compound in their blood. High levels of this compound can be one of the first warning signs of skin cancer, which is almost always caused by excessive exposure of the skin to sunlight.

Which one of the following, if true, would cast doubt on the study's implication that exercising more than three hours per week increases the odds of contracting skin cancer?

- ◯ Lack of exercise increases the rate of absorption of many dangerous chemical compounds into the blood stream.
- ◯ Exercise increases the rate of blood flow through the circulatory system, thereby increasing the rate at which contaminants spread through the body.
- ◯ The most common form of exercise among the women in this study was swimming in an indoor pool.
- ◯ Women contract skin cancer at a significantly higher rate than men do.
- ◯ Women who exercised more than three hours per week also spent more time outdoors than did women who exercised fewer than three hours per week.

14. **E** The answer is E. The argument is implying some causal link between exercising more than three hours per week and contracting skin cancer. We need to weaken this by coming up with an alternate cause for the skin cancer. In A, lack of exercise is outside the scope, since this argument is about women who do exercise. In B, how fast contaminants spread isn't relevant to the argument. In C, just because the women were exercising indoors, doesn't mean they weren't spending other time outdoors, where they could contract skin cancer. In D, we don't care about women in general, we only care about the women in this study. That leaves us with E, which gives us a nice alternate cause for the skin cancer; the women who exercise more than three hours per week (the ones we care about) ALSO spend more time outdoors. So maybe it's the time they spend outdoors that's causing the skin cancer, and NOT just the exercising. A classic weakener. We like it.

15. To many environmentalists, the extinction of plants — accompanied by the increasing genetic uniformity of species of food crops — is the single most serious environmental problem. Something must be done to prevent the loss of wild food plants or no-longer-cultivated food plants. Otherwise, the lack of genetic food diversity could allow a significant portion of a major crop to be destroyed overnight. In 1970, for example, southern leaf blight destroyed approximately 20 percent of the United States corn crop, leaving very few varieties of corn unaffected in the areas over which the disease spread.

Which of the following can be inferred from the passage above?

- ○ Susceptibility to certain plant diseases is genetically determined.
- ○ Eighty percent of the corn grown in the United States is resistant to southern leaf blight.
- ○ The extinction of wild food plants can in almost every case be traced to destructive plant diseases.
- ○ Plant breeders should focus on developing plants that are resistant to plant disease.
- ○ Corn is the only food crop threatened by southern leaf blight.

15. **A** The answer is A. Okay, we need to do something to prevent the loss of food plants. And we need to find an answer that we KNOW is TRUE from the information given. Let's check out the answers. In A, do we know that susceptibility to certain plant diseases is genetically determined? Yes, because the argument tells us that the lack of genetic food diversity could allow a significant portion of a major crop to be destroyed overnight. In B, don't let that 20 percent figure throw you off. Just because 20 percent of the U.S. corn crop was destroyed in 1970, doesn't mean that 80 percent is resistant now. In C, do we know that it can be traced to plant diseases in ALMOST EVERY CASE? Sounds extreme, doesn't it? In D, do we know anything about what plant breeders do? Nope. In E, isn't it extreme to say that corn is the ONLY plant affected by southern leaf blight? It was just an example, but we don't know it's the ONLY one. That leaves A.

HARD VERBAL BIN EXPLANATIONS

1. FLAG:

   ○ break down
   ○ regain energy
   ○ resume course
   ○ push forward
   ○ show pride

1. **B** The answer is B. FLAG is not being used as a noun here; we can see this by looking at the answer choices, which are verbs. Okay, so we know flag is a verb here. We may have heard it used as in "to mark" something, or "flag down" a taxicab. But these meanings don't have clear opposites. Here FLAG means to become worn down, to lose energy. B is the best opposite of that.

2. SYNOPSIS : CONDENSED ::

   ○ digression : repeated
   ○ mystery : enticing
   ○ excursion : pleasant
   ○ antiquity : forgotten
   ○ plagiarism : pirated

2. **E** E is the answer. SYNOPSIS is something that's CONDENSED. Choice A? Digressions are wanderings, not repetitions. Eliminate it. B and C are not good relationships. D—ANTIQUITY isn't something FORGOTTEN, just old. Dump D. Hope it's E! PLAGIARISM is something that's PIRATED? Bingo. Not that any of us would know from first-hand experience.

3. To examine the _____ of importing concepts from one discipline to enhance another, merely look at the degree to which words from the first may, without distortion, be _____ the second.

- ○ danger. .meaningless for
- ○ popularity. .created within
- ○ etiquette. .revitalized by
- ○ pace. .supplanted by
- ○ validity. .employed by

3. **E** This is E. Which blank first? Maybe the second, but you can do whichever you feel more comfortable with. For the second blank, the phrase "from one discipline to enhance another" is a helpful clue. That's what will happen in the second part of the sentence. "Words from the first may" be *used to enhance* the second? Look for something like "used to enhance." It doesn't matter that it's not just one word, or more words than there are in the answer choices. We just want the meaning to be similar. So A stinks, based on this second blank. B isn't much good either. C—"revitalized by" isn't at all bad; this is something like used to enhance. D—"supplanted by" isn't terrible either; it would be something like replace. And E—"employed by" would also be a lot like replaced. So we still have C, D, and E going into the other blank. How about something like "possibility" for the first blank? C—"etiquette"? Nonsense. D—"pace"—is garbage. That leaves E—"validity," which isn't at all bad. Sometimes we need to settle for the best of a so-so bunch.

4. CONSUMMATE:
   ○ refuse
   ○ undermine
   ○ satiate
   ○ abrogate
   ○ suspect

4. **D** It's D. CONSUMMATE is used as more than one part of speech. Here it's used as a verb. You may not know exactly what it means, but there's a phrase that you've probably heard that uses it: to consummate a marriage. What does that mean? Really, to make it official, partners must engage in traditional wedding night/honeymoon activity. The opposite of this is not to not have sex, but rather to declare not official, to cancel, declare null and void. And whatever the answer is, it should be something that can be done to a marriage. A—REFUSE? Well, you could do this to a marriage, but it doesn't really sound great, and there are four more answers to look at. Choice B—UNDERMINE? One could certainly do this to a marriage, and it has a negative connotation, whereas if anything, the stem is positive. So, not bad. C—SATIATE. Well. We'll just skip the jokes, but somebody might make the association. Anyway, it can't really be done to a marriage, and it's not negative. D—ABROGATE is the answer choice that we're least likely to know, which makes it immediately suspect. We can't get rid of it if we don't know the word. E—SUSPECT is very weird with marriage, and what's the clear opposite of suspect, to "not suspect"? So we have A, B, and D. And we really wish we had learned more words. We can take a shot at this point, but it is choice D—ABROGATE—that is the correct opposite. It means to void, cancel, declare null and void.

5. ADMONISH : COUNSEL ::
   ○ mollify : intensity
   ○ necessitate : generosity
   ○ enervate : vitality
   ○ manufacture : opinion
   ○ remunerate : payment

5. **E** It's E. If you know the stem words, a good sentence is ADMONISH is to provide COUNSEL. A) MOLLIFY is to provide INTENSITY? No, it's to lessen it. B) totally non-related. C) ENERVATE is to provide VITALITY? No, it's to deprive of it. So lose it. D) not related. E) REMUNERATE is to provide PAYMENT? Yes indeed. And if you don't know most of these words, good counsel would be to study vocabulary!

Our visual perception depends on the reception of energy reflecting or radiating from that which we wish to perceive. If our eye could receive and measure
5 infinitely delicate sense-data, we could perceive the world with infinite precision. The natural limits of our eyes have, of course, been extended by mechanical instruments; telescopes and microscopes,
10 for example, expand our capabilities greatly. There is, however, an ultimate limit beyond which no instrument can take us; this limit is imposed by our inability to receive sense-data smaller than those
15 conveyed by an individual quantum of energy. Since these quanta are believed to be indivisible packages of energy and so cannot be further refined, we reach a point beyond which further resolution of the
20 world is not possible. It is like a drawing a child might make by sticking indivisible discs of color onto a canvas.

We might think that we could avoid this limitation by using quanta with extremely
25 long wavelengths; such quanta would be sufficiently sensitive to convey extremely delicate sense-data. And these quanta would be useful, as long as we only wanted to measure energy, but a
30 completely accurate perception of the world will depend also on the exact measurement of the lengths and positions of what we wish to perceive. For this, quanta of extremely long wavelengths are
35 useless. To measure a length accurately to within a millionth of an inch, we must have a measure graduated in millionths of an inch; a yardstick graduated in inches is useless. Quanta with a wavelength of one
40 inch would be, in a sense, measures that are graduated in inches. Quanta of extremely long wavelengths are useless in measuring anything except extremely large dimensions.

45 Despite these difficulties, quanta have important theoretical implications for physics. It used to be supposed that, in the observation of nature, the universe could be divided into two distinct parts, a
50 perceiving subject and a perceived object. In physics, subject and object were

supposed to be entirely distinct, so that a description of any part of the universe would be independent of the observer. The quantum theory, however, suggests otherwise, for every observation involves the passage of a complete quantum from the object to the subject, and it now appears that this passage constitutes an important coupling between observer and observed. We can no longer make a sharp division between the two in an effort to observe nature objectively. Such an attempt at objectivity would distort the crucial interrelationship of observer and observed as parts of a single whole. But, even for scientists, it is only in the world of atoms that this new development makes any appreciable difference in the explanation of observations.

6–7   Don't forget to find the main idea before doing the questions. This passage is about quanta and the limits of visual perception.

6. The author employs the metaphor of a child's drawing (lines 20–22) mainly to

- ⭕ highlight the eventual limitation of the resolution of sense-data using quanta
- ⭕ reveal the sense of frustration scientists feel when confronted by the limits of accurate measurement
- ⭕ reply to the criticisms of certain skeptics who hold the view that any mechanical extensions of perception necessarily introduce distortions of the sense-data
- ⭕ explain the relationships between discs of color and units of energy
- ⭕ discredit those scientists who argue that precise perception of the world is possible through the use of quanta

6. **A** The answer is A. The question sends us to lines 20–22; make sure to read around that as well, since the answer is probably not completely located in the lines they mention. And it's not. The metaphor is used to describe the "limitation" (line 24) of our perception. Our visual resolution is only so good. A child sticking discs of color onto a piece of paper is not going to be able to create a work of art with great detail, because all he has are these little circles to use. Similarly, our perception is limited to the level of quanta, our own little dots. We need to try to come up with this stuff on our own before looking at the answers. This way we need only match our already correct answer to the junk ETS throws at us. Which answer is best? Choice A says that the metaphor is used to highlight limitations of perception. Sounds good. B—Oh yes, scientists are frustrated like little kids playing with discs of color. Not likely. C has nothing to do with the metaphor. D is no good. We're talking metaphor here, and choice D suggests that there is a literal relationship between quanta and discs of color. Choice E? Again, this is not what the metaphor is used for. The passage never says that there's anybody who thinks that we can have precise perception of the world and who understands quanta. A is indeed best.

7. According to the passage, previous theories in theoretical physics differed from quantum theory in that these theories assumed that

- ○ the natural limits of human perception cannot be overcome by using quanta of extremely long wavelengths
- ○ the observer and the object perceived can be separately identified
- ○ the use of mechanical instruments is more useful to physics than theoretical speculation
- ○ the interrelationship between the perceiver and perceived makes no difference in observations of the world of atoms
- ○ scientific method is independent of the actual practices of physicists

7. **B** The answer is B. How do the previous theories in physics differ from quantum theory? Let's look for where previous theories are discussed. It shows up around lines 47–48, right near the "however,"—a trigger word that marks the comparison. The passage says that in physics, object and observer were thought to be separate; however, quantum theory is different. And there it is. Previous theories separated the two; let's find it. Choice A doesn't work; it would be quanta of extremely *short* wavelengths, anyway. B is lovely, ain't it? C goes against common sense. Not many scientists would ever have wanted to go on record as saying that theoretical speculation isn't particularly useful. D has two problems: The previous theory or theories didn't even think there was a relationship between the observer and the observed, and, limiting things to the world of atoms is not what goes on. E is silly. Physicists don't use the scientific method, and it's not relevant to physics? Guess that's why they call it the scientific method. So we like B.

8. HYPERBOLE:

- ◯ dietary supplement
- ◯ strange sensation
- ◯ direct route
- ◯ employee
- ◯ understatement

9. Just as midwifery was for hundreds of years _____ practice, something that women retained control over for themselves, so too the increasingly independent role of the midwife in the process of childbirth is a _____ domination by institutional medicine.

- ◯ a personal. .reaction of
- ◯ a controversial. .tolerance of
- ◯ an autonomous. .liberation from
- ◯ a communal. .celebration of
- ◯ a dangerous. .protection from

8. **E** E is correct. Here's a word you might remember from high school English classes. HYPERBOLE means exaggeration. The opposite of that would be "not exaggerating," or "understating." And whaddya know—there's choice E—UNDERSTATEMENT. Even if we didn't remember the meaning of HYPERBOLE, we can eliminate at least a couple of answers. Choices A and D have no clear opposites. What the heck is the opposite of an employee? Don't forget that elimination is just as good a way to get close to the correct answer as is actually knowing the word. Another thing we might have made use of here is the prefix "hyper," which suggests a lot of something, or too much of it. The opposite should then be something that is a little of something— like UNDERSTATEMENT.

9. **C** It's C. There's an excellent clue for the first blank, which describes what kind of practice midwifery is. We're told it's "something that women retained control over for themselves." This is in the sentence to tell us to put something very much like it in the first blank. Do any of the first words mean anything like "something. . . retained control over themselves"? Choice A has "a personal"—not bad. Choice B—"a controversial"—is not very good. C—"an autonomous" is excellent. "A communal"— choice D, isn't awful. But E—"a dangerous" is. So we have A, C, and D. Next blank. The "independent role of the midwife. . . is a ____ domination by institutional medicine." An exception to? Choice A says "reaction of," but this would be a "reaction of domination," which doesn't make much sense. We would prefer something like reaction against, which this isn't, so lose it. On to C. "Liberation from" is a lot like exception to. We like it. Be sure to look at D, though. "Celebration of"? Don't think so. So C it is, with its lovely definition of autonomous as retaining control over something for themselves.

10. EPIDEMIOLOGY : DISEASE ::
    ○ radiology : fracture
    ○ paleontology : behavior
    ○ epistemology : knowledge
    ○ ichthyology : religion
    ○ numerology : formulas

10. **C** It's C. Once again process of elimination will save the day. EPIDEMIOLOGY is the study of DISEASE. How's A? That's right, it stinks. B? If you think PALEONTOLOGY is the study of BEHAVIOR, go see *Jurassic Park*. C—EPISTEMOLOGY is the study of KNOWLEDGE. Either we know that it is, or we don't know the word. Either way, it's a keeper. D—ICHTHYOLOGY is the study of RELIGION? Well, we might not know what ICHTHYOLOGY is, but we'd likely know that it wasn't the study of religion; that would probably be a word we were more familiar with. If you're not sure, keep it. E—NUMEROLOGY is the study of FORMULAS? Yikes. It's like horoscopes; we can find it on the back page of *Cosmopolitan* magazine. C is the best answer. Incidentally, ICHTHYOLOGY is the study of fish. Ich!

11. Modernity appears to be particularly _____ mistaken notions, perhaps because in breaking free from the fetters of convention, the result is that we are very likely to be _____ unexamined hypotheses and unprepared actions.

- ◯ immune to. .accepting of
- ◯ contrary to. .reliant on
- ◯ fraught with. .susceptible to
- ◯ disposed of. .suspicious of
- ◯ insensitive to. .liberated from

11. **C** It's C. Here the two parts of the sentence are continuous, because of the "because" acting as a trigger. It's probably easier to deal with the first blank first. The "mistaken notions" in the first part of the sentence are similar to the "unexamined hypotheses" and "unprepared actions" of the second part. And modernity and "breaking free . . . of convention" also seem to be linked. So, if that's what's going on when we are playing around with modernity, it is probably full of, connected to, or leading to those mistaken notions. Look for something like that in the first words. Choices A, B, and E are all very much not like connected to. Lose them. C's "fraught with" is just a fancy schmancy way of saying full of, and "disposed of,"—choice D,—just really isn't clearly like linked or different from it. Let's let the other blank do the work for us. When breaking those fetters, we are probably using or doing something positive with those unexamined hypotheses. We should be suspicious of choice D, since it's negative. C is the best answer, and "susceptible" is much closer to using or doing or open to using.

12. PUISSANCE:

- ○ impotence
- ○ poverty
- ○ flexibility
- ○ grace
- ○ vigor

12. **A** A is correct. Here's another stem word that we're unlikely to know. And it doesn't look particularly positive or negative. In a case such as this, make opposites for the answer choices. This is unlikely to shake loose a recollection of the meaning of the word PUISSANCE, but it will help us spot answer choices that don't have clear opposites. Choice A—IMPOTENCE—has got an opposite—potency. B's opposite would be wealth, C's inflexibility, D's clumsiness, and E's lack of vigor, or no strength. They all have decent opposites, so we'll just pick one. It's nice to know that puissance means power, as opposed to say, A—impotence. Eat those vocab words for breakfast, but on the test, if stumped, take your best shot, and move on.

13. OFFICIOUS : OBLIGING ::

- ○ dubious : peculiar
- ○ malevolent : corrupt
- ○ effusive : demonstrative
- ○ placid : merciful
- ○ radical : cautious

13. **C** C is the correct answer here. The stem sentence is OFFICIOUS is overly OBLIGING. Choice A is not a good relationship, and in B, somebody malevolent isn't necessarily corrupt, much less overly corrupt. So they're out. Choice C—EFFUSIVE is overly DEMONSTRATIVE? Oh dahhhling, it certainly is. How about D? PLACID is overly MERCIFUL is lame, and not related. E—RADICAL is overly CAUTIOUS? No way. So C looks best. If you couldn't make a sentence for the stem, you still should have been able to eliminate at least A and D as bad relationships, and then work backwards with the other choices you knew the words in.

14. The _____ issues that arise inherently from the very nature of social scientific investigation must be judged separately from the solely _____ issues, which are hotly debated one moment and forgotten the next.

- ⃝ reiterated. .pragmatic
- ⃝ innate. .realistic
- ⃝ habitual. .discerning
- ⃝ theoretical. .arbitrary
- ⃝ perpetual. .temporal

14. **E** E is the answer. Okay, we've got two kinds of issues that we know are different from each other. We know they are different because the sentence emphasizes that they must be judged separately. Which issues do we know more about? The ones in the second blank are "hotly debated one moment and forgotten the next." That's lovely. We want a word that sums that up. Exercise your vocabulary if possible. Something like transitory, fleeting, ephemeral, temporary. Looking at the second words in the answer choices, we see that A, B, and C are way off the mark. D and E look like "temporary." And now for the first blank. We know the second bunch of issues are the temporary ones, so the first must be the real or permanent ones. Choice D's "theoretical" is too fuzzy, but choice E's "perpetual" is a lot like permanent. So we dig E.

15. EFFERVESCENT:
- ○ vapid
- ○ intercepted
- ○ dispersed
- ○ disaffected
- ○ disconcerted

15. **A** It's A. EFFERVESCENT means bubbly, bouncy, energetic. We want the opposite of that: not bubbly, not bouncy, not energetic. How about something like "blah"? Sure, it's not a pretty vocab word, but it doesn't have to be; let's see what happens. A) VAPID, is like not having energy, not bouncy, kind of "blah." We'll keep it. B) INTERCEPTED, is not like "blah" at all. Lose it. C) DISPERSED, isn't like "blah," and is in fact closer to being a synonym for our stem than an antonym. Eliminate it. D) DISAFFECTED, is probably the hardest word among the answer choices. If you don't know it, you can't eliminate it. Choice E, DISCONCERTED, means confused. Is this anything like "blah"? Not really, so dump it. So now we have two left, A and D. If you know what DISAFFECTED means (unfriendly, antagonistic), then you already know the answer is A. But if you didn't, at least you got it down to two choices on a hard antonym. Learn that vocab!

HARD MATH BIN EXPLANATIONS

Column A

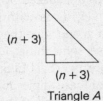

(n + 3)

(n + 3)

Triangle A

Column B

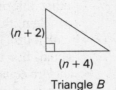

(n + 2)

(n + 4)

Triangle B

1. The area of Triangle A

The area of Triangle B

○ the quantity in Column A is always greater

○ the quantity in Column B is always greater

○ the quantities are always equal

○ it cannot be determined from the information given

1. **A** It's A. Write down A, B, C, D. This is a great place to plug in and avoid messy algebra. Instead of multiplying icky stuff like $(n + 3)$ and $(n + 3)$, let's just pick some values for n. Say $n = 5$. Okay, then the area of triangle A is and 8 times 8, and the area of triangle B is $\frac{1}{2}$ times 7 times 9.

We're just comparing the values for the two columns (remember this is called quantitative *comparison*, not calculation).

So we can disregard the $\frac{1}{2}$ on both sides.

Column A is 64 and Column B is 63—this time. Column B isn't always bigger, so eliminate B, and they're not always equal, so eliminate C. We have two choices left, so we plug in again. Try something weird this time, like 0, 1 or –1.

Let's use –1 for n. Now Column A is $\frac{1}{2}$ times 2 times 2, and Column B is $\frac{1}{2}$ times 1 times 3. Ignoring the $\frac{1}{2}$ on both sides gives us 4 for Column A and 3 for Column B. Column A is still bigger, so A is the answer.

Column A   Column B

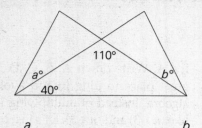

2. a b

○ the quantity in Column A is always greater
○ the quantity in Column B is always greater
○ the quantities are always equal
○ it cannot be determined from the information given

2. **D** The correct answer here is D. Watch out. This is nastier than it looks. Sometimes we can eyeball pictures, and get a fair idea of approximate lengths and angles. But unless our notions are backed up by other information given to us with the problem, that notion is spurious (hey— look it up). In this case, some things look equal, but the picture never TELLS us they're equal. Some of these angles must be certain measures, but not all of them. The angle on the lower right corner of the middle triangle must be 30. We know two other angles of that triangle, and they total 150 degrees, and all triangles have a total of 180 degrees, so there's 30 left for that angle. Okay. We also know that the angles adjacent to the 110 degree angle at the top of the middle triangle are each 70 degrees. Why? Because straight lines have a total of 180 degrees, and each of those angles plus the 110-degree angle form straight lines. And not that we need it, but the vertical angle on top of the 110-degree angle is also 110, because vertical angles are equal. That's everything we know exactly. We know that the two angles in the left triangle (the ones besides the 70 we just found) must add up to 110 degrees. That 110 can be broken up any way we like. We can say that angle a is 50 degrees, and the other is 60. The right-hand triangle works the same way. We know that the other two angles must equal 110, and we can break it down however we like. If we make angle b 50 degrees, Column A and Column B will be equal. But there is no reason angle b couldn't be 60 degrees, and the other angle in that triangle be 50. That would make the answer B. Since we just got two different answers depending on what we used for angle measures, the answer is D. Even though angles a and b look equal, they don't have to be.

3. How many square tiles, each with a perimeter of 64 inches, must be used to completely cover a bathroom floor with a width of 64 inches and a length of 128 inches?

- ⦿ 2
- ⦿ 4
- ⦿ 8
- ⦿ 32
- ⦿ 128

Column A   Column B

a is a positive number and $ab < 0$.

4. $a(b + 1)$ $a(b - 1)$

- ⦿ the quantity in Column A is always greater
- ⦿ the quantity in Column B is always greater
- ⦿ the quantities are always equal
- ⦿ it cannot be determined from the information given

3. **D** It's D. Draw yourself a picture, and be careful. If the tiles have a *perimeter* of 64, then they have sides of 16. Perimeter is the sum of the four sides, right? So we have tiles 16 inches on each side that we are using to cover a floor that's 64 by 128 inches. How many will we need along each side? On the 64-inch side, the width, four tiles will do it. On the 128-inch side we will fit eight tiles. So the width will be 4 tiles and the length 8 tiles. That makes 4 rows of eight tiles (or we can think of it as 8 rows of 4 tiles). Either way, that's a total of 32 tiles, choice D.

4. **A** It's A. A nice, classic plug-in quant comp. Write down A, B, C, D to use process of elimination. We're told that a is a positive number, while ab is less than 0. Pick some numbers that go along with this. Our a can be 3, and b, which looks like it needs to be negative, can be –4. So now we evaluate the columns. Column A is $3(-4+1) = -9$. Column B is $3(-4-1) = -15$. For now Column B is larger. Remember that –9 is bigger than –15, since it's closer to 0. Anyway, we can eliminate B and C. Now, plug in again. Try something a little weirder this time. Maybe make $a = 1$, and $b = -1$. Now Column A is $1(-1 + 1) = 0$. And Column B is $1(-1-1) = -2$. Column A is still bigger, so the answer is A.

5. Which of the following CANNOT be an integer if the integer k is a multiple of 12 but not a multiple of 9?

○ $\dfrac{k}{3}$

○ $\dfrac{k}{4}$

○ $\dfrac{k}{10}$

○ $\dfrac{k}{12}$

○ $\dfrac{k}{36}$

5. **E** It's E. We are being asked which of the fractions in the answer choices WILL NOT be an integer if k is a multiple of 12 but not a multiple of 9. This CANNOT question is a good place to remember some of what we learned on "Sesame Street": One of these things is not like the others. See which four are alike, and the answer will be the one that's different.

So, we'd better come up with some ks to PLUG IN on this handsome question with variables in the choices. Twelve and 24 are multiples of 12 that are not multiples of 9. But we can't use 36, since that is a multiple of 9, even though it's the next multiple of 12. Let's play with 12 and 24 and see where we are. If we use $k = 12$, then choice A equals 4. That's an integer. So A is okay. If we use 12 in B, then we get 3, so that's an integer too. We should put checks next to A and B so we know that whatever they are, they're the same as each other (either both work or both don't). When we try 12 in choice C it doesn't work. But that doesn't mean it doesn't ever work. We'll come back to it. Put $k = 12$ into D and we get 1, definitely an integer. Try $k = 12$ in E and we get junk. So, we have C and E as holdouts. Can we come up with a multiple of 12 that's not a multiple of 9 that will make one of those choices an integer? Let's try some more possible k values. Forty-eight and 60 are okay; 72 is not. We want a value for k that is divisible by 10 or 36. Well, 60 is good. And guess what? We will never find an acceptable value for k that will be divisible by 36. That's why choice E is the odd man out, and thus the answer.

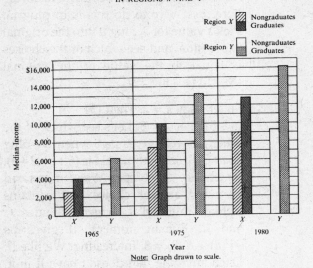

MEDIAN INCOME OF
COLLEGE GRADUATES *VS.* NONGRADUATES
IN REGIONS *X* AND *Y*

Note: Graph drawn to scale.

6. For how many of the four categories given did the median income increase by at least 30 percent from 1975 to 1980?

○ None
○ One
○ Two
○ Three
○ Four

6. **A** It's A. This question is a bit of work. We're asked how many of the categories of workers had a 30% or higher increase from 1975 to 1980. One way to do this would be to start with the 1975 figures, add 30% to each, and see how that compares with the 1980 figures. For Region *X* nongrads, 1975 was $7,500. Find 30% of this using translation, then add it to the 1975 amount. That would be 30% higher. Is the 1980 amount that or larger? 30/100 times 7,500 = 2,250. Added to the original, that would be 9,750. And the 8,500 in 1980 is less than that. So that's one of the four groups that DIDN'T have a 30% increase. Repeat for Region *X* grads. They went from $10,000 to $12,800. Thirty percent of the $10,000 would be $3,000, which would be $13,000, but the 1980 amount falls short of this by about $200. Oh well. For Region *Y* nongrads, 1975 was $7,800. Thirty percent of that would be $2,340. Added to the $7,800, that would give $10,140. But 1980 was only about $9,300. So, no 30% increase here either. Last chance is for Region *Y* grads. They made about $13,200 in 1975; an increase of 30% would be $4,960, yielding a total of $18,160. But they were really only making $16,100 in 1980. So, none of the groups saw an increase of 30% or more between 1975 and 1980. Too bad for them, but that's choice A.

7. Which of the following is equivalent to $(3a - 5)(a + 6)$?

  I. $(3a + 5)(a - 6)$

  II. $-5(a + 6) + 3a(a + 6)$

  III. $3a^2 - 30$

  ○ II only
  ○ III only
  ○ I and II only
  ○ II and III only
  ○ I, II, and III

7. **A** A is correct. Don't be chumped into messing around with FOIL and factoring here. Best way to do this is to plug in. Pick a value for a, plug it into the original expression, and see which of the choices is equal to the value of the original $(3a - 5)(a + 6)$.

So let's say $a = 2$. Then $(3a - 5)(a + 6)$ is $(6 - 5)(2 + 6) = 8$. Let's see which of the other answers gives us 8 when we plug in $a = 2$. Roman numeral I is $(6 + 5)(2 - 6)$, which is −44. Nope. We can get rid of every answer choice that contains Roman numeral I, which includes C and E. Roman numeral II gives us $-5(8) + 6(8) = 8$. Interesting. We like II. Ditch anything that doesn't have II in it, like B. So what's up with III, then? It givesus $3(4) - 30$, which is −18. So III stinks. Only II worked, so A is the answer.

A rectangular bathroom measures
$9\frac{1}{2}$ feet by 12 feet. The floor is
covered by rectangular tiles
measuring $1\frac{1}{2}$ inches by 2 inches.

8. The number of $6 \times 48 \times 19$
    tiles on the
    bathroom floor

- ◯ the quantity in Column A is always greater
- ◯ the quantity in Column B is always greater
- ◯ the quantities are always equal
- ◯ it cannot be determined from the information given

8. **C** This is C. Draw the floor, a rectangle $9\frac{1}{2}$ feet by 12 feet. The tiles are $1\frac{1}{2}$ by 2 INCHES. How many fit along the sides of the rectangle? Suppose we line the $1\frac{1}{2}$ inch sides along the side of the floor that will be 9 feet. In one foot, there will be 8 tiles, because $1\frac{1}{2}$ inches times 8 = 12 inches. So, on that side of the floor, there will be 8 times $9\frac{1}{2}$ tiles. Leave it that way; don't multiply it out. If you wanted to multiply it, looking at the ugly numbers in Column B should discourage you. Multiplication is not what this test is about. Okay, back to the floor. The 2-inch sides will be along the side of the floor that will be 12 feet long. There will be 6 tiles in each foot, so 12 times 6 tiles along that side. In order to find the number of tiles in the whole floor, we need to multiply the number in the length times the number in the width. This will be 8 times $9\frac{1}{2}$ times 12 times 6. Again, don't multiply it all out. We can knock the same numbers out of both sides of the question. Column A is the number of tiles, and Column B is 6 times 48 times 19. We can certainly divide 6 out of each side, knocking that out. So now we have:

Column A   Column B

$$8 \times 12 \times 9\frac{1}{2} \qquad 48 \times 19$$

We can divide each side by 12 now, getting rid of a 12 on the left, and changing the 48 on the right to a 4. So now there's:

Column A   Column B

$$8 \times 9\frac{1}{2} \qquad\qquad 4 \times 19$$

We can also divide both sides by 4 again:

$$2 \times 9\frac{1}{2} \qquad\qquad 19$$

Now it's not so annoying to actually do the multiplication, and lo and behold, we find that Column A and B are equal. So C it is. Careful canceling sure beats multiplying all that junk out, doesn't it?

9. An office supply store charged $13.10 for the purchase of 85 paper clips. If some of the clips were 16¢ each and the remainder were 14¢ each, how many of the paper clips were 14¢ clips?

- ◯ 16
- ◯ 25
- ◯ 30
- ◯ 35
- ◯ 65

9. **B** It's B. If we are being asked how many of the paper clips were the 14¢ clips, why not Plug In the answers, and see if they work out? Start in the middle with C. Say there were 30 14¢ clips. If there were 85 clips altogether, then 55 of them were the 16¢ clips. Will this give us the $13.10 total mentioned in the question? We'd have 30 clips times 14¢, which is $4.20, and 55 clips times 16¢, which is $8.80. That would total $13.00 exactly, which is not enough money. What do we do now? The office spent more money, and the number of clips has to stay at 85, so they must have bought more of the expensive ones. We want fewer 14¢ clips and more 16¢ ones. Go to choice A or B. B seems a good choice to try next because C was only off by 10¢. Let's do it. If we have 25 14¢ clips, then we'll have 60 16¢ clips. That's $3.50 plus $9.60, which, that's right, equals $13.10. We are pleased to introduce B, the correct answer.

<u>Column A</u>   <u>Column B</u>

_k_ is an integer such that
$9(3)^3 + 4 = k.$

10. The average   16
     of the prime
     factors of _k_

○ the quantity in Column A is always
  greater
○ the quantity in Column B is always
  greater
○ the quantities are always equal
○ it cannot be determined from the
  information given

10. **C** It's C. We're not going to be able to get
     away without doing some arithmetic
     here. We need to find out what _k_ is. Just do
     it carefully, remembering PEMDAS. So,
     parentheses and exponents first: 3 to the
     third power is 27. Now multiply: 9 times
     27 = 243. That plus 4 = 247. Eek. But that's
     _k_. Now we need to find its factors, since
     that's what they're talking about in Col-
     umn A. Trial and error is the way to go
     here. Not divisible by 2, or any even num-
     ber, for that matter. Anyway, we need
     prime factors. Try 3—no good. Doesn't
     end with 5 or 0, so not 5 either. Keep
     going. Seven's no good, and 9 isn't prime
     so there's no need to even try it. Eleven is
     useless. Thirteen is the first thing we find
     that goes in. In fact, 247 is 13 times 19.
     Those are the prime factors. Pretty hid-
     eous ones, too. Okay: Column A asks us
     for the average of the prime factors of _k_.
     Add them and divide by 2; we get 16. It's
     C. Just bite the bullet here, and take the
     time to get it right.

Column A   Column B

$$y > 0 \text{ and } (-1)^y = 1$$

11. y 2

- ○ the quantity in Column A is always greater
- ○ the quantity in Column B is always greater
- ○ the quantities are always equal
- ○ it cannot be determined from the information given

Column A   Column B

$$a = b + 2$$

12. $a^2 - 2ab + b^2$ $2a - 2b$

- ○ the quantity in Column A is always greater
- ○ the quantity in Column B is always greater
- ○ the quantities are always equal
- ○ it cannot be determined from the information given

11. **D** It's D. Don't forget to write down A,B,C,D. We're being asked to compare y with 2. Pick a "normal" number for y. Hmm . . . how's 2? (–1) squared = 1, so that's okay. So Column A and Column B can be equal, so strike A and B, since neither column is always bigger. But we have to plug in for y again. Can we mess this up? We can't plug in 0 or a negative number because the problem says y has to be greater than 0. One doesn't work with the other requirement, that $(-1)^y = 1$, but another even number, like 4, does work. Column A is bigger now, so lose C. All that's left is D, a fitting end since we were able to get two different answers when we used different values for y.

12. **C** It's C. Write down A, B, C, D! We've got variables, so plugging in is the way to go here. First, pick a set of easy numbers for a and b. The values $a = 5$ and $b = 3$ work with the information we're given. Now evaluate Column A. a^2 is 25, $-2ab$ is $(-2)(5)(3) = -30$, and $b^2 = 9$. So 25 – 30+9 = 4. That's Column A. Column B is $2(5) - 2(3) = 10 - 6 = 4$. Column B is also 4. They're equal this time, so cross out A and B. But you have to make sure to plug in at least twice. Let's pick a wackier set of values for a and b. We can make $a = 0$ and $b = -2$. Column A is 0 squared minus 2 (0) (–2), which is 0, plus (–2) squared, which is four. Column B is 2 (0) – 2 (–2), or 0 minus –4, which is also 4. They're equal again. It's beginning to look a lot like C.

13. If the dimensions of a rectangular crate, in feet, are 5 by 6 by 7, which of the following CANNOT be the total surface area, in square feet, of two sides of the crate?

- ○ 60
- ○ 70
- ○ 77
- ○ 84
- ○ 90

13. **E** The correct answer is E. We are being asked for the answer that CANNOT be the sum of the surface areas of two sides of the solid. How do we find surface area? Surface area is the areas of the sides of the box added together. But that's not necessary to do here. We just want to know which of the answers can be two sides added together. We will have 2 sides that will have dimensions 5 by 6, two sides with dimensions 6 by 7, and two sides with dimensions 5 by 7. So, we have two sides of area 30, two that are area 35, and two that are 42. Now let's take each of the answers and see if we can make them by adding two of the same or different sized sides. A can be made with 30 + 30. B can be made with 35 + 35. C can be made with 42 + 35. D can be made with 42 + 42. But E CANNOT be made with two sides. The largest number we can get that is a sum of two sides is 84. So E is the bad seed.

Column A	Column B

Tommy's average after 8 tests is 84. If his most recent test score is dropped, Tommy's average becomes 85.

14. Tommy's most recent test score   83

- ○ the quantity in Column A is always greater
- ○ the quantity in Column B is always greater
- ○ the quantities are always equal
- ○ it cannot be determined from the information given

14. **B** The answer is B. Remember, average is equal to total divided by number, so always think TOTAL. First, we're told that Tommy has an 84 average after 8 tests. To get his total, multiply the average, 84, by the number, 8. We get 672. Then we're told if one test score is taken away (they tell us it's the most recent just to be obnoxious; we actually don't care which one it is!), Tommy's average is an 85. Let's figure out his new total: multiply his new average, 85, by his new number, which is 7 (8 minus the score that was dropped). That's 595. The difference between his old total, 672, and his new total, 595, will be the score that was dropped (his "most recent test score," or Column A). So, 672 minus 595 is 77. Column A is 77, Column B is 83, and the answer is B.

<u>Column A</u>   <u>Column B</u>

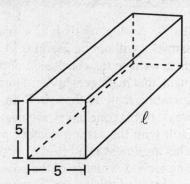

A rectangular box has a surface
area of 190 square feet.

15. The length, ℓ,   7 feet
    of the box

   ○ the quantity in Column A is always
      greater
   ○ the quantity in Column B is always
      greater
   ○ the quantities are always equal
   ○ it cannot be determined from the
      information given

15. **C**   It's C. We're given two of the three dimensions of the box, and asked about the
third. We also know the surface area of
the box. We find surface area by finding
the areas of the six sides of the box (top,
bottom, left side, right side, front and
back) and adding them together. Here
we really only know the area of the front
and back, which are each 5 times 5 = 25
square feet. The whole box has a surface
area of 190, so the front and the back
account for a total of 50 of that 190. That
leaves another 140. Each of the long
sides of the box—the top, bottom, left
and right sides—has dimensions of 5
times l. And four of these must equal the
140 square feet we have left. If we take
the 140 and divide it by 4, dividing it
among the four equal sides, we find that
each has an area of 35. We know one
dimension of each of those sides is 5. In
order to get area to equal 35, the value of
l must be 7. So it's C, since Column A
and Column B will both be 7. Phew!

HARD ANALYTIC BIN EXPLANATIONS

1. On the basis of a study it conducted, a research group concluded that managers in division A of a certain company authorize more discretionary spending than do managers in division B. These conclusions are based on an analysis of the number of non-budgeted expense reports that each manager approved.

The statistics used by the group will not be useful as a measure of which division spends more on non-budgeted expenses if which of the following is true?

- ⬭ The group counts each expense report equally, regardless of the dollar value of the report.
- ⬭ The group records all expenses, including those made by the managers themselves.
- ⬭ Most expense reports submitted to managers for approval are in fact approved.
- ⬭ Most non-budgeted expenses are incurred by the managers themselves.
- ⬭ All non-budgeted expense reports are subject to approval by someone who works for neither division.

1. **A** It's A. Asking us to find a reason the statistics will not be useful is like asking us to weaken the conclusion of the argument, that managers in A authorize more spending than do those in B. In order to weaken this conclusion, we need to find fault with the assumptions or premises. This argument is a bit of a word game. The second sentence of the passage tells us that the conclusion is based on an analysis of the NUMBER of expense reports. It looks like the study considered the NUMBER of reports to be the basis on which their pronouncement was made, rather than the AMOUNT OF MONEY that was authorized. These are not the same thing, but the argument has us thinking of them as the same thing. This is the flaw in the study, perhaps. Choice A nails it home, telling us that the group counts each report the same despite how much money it may involve. Choice B, while it does not do so particularly strongly, helps SUPPORT the study, saying it was "all-inclusive." Choices C, D, and E all have that "who cares?" element; the information they supply is irrelevant to what we are asked to do, giving us unimportant details about who submits reports, who approves them, etc. Choice A, if true, does the most to undermine the methodology of the study.

2. Geographers and historians have traditionally held the view that Antarctica was first sighted around 1820, but some sixteenth-century European maps show a body that resembles the polar landmass, even though explorers of the period never saw it. Some scholars, therefore, argue that the continent must have been discovered and mapped by the ancients, whose maps are known to have served as models for the European cartographers.

Which of the following, if true, is most damaging to the inference drawn by the scholars?

- ◯ The question of who first sighted Antarctica in modern times is still much debated, and no one has been able to present conclusive evidence.
- ◯ Between 3,000 and 9,000 years ago, the world was warmer than it is now, and the polar landmass was presumably smaller.
- ◯ There are only a few sixteenth-century global maps that show a continental landmass at the South Pole.
- ◯ Most attributions of surprising accomplishments to ancient civilizations or even extraterrestrials are eventually discredited or rejected as preposterous.
- ◯ Ancient philosophers believed that there had to be a large landmass at the South Pole to balance the northern continents and make the world symmetrical.

2. **E** It's E. Here we need to damage the scholars' inference that ancients must have discovered and mapped Antarctica, just because a polar landmass appeared on the ancient maps. Right next to "here be dragons," no doubt. So we need to find another reason why it appeared on their maps, even if they didn't really know it existed and hadn't been there. Choice A, if anything, just reinforces the notion that we're not so sure who did discover the continent. As for choice B, it would be all the more remarkable if Antarctica was smaller, and on the map. And we're looking to weaken the inference, so this is no good. Choice C repeats something already in the passage, that some maps show a polar landmass. Whoop de doo. D? Um, extraterrestrials? Use the telescope. E—Yes, that's right, the ancients had another reason the polar landmass had to be there, or else the world would fall apart. They never saw the thing. This will weaken the smartypants' inference, all right. So E it is.

Seven foods—A, B, C, D, E, F, and G—are to be chosen for the creation of a menu which is to include either three or four foods. A, B, C, and D are hot foods, and E, F, and G are cold foods. There must be at least one hot food and at least one cold food on the menu, but there cannot be an equal number of hot and cold foods. The entree on the menu must be a food whose temperature is not the temperature of the majority of the other foods on the menu. The following conditions must also be met:

If A is on the menu, then D cannot be on the menu.

If B is on the menu, then E cannot be on the menu.

D and F cannot be on the menu unless they are both on the menu.

If G is on the menu, then E must be on the menu.

3–5 Okay, let's set this up. We have lots of conditional (if/then) clues. Make sure you include the contrapositives with each if/then clue. The "entree" issue may seem annoying at first, but we can deal with it when we must. It would not be easy to incorporate the entree into the diagram, since it could be either a hot or cold food. Perhaps when necessary, we can circle or somehow mark which item can be the entree. We want to be able to tell the hot and cold foods on sight, maybe using upper and lower case letters. And look for those deductions.

$$A\ B\ C\ D\ e\ f\ g \qquad \underline{on} \quad \big|\quad \underline{off}$$

$$A \rightarrow \sim D\ (D \rightarrow \sim A)$$
$$B \rightarrow \sim e\ (e \rightarrow \sim B)$$
$$D \rightarrow \boxed{Df}$$
$$f \rightarrow \boxed{Df}$$
$$g \rightarrow e\ (\sim e \rightarrow \sim g)$$

Some stuff we might realize includes that since there are to be three or four foods, one of which is an entree (and in the minority temperature category), AND since there cannot be an equal number of hot and cold foods, yet must be at least one of each, there are only a couple of ways the numbers can work out. If there are three foods, there must be two of one temperature and one of the other, which would be the entree. If there are four foods, it has to be three and one, with the one as the entree. That's nice to realize. Now on to the real fun.

3. Which one of the following represents an acceptable menu?

   ○ A, B, C
   ○ C, E, G
   ○ D, F, G
   ○ A, C, D, F
   ○ B, D, E, F

4. If B is on the menu, which one of the following must be true?

   ○ There are three foods on the menu.
   ○ There are four foods on the menu.
   ○ B is the entree on the menu.
   ○ D is the entree on the menu.
   ○ F is the entree on the menu.

3. **B** B is the answer. An acceptable line-up question means we need to go through the clues one by one, including any clues that are really in the setup of the game. So we must have three or four foods, with at least one hot and one cold. Let's see if anything is history yet. Choice A is out because it only has hot food. Choices B, C, D, and E are okay so far. And there can't be an equal number of hot and cold. That will kill E. The question doesn't bring up the entree issue, so we'll just skip it here. Next, if A then no D. Oops. There goes choice D. B and C are left. Next clue, if B then no E does nothing for us, nor does the next clue. But the last clue takes care of it. If G then E is violated in choice C. That leaves choice B.

4. **E** E it is. If B is on, let's see what happens. No E is what happens. And if we made our contrapositives, the one for the last clue is a help. If G then E has the contrapositive: if no E then no G. So, no G. We have to have a cold food, so it will have to be F. It's the only cold, and will thus be the entree. That's choice E. We also know that D is on the menu, but it's not necessary to answer the question. Make those contrapositives, folks!

5. Which one of the following could NOT be the entree on the menu?

○ C
○ D
○ E
○ F
○ G

5. **E** E is the correct answer. The question is which, in general, *can't* be the entree? Don't forget that we just did two questions. In question 4, F was the entree, so we can cross off choice D. We also had a good setup in number 3. That entree was C, so eliminate choice A. This is why you should NEVER erase any work!

Now we have choices B, C, and E left, and we'll just have to try them. In choice B, can we have D as the entree? If D, a hot food, were the entree, we would need two or three cold foods as the rest of the selections. We would have to have F, because we can't have D without F. And we can also have E and G. So that's okay. We can now eliminate choice B. Can E (choice C) be the entree? E is a cold food, and it would need to be the only cold food. We now need two or three hot foods. We couldn't use D, because it would drag F along with it. But we could use A and C, and that would make an acceptable selection. So now we can eliminate choice C. Looks like the answer is E. You don't have to check it, but let's: G cannot be the entree, because the entree must be the only food of that temperature, and if we use G, we must also take E. No good. So choice E (food G) is the one that cannot be the entree.

6. The Natural Bounty Market, an organic food cooperative, solicits two-thirds of its new members by running ads on the local public radio station between the hours of 6 a.m. and noon. The Natural Bounty's membership committee, in an effort to increase its member base, resolves to run radio ads around the clock. The committee expects that, because of the increased number of radio ads, the number of new members will increase by at least 100 percent.

The membership committee's expected goal would be most strongly supported if which of the following were true?

○ The ads run between 6 a.m. and noon were heard by fewer than 40 percent of the listeners of the public radio station who would be interested in joining The Natural Bounty Market.
○ Grocery shoppers typically listen to the radio in the morning hours.
○ Most of the public radio station listeners with an interest in The Natural Bounty Market are already members of that cooperative organization.
○ The majority of those who become members of The Natural Bounty Market do so as a result of the solicitations on the public radio station.
○ The total number of listeners to the public radio station is fairly constant throughout the day and evening.

6. **A** The correct answer is A. What, if true, will most likely get the Market more members? The thinking of the committee is that since their advertising is effective at one time of day, it will be equally effective at other times. This is a sort of argument by analogy, which assumes that the time period from 6 A.M. to noon is analogous to other time periods. The membership committee's goal is most strongly supported if this is true; their goal is realistic if the audience is the same or larger at other times of day. Check out the answers: Choice A covers it, saying that other time periods have more listeners who should be interested in the Market. We like A. Choice B, if true, would not help the committee's strategy. Similarly, choice C suggests that the committee would be wasting its money; they will already have most of the members they are likely to get from the station. Choice D is harmless, but it doesn't address the issue of advertising times. We also don't know about the listenership's variations throughout the day. Choice E might seem to suggest that the ads would not improve the likelihood of reaching more listeners, but we really don't know that. It doesn't tell us anything about whether the makeup of the audience is the same even if the number of listeners is the same. Choice A gives the possibility that there are many listeners who might be interested in the Market, who don't already hear its ads, thus making it more likely that the committee will be able to see an increase in membership.

In the English department at a certain university, a final paper's grade is determined after one full week, Sunday to Saturday, of consideration by the staff. Each day one member of the staff—Professor X, Professor Y, Professor Z, Teaching Assistant (TA) K and Teaching Assistant L—reads the paper and passes it on to the next person to read the next day.

Teaching assistants each use two consecutive days to read final papers, and professors each use one day.

The final paper is handed in on Sunday.

If, on any day, a final paper is determined to be a failure, it is no longer passed on to the next person.

Only a professor can determine that a final paper is a failure. However, a final paper cannot be determined to be a failure on Sunday.

7–11 The days of the week (with their natural order) will top this assignment grid, and in case you had any doubt, look at the answer choices for question 7! We have professors, who take up one day each, and teaching assistants, who use two consecutive days. We should consider each of the TAs as a block of kk or ll. The last two clues are difficult or impossible to symbolize. Just copy them down briefly or do something to remember that they are there. And the diagram will look like this:

X Y Z k l

| kk |
| ll |

	S	M	T	W	T	F	S

Now on to the show. . .

7. Which one of the following is an acceptable sequence of staff members to read the final paper?

	Sun	Mon	Tue	Wed	Thu	Fri	Sat
○	L	L	Y	X	Z	K	K
○	K	L	Z	K	L	X	Y
○	Z	K	K	X	L	Y	L
○	Y	Z	L	K	L	K	X
○	X	Y	K	K	L	Z	Y

8. If Professor Z reads the paper on Friday, which one of the following must be true?

○ Professor X reads the paper on either Sunday or Saturday.

○ Professor Y reads the paper on either Tuesday or Thursday.

○ Either Professor X or Professor Y must read the paper on either Monday or Wednesday.

○ Professor X and Professor Y must read the paper on consecutive days.

○ Professor Y does not read the paper on either Monday or Wednesday.

7. **A** A is the answer. Here is our pal, the possible line-up question. Just take the clues, one by one, not forgetting the clues that may be imbedded in the setup, as well. In the setup, it says that each person reads the paper once, and then passes it on. The first clue is that the TA's use two consecutive days, and the professors use one. Is that violated anywhere? Yes, in B, C, D, and E. E also uses Professor Y twice, which is a no-no. It's A.

8. **E** The answer is E. If Professor Z reads a paper on Friday, where does that leave us? A professor must read the paper on Saturday, because a TA's two days won't fit at the end of the week. Where can we put the TA's blocks? There are a few arrangements, and it helps to notice that the question's answers focus on the professors, so we don't actually care which TA is on any particular day. We need room for two TA blocks and one professor. We can start with TAs, so they'd be on Sunday/Monday and Tuesday/Wednesday, and a professor on Thursdays. Or we can have a TA block Sunday/Monday, a professor on Tuesday, and another TA block on Wednesday/Thursday. The third possibility is that we can have a professor read on Sunday, a TA block on Monday/Tuesday, and another on Wednesday/Thursday. What must be true is that a professor (either X or Y, since Professor Z's locked in on Friday) reads the paper on either Sunday, Tuesday, or Thursday, and a TA reads it on Monday and Wednesday. Choice A CAN be true, but doesn't have to be. Same is true for choice B. Choice C is impossible—it will always be a TA reading on Monday or Wednesday. Choice D in fact can't ever be true—either X or Y will read on Saturday, and the other will read before Friday. E is the one that must be true. Y (or X for that matter) will never read the paper on Monday or Wednesday. It will always be a TA on those days. Whew!

9. If Teaching Assistant L notices a problem with a paper on Wednesday, and the paper is determined to be a failure on Friday, Professor Y could have read the paper on any of the following days EXCEPT

- ◯ Sunday
- ◯ Monday
- ◯ Tuesday
- ◯ Thursday
- ◯ Friday

9. **B** It's B. If Teaching Assistant L notices a problem with a paper on Wednesday, he is reading the paper on either Tuesday/Wednesday or on Wednesday/Thursday. We can try both of those out at the same time. And in order for the paper to be determined a failure on Friday, a professor had to be reading it that day. So we have:

	S	M	T	W	R	F	S
⑨			I	I		X/Y/Z	
⑨				I	I	X/Y/Z	

This means we have to worry about where we can fit the kk block. In the first variation, kk could only be Sunday/Monday. In the second variation, kk can be Sunday/Monday, or Monday/Tuesday. So in the first variation, the professors (including Y) are on Thursday, Friday, and Saturday. But we want to know where Y CANNOT be. Since he CAN be on Thursday or Friday, we can eliminate choices D and E. In the second variation, we need a professor on Friday and Saturday, again, and one on either Sunday or Tuesday to accommodate the kk block. So we can have a professor, let's call him Y, on Sunday or Tuesday. Those are choices A and C, which can now be eliminated. It's B who's the odd man out, and the answer. Y can't be there.

10. If Teaching Assistant K reads a paper on Tuesday, and Professor X is the only member of the staff who can fail a paper after it is passed on by Teaching Assistant K, which one of the following must be true?

- ○ Professor X reads the paper on Wednesday.
- ○ Professor X reads the paper on Thursday.
- ○ Professor Y reads the paper on Sunday.
- ○ Teaching Assistant K reads the paper on Wednesday.
- ○ Teaching Assistant L reads the paper on Thursday.

10. **D** D is correct. In order for Professor X to be the only person who can fail the paper after K reads it on Tuesday, we need for Professor X to be the ONLY professor who reads after Tuesday. That means we want to plug up the end of the week with TAs. If K reads on Tuesday/Wednesday, L could read on Thursday/Friday, and X on Saturday. That would be one way to do it:

	S	M	T	W	R	F	S
⑨			l	l		X/Y/Z	
⑨				l	l	X/Y/Z	
⑩			k	k	l	l	x

The question asks us which MUST be true, so let's try to prove the answers false. Choice A says X on Wednesday. This isn't true in our perfectly acceptable setup, so it need not be true always. Choice B? Same as A. Lose it. Choice C—that Y reads on Sunday, can be true, but doesn't have to be true. Y and Z are interchangeable for Sunday and Monday. So we can ditch C. Looks like D and E are true for this setup. But we need to get rid of one of these choices. So let's try another acceptable setup. Try moving L to Friday/Saturday, then a professor on Thursday:

	S	M	T	W	R	F	S
⑨			l	l		X/Y/Z	
⑨				l	l	X/Y/Z	
⑩			k	k	l	l	X
⑩			k	k	X	l	l

Hey, that eliminates choice E. So, choice D is the only one left, and therefore will always be true.

11. Suppose it is known that Teaching Assistant K reads a paper on either Tuesday or Wednesday, but not both days, and that Teaching Assistant L reads the paper on either Thursday or Friday, but not both days. All of the following are possible schedules for the teaching assistants EXCEPT:

○ Teaching Assistant K reads the paper on Monday, and Teaching Assistant L reads the paper on Wednesday.
○ Teaching Assistant K reads the paper on Tuesday, and Teaching Assistant L reads the paper on Thursday.
○ Teaching Assistant K reads the paper on Tuesday, and Teaching Assistant L reads the paper on Friday.
○ Teaching Assistant K reads the paper on Wednesday, and Teaching Assistant L reads the paper on Thursday.
○ Teaching Assistant K reads the paper on Thursday, and Teaching Assistant L reads the paper on Friday.

11. D It's D. We want the schedule that DOESN'T work—the bad one. If K reads on either Tuesday or Wednesday but not both, he's doing either Monday/Tuesday or Wednesday/Thursday. If L reads on Thursday or Friday but not both, he's doing either Wednesday/Thursday or Friday/Saturday Here's what it all looks like:

	S	M	T	W	R	F	S
⑨			I	I		X/Y/Z	
⑨				I	I	X/Y/Z	
⑩			k	k	I	I	X
⑩			k	k	X	I	I
⑪		k	k	[I	I]/	[I	I]
				k	k	I	I

Look at the answer choices—which are covered by our diagram? All but D, so D is the answer.

How does an architect most easily maintain a client base interested in commissioning her for new projects? She relies on the design features and building materials utilized in the projects with which she initially won her following. Unfortunately, the result is that she will never experience measurable artistic development as an architect.

12. The argument depends upon which of the following assumptions about an architect's maintenance of a client base?

   ⬭ An architect is never more interested in artistic development than with reliance on the design features and materials with which she developed her following.

   ⬭ An architect is always careful to replicate a part of her original design when commissioned by a former client for a new project.

   ⬭ An architect pays scant attention to the artistic development of her contemporaries in the field.

   ⬭ An architect talks with her clients specifically about the design features and building materials that drew them to the architect's work in the first place.

   ⬭ An architect is capable of predicting any trends or shifting preferences in the field before turning in final designs for a new project.

12. **A** It's A. We need to find what the assumption is that's been made here. Remember the assumption won't be explicitly stated, but will be needed to come to the conclusion that the artist "will never experience measurable artistic development as an architect." The argument equates keeping a client base won over by her earlier work and designs with continuing to employ the same designs and materials. Suggesting that these two are connected is the assumption made here, and it's not necessarily the case. Let's look for a version of that assumption in the answers. Choice A says that an artist isn't ever going to be more interested in developing her art than she will be with maintaining a client base. This seems to sum up the assumption. The author of the argument seems to think that because the people chose this architect based on her previous work, they want her to build the exact same buildings for them. There really is nothing to support that in the argument, unless you make this assumption. This looks good. In B, replicating part of the previous work isn't necessary for the argument to work. Choices C, D, and E are out of scope, each addressing a different point not closely related to the argument, such as trends, what other people are doing, etc.

13. Which of the following, if true, is most damaging to the conclusion above?

- ○ Frequently among those in an architect's client base are former architects and students of architecture.
- ○ Those commissioning architects for new projects are pressured to commission works of broad-based appeal.
- ○ Former clients commissioning architects for new projects most frequently cite "innovative design" as their most desired attribute for the new project.
- ○ Alienation of a client base through refusal to draw upon signature design features and building materials can cost an architect a great deal of income.
- ○ The favored design features and building materials of one nation's architectural industry can be widely divergent from those of another nation.

13. **C** The answer is C. We're being asked to weaken the conclusion from the previous argument. Let's bust on the assumption. The argument assumed that keeping a client base was analogous to keeping the styles and building materials that originally won that client base. Ruin this by saying that they needn't be connected. Just because somebody admired the architect's work doesn't mean they want a carbon-copy of that building. Let's see what they've got for us here. Choice A is from out-of-scope city. Who cares that they might be former students of architecture? Choice B doesn't do it; nobody ever said this architect had broad-based appeal. Hey, but in choice C, clients like when their architects come up with something innovative. It wouldn't be innovative if they kept designing the same "innovative" building, would it? So apparently, she could continue to expand her range, especially if she's been identified as "innovative." Those clients want to see what kind of wacky stuff she'll come up with for them! Choice D—Income? Out of scope. Choice E— one nation or another also is out of scope.

14. Several large steel companies in the United States have requested that tariffs be imposed on imported foreign steel. These companies usually incorporate high-tech refining processes in their steel production, which, while creating a higher grade of steel, also cause significant price increases. These companies fear they will lose a substantial portion of the domestic market to foreign competitors in the next few years. They contend that foreign steel, while generally of a lower grade, will be highly competitive in the United States due to its low price. Those companies requesting the tariffs should instead consider a return to more primitive, and profitable, refinement techniques.

Which of the following, if true, would most seriously weaken the conclusion drawn above?

- ○ An increase in the quality of steel used in an industry tends to result in higher customer satisfaction and assurance levels.
- ○ Tariffs have been shown to be an ineffective method of stymieing foreign competition in the electronics industry.
- ○ Domestic purchasers of steel will not buy low-grade foreign steel if strict tariffs are applied to its importation.
- ○ The United States automotive industry, which accounts for almost all domestic steel purchases, only uses steel of the highest grades.
- ○ The technologically advanced refining processes used in the production of American steel tend to be less environmentally sound than the processes used to produce low-grade steel.

14. **D** It's D. We need to weaken the argument that there shouldn't be tariffs on imported steel, but should instead be "primitive" refinement techniques on domestic steel. D says that the major purchaser of steel, the automotive industry, only buys high-grade steel. The author's suggestion that steel companies requesting the tariffs should consider a return to more primitive, and profitable, refinement techniques is now illogical because these primitive techniques will produce steel of a lower grade that will not be purchased by the automotive industry. In A, customer satisfaction and assurance levels are outside the scope. So is the electronics industry in B. And so is the environment in E. Answer choice C does weaken the author's argument by suggesting that the tariff might have its intended effect IF implemented (of course, we have no information on the probability of the tariff actually being implemented). But, this doesn't address the author's suggestion that the steel manufacturers ditch their technology, and as such, is not as strong a weaken answer as D.

15. At a certain university, of the last fifty women considered for full-time positions, only eighteen percent of them held these positions at the university after three years. Comparably, of the last fifty men considered, sixty percent of them are still working full-time after three years. Over forty percent of all full-time positions in the academic profession are currently held by women. An examination of these statistics makes it clear that this university's hiring practices are gender-biased and should be altered to promote the full-time employment of women.

Which of the following, if true, most seriously weakens the force of the evidence cited above?

- ○ Almost all of the women who were considered for full-time positions at the university were hired, then left of their own accord after a few months.
- ○ When compared with the overall academic profession, the board of directors of the university seems to have an unbiased attitude toward women.
- ○ The definition of full-time employment has been altered several times over the last decade.
- ○ Most women who hold full-time academic positions have received multiple degrees.
- ○ Forty percent of the women who were not retained for full-time employment have expressed outrage at what they consider unfair hiring practices.

15. **A** It's A. We need to weaken the argument that the university's hiring practices are gender-biased. Choice A weakens it by pointing out that the women left of their own accord before the three-year period in question, so the hiring practices cannot be called gender-biased. B really isn't strong enough; it just says the university seems to be unbiased compared to the whole profession, but that doesn't mean it isn't biased at all. C doesn't even mention gender-biased hiring practices. D's multiple degrees is outside the scope. And E may be true, but it does nothing to weaken the conclusion about gender-biased hiring practices.

APPENDIX

Installing and Using Your GRE Diagnostic Software

ABOUT THE SOFTWARE

The diagnostic tests on the CD-ROM are designed to help you practice your test-taking skills, pacing, and techniques in a setting that is very much like the real GRE. We want to make sure your testing experience is as realistic as possible. Each test has a pool of questions, and each question drawn from that pool depends on how you answered the previous question—just like an actual GRE.

In addition to the four full-length GREs on the disc, you can practice specific question types with drills. The drill questions come out of a pool of questions that will not show up on the tests. However, when you have completed all four full GREs, the entire question pool (over 2,000 questions) is opened into the drills. So, although you may see some repeat questions at that point, you can drill as much as you need to. We've even included some suggestions for using the drills (see below).

Although the software allows you to take a single section of the test on its own, we recommend trying an entire test in one sitting. Remember—you want to simulate real testing conditions. And don't forget to use scratch paper—that screen-to-scratch paper conversion is very important. We also advise that you make good use of the review features—look at the explanations for questions you missed, and determine which sections are giving you the most trouble.

SYSTEM REQUIREMENTS

WINDOWS™

486/66 MHz or higher

Windows 3.1, 95, 98

16 MB RAM

10 MB Hard Disk space

SVGA Monitor (256 Colors)

Double-speed CD-ROM or faster

Mouse

MACINTOSH®

Power PC

System 7.0 or higher

16 MB RAM

10 MB Hard Disk space

256 Color Monitor (640 × 480 pixels)

Double-speed CD-ROM or faster

Mouse

INSTALLATION AND START-UP

WINDOWS:

Close all other applications.
Check that your monitor is set to 256 colors.

1. Insert the CD in your CD-ROM drive.

2. From your Start Menu (or File menu if using Win 3.1), select **Run**.

3. Type D:setup and press **Enter**. (If your CD-ROM drive is not drive D:, type the appropriate letter)

4. Follow the onscreen instructions until installation is complete.

5. Once setup is complete, if you want to begin immediately, you can check "Yes, I want to run GRE Diagnostic now" and select **Finish.** Otherwise, just select Finish.

To run the software later, make sure the CD is in your CD-ROM drive, and simply select **GRE Diagnostic** from the *Princeton Review* folder in Programs from the Start Menu (or in the *Princeton Review* Program Group, if you are using Win 3.1).

MACINTOSH:

1. Insert the CD in your CD-ROM drive

2. Double click the GRE Diagnostic Installer icon

3. Follow the onscreen instructions until installation is complete.

To run the software, make sure the CD is in your CD-ROM drive, and simply double click the *Tester* icon located in the *GRE Diagnostic* folder on your hard drive.

USING GRE DIAGNOSTIC TESTS

THE MAIN MENU

Each time you launch your GRE Diagnostic, you will begin with the main menu screen. From this screen, you can **Take a Test**—one of four GRE Diagnostics (which can be taken section by section or as a whole test), **Review a Test** you've already taken, or **Practice a Section** with drills. You can also exit the software by clicking **Quit** on the upper-right corner.

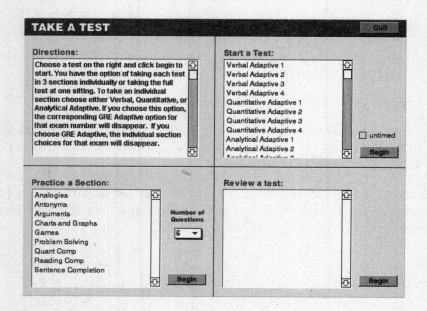

TAKING A TEST

Each full-length GRE consists of four sections: Verbal, Quantitative, Analytical, and an unscored Experimental section. In an actual GRE, you will not know which section is experimental, but in this software you do. You can skip this section by clicking Exit Section—see TOOLBAR for explanation.

If you choose to take an individual section, you can only take the corresponding sections separately as well. Likewise, if you take a full test, the corresponding sections become unavailable.

You also have the option of taking an untimed test by clicking the "untimed" box above the Begin button. This option is only recommended if you have a documented learning difference and will be taking the real GRE untimed.

To start a test, select one from the list and click **Begin**. You will go directly to the Directions screen of the first section of your selected test.

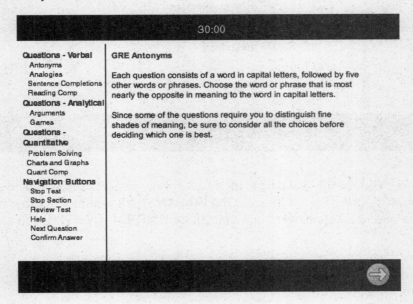

This is also the **Help** screen. If you need to review the directions for any type of question or the functions of any of the buttons on your screen, simply click the **Help** button at the bottom of any active testing screen and this screen will reappear. You can then click on the topic with which you need help.

Since the timer starts as soon as you click **Begin**, you should not spend unnecessary time on the Directions screen. Please review all of the section directions (provided in the book) before taking the diagnostic tests. The buttons on the actual GRE are also explained in the book on page 12, but please read the TOOLBAR section below because the buttons on these diagnostic tests are slightly different.

Unlike the actual GRE, there is no warning that you are nearing the end of a section, so pay attention to the timer.

Here is a sample test question screen:

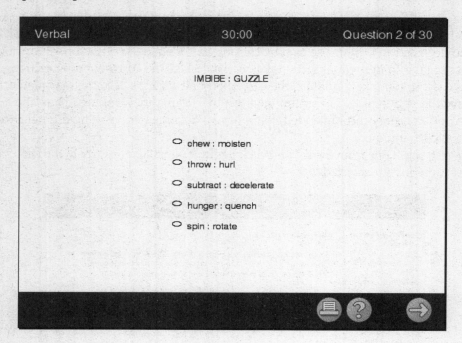

IMBIBE : GUZZLE

○   chew : moisten

○   throw : hurl

○   subtract : decelerate

○   hunger : quench

○   spin : rotate

To select an answer, click on the oval next to the answer or the answer itself, and then click the **NEXT QUESTION** button, which will turn into a **CONFIRM ANSWER** button. Click that button again to move to the next question. Remember, once you click **CONFIRM ANSWER,** you cannot return to that question.

THE TOOLBAR

 Clicking **STOP TEST** will give you the following warning:

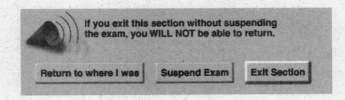

Return to Where I Was does exactly what you think it does.

Quit Exam will end the exam and erase all your results. We have included this button for emergency purposes, but we recommend that you never use it because you will not be able to review any of your work on that test. Furthermore, when you start a new test, it is possible that there will be questions repeated from the test that you quit, which will compromise the validity of your score. Clicking this button is equivalent to clicking **Test Exit** from the toolbar of an actual GRE.

Exit Section ends the present section of the test. Once you have exited a section, you cannot return to it. Clicking this button is equivalent to clicking **Section Exit** from the toolbar of an actual GRE.

The **Stop Test** button does not appear until after you select an answer and click the **Next Question** button. It does not appear at all on the first question of any section.

 Clicking **PRINT** will print the question presently on the screen. You cannot print out the entire test. This feature is not available during a real GRE.

 Clicking **HELP** will bring you to the Directions screen (see above), just as it does on an actual GRE.

 Clicking **NEXT** will change the button into **CONFIRM.** In the actual GRE, these are two separate buttons.

 Clicking **CONFIRM ANSWER** will record your answer and bring you the next question. Before confirming, you have one last chance to change your answer.

ENDING A SECTION AND FINISHING THE TEST

When you reach the end of a section, you will see this message:

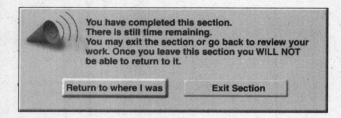

Return to where I was allows you to continue working on the last question in the section only. You cannot review the test at this time.

Exit Section will end your time on the section. Choose this option if you are finished with the section. If you have another section remaining, you will have a short break (2 minutes after section 1 and 3, 10 minutes after section 2) and then the computer will start the next section. (In an actual GRE you will only have 1 minute after section 1 and 3.) If you would like a longer break, you can also wait until time runs out on this section.

When you reach the end of the last section of the test and choose **Exit Section**, you will receive a message that reads, "You have reached the end of the exam."   Select **Exit** to proceed.

THE SCORE REPORT

When you have completed a test, you will see a screen that asks you to wait while your exam is scored. Then you will see your **SCORE REPORT**. This report gives you detailed information about your test. You can view the results of each section by selecting a section from the pull-down menu in the upper-right corner, or you can print the full report by clicking the **Print** button.

SCORE REPORT   Print   Exit Review

Exam Name Computer Adaptive Test 1   Date 3/12/99   Subject Verbal

Scores   Verbal=220

Section Performance (Click on a question to review.)

Q#	Corr Ans	Your Ans	Category	QID	Time Spent
1	D	E	ANT	9052	00:17
2	B	E	ANA	9024	00:14
3	A	A	ANA	9070	00:06
4	C	D	ANT	9106	00:10
5	E	D	SC	9016	00:03
6	D	A	ANA	9023	00:01
7	A	C	RC	9036	00:02
8	A	D	RC	9035	00:01
9	B	C	RC	9034	00:01
10	C	C	ANA	9021	00:18
11	A	C	ANT	9047	00:02

Performance Summary

Category	#Right	#Wrong	%Right	Average Time
Antonyms..(ANT)	2	6	25	00:06
Analogies..(ANA)	5	3	62	00:06
Sentence Completion..(SC)	1	5	16	00:03
Reading Comp..(RC)	1	7	12	00:02

You can view this **SCORE REPORT** at another time by selecting this test from the **Review a Test** section of the Main Menu.

REVIEWING YOUR TEST

You may review any question from your test by clicking on the question number in the **SCORE REPORT**. This will display the correct and incorrect answers. The review mode will show you a green checkmark to indicate the credited response, and show your answer as the darkened oval. To view an explanation for an answer choice, click on the answer (the words in the answer, not on the oval). These explanations do not print. To return to the **SCORE REPORT**, click on the **STOP SECTION** button.

PRACTICE A SECTION—TAKING DRILLS

To take a drill, select a question type from the **Practice a Section** menu, select whether you want 5 or 10 questions, and click **Begin.**
The drill screens look the same as the testing screens, with the following functional differences:

- The questions are untimed.

- You are shown the correct answer as soon as you select an answer. So, while there is no need to confirm answers, you cannot change answers while using the drills.

- You can view explanations immediately once you've answered by clicking on the answer choice—not the oval. But unlike **Reviewing a Test**, you cannot go back to a question once you have moved onto the next.

We've designed our drills so that you will not jeopardize the accuracy of any of your practice tests by seeing questions early. We have secured a group of about 400 questions for you to drill before you complete the tests. Once you have completed all four tests, you may see questions you saw previously in a test or drill (we want you to be able to drill to your heart's content), but at this point seeing questions again will not affect the utility of these drills. Remember that questions tend to fall into predictable patterns—that's part of what makes the GRE a standardized test.
You can use the drills to increase your familiarity with a particular question type, to target specific weaknesses, or to increase your speed or accuracy. Here are some suggestions:

Building accuracy

After you've taken a test, look at the **Performance Summary** on your **Score Report** and find a question type you need to improve on. Note the average time per question. To increase your accuracy on that type of question, double the average amount of time spent per question and try to get each drill question right. Then decrease the time slightly, while staying at 100% accuracy. This drilling method helps you improve your performance in the first third of the test, where accuracy is more important than speed.

Building speed

From the **Performance Summary** of your **Score Report**, choose a question type you will do well on. Note the average time spent per question. When drilling that question type, decrease that time slightly and challenge yourself to maintain the same level of accuracy. This drilling method helps you build speed for the middle of the test, where you need to move more quickly without sacrificing accuracy.

Practicing pacing

You can choose the appropriate number of drill questions to simulate the pacing of an actual test. For example, if your target score is 700 on the Quantitative section, aim for 100% accuracy on the first 10 questions in the first 15 minutes of the test. You can simulate this in a drill by working 5 Quant. Comp. questions and 5 Problem Solving questions in 15 minutes.

Mini-test

You can simulate the experience of taking a portion of the test by choosing an assortment of questions and working them within a set amount of time. A Verbal Mini-test might consist of 5 of each of the four question types in 20 minutes. You can use a Mini-test drill to help build your stamina through the most crucial part of the test.

If you have any questions, please call our Technical Support Center at (800) 546-2102.

ABOUT THE AUTHOR

Karen Lurie lives in New York City. The world of the Graduate Record Examination has been orbitting her for about ten years. She has written five books, including the *LSAT/GRE Analytic Workout* and *GRE Crash Course*.

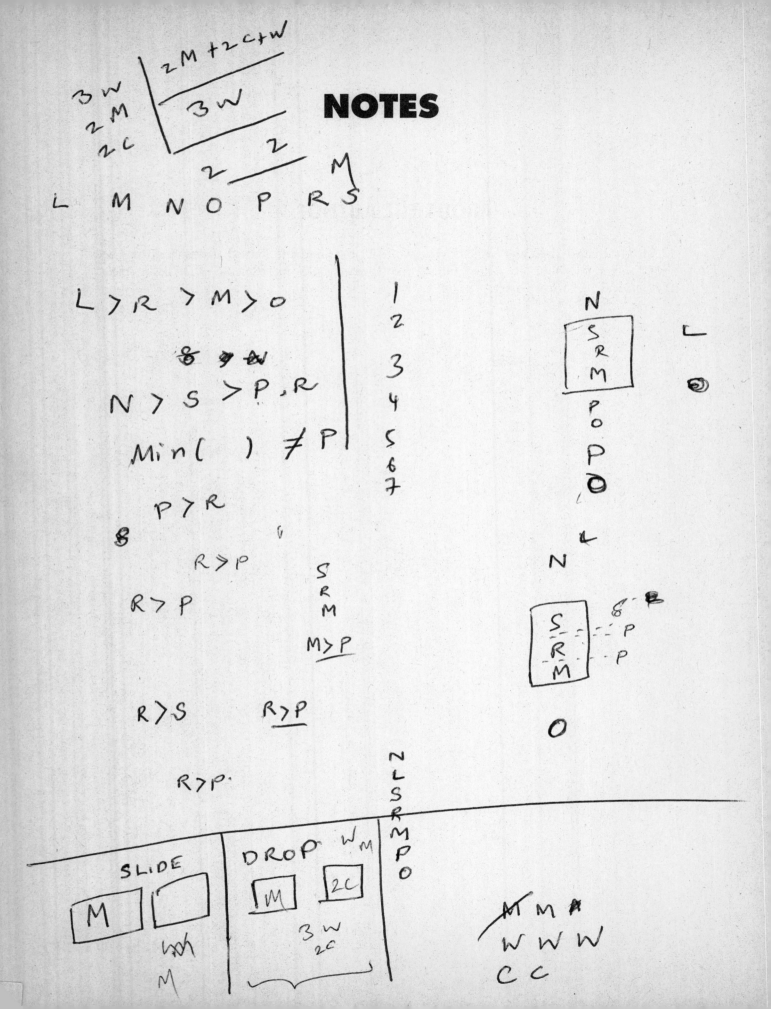

NOTES

NOTES

NOTES

E F G H L M S | eased – (E L M)

$\#\ S \neq H + 1$

1	2	3	4	5	6	7
G	E	H		S	F	M
G	E	L	F	M	H	
G		M	L			

1	2	3	4	5	6	7
G	E	L	M		M	M

S	H	

	3	4	5

F G H

I J K

M N P

M $\#$ G H P

K $\neq$ G N //

NOTES

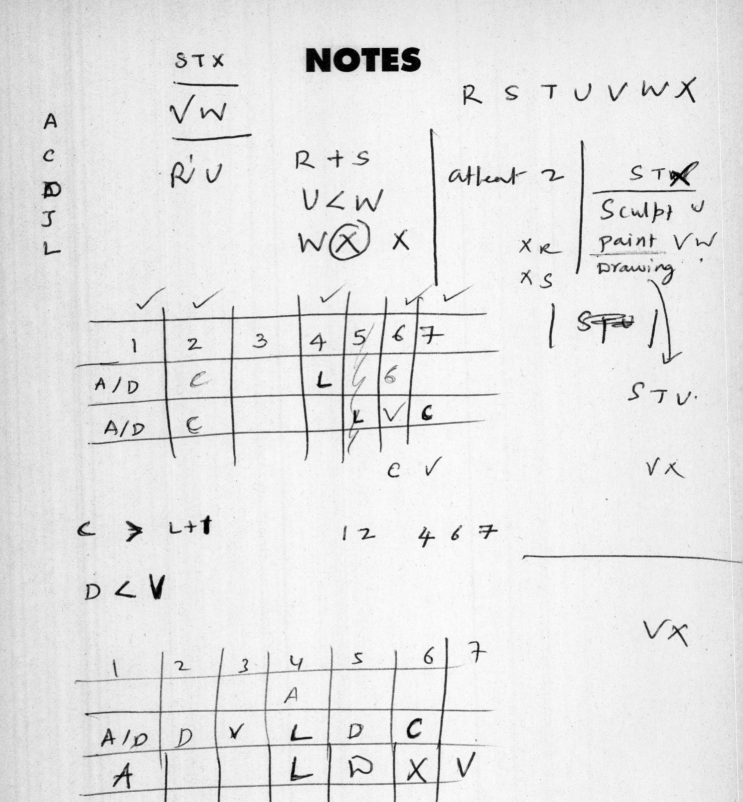

NOTES

NOTES

NOTES

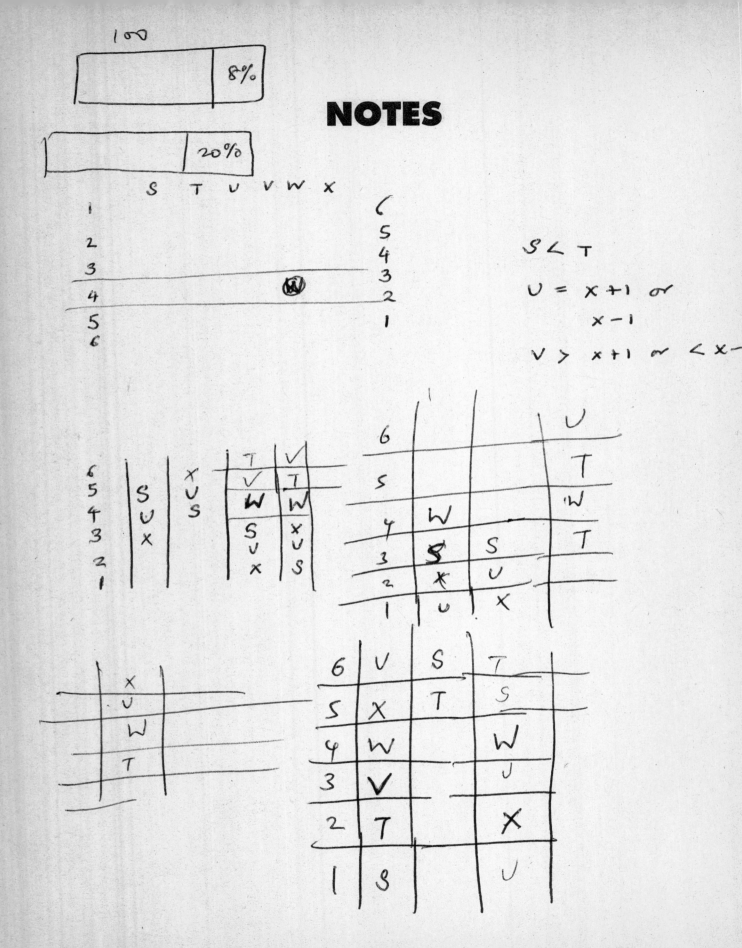

NOTES

FIND US...

International

Hong Kong
4/F Sun Hung Kai Centre
30 Harbour Road, Wan Chai,
Hong Kong
Tel: (011)85-2-517-3016

Japan
Fuji Building 40, 15-14
Sakuragaokacho, Shibuya Ku,
Tokyo 150, Japan
Tel: (011)81-3-3463-1343

Korea
Tae Young Bldg, 944-24,
Daechi- Dong, Kangnam-Ku
The Princeton Review- ANC
Seoul, Korea 135-280,
South Korea
Tel: (011)82-2-554-7763

Mexico City
PR Mex S De RL De Cv
Guanajuato 228 Col. Roma
06700 Mexico D.F., Mexico
Tel: 525-564-9468

Montreal
666 Sherbrooke St.
West, Suite 202
Montreal, QC H3A 1E7 Canada
Tel: (514) 499-0870

Pakistan
1 Bawa Park - 90 Upper Mall
Lahore, Pakistan
Tel: (011)92-42-571-2315

Spain
Pza. Castilla, 3 - 5° A, 28046
Madrid, Spain
Tel: (011)341-323-4212

Taiwan
155 Chung Hsiao East Road
Section 4 - 4th Floor,
Taipei R.O.C., Taiwan
Tel: (011)886-2-751-1243

Thailand
Building One, 99 Wireless Road
Bangkok, Thailand 10330
Tel: (662) 256-7080

Toronto
1240 Bay Street, Suite 300
Toronto M5R 2A7 Canada
Tel: (800) 495-7737
Tel: (716) 839-4391

Vancouver
4212 University Way NE,
Suite 204
Seattle, WA 98105
Tel: (206) 548-1100

locations

National (U.S.)
We have over 60 offices around the U.S. and
run courses in over 400 sites. For courses and locations
within the U.S. call 1 (800) 2/Review and you will be
routed to the nearest office.